BUSINESS OPPORTUNITIES IN THE PHILIPPINES

WE ARE INDEED delighted to have this important publication on the various business opportunities in the Philippines. We view the timely production of this book as a strong manifestation of the region's sustained confidence in the Philippine business environment.

The authors have succeeded in presenting an extensive but accurate picture of the local business climate. Potential investors would certainly find details on economic policies, the banking system, investment opportunities, most useful.

BENITO C. BENGZON JR. (DIRECTOR, OFFICE OF TOURISM COORDINATION/INVESTMENT PROMOTION UNIT)

Titles in the Nanyang Business Report Series

Business Opportunities in Penang, Malaysia

Business Opportunities in Sichuan Province, China

Business Opportunities in India

Business Opportunities in the Philippines

Business Opportunities in Myanmar

Business Opportunities in the Yangtze River Delta, China

For further enquiries, information or feedback on the series, please write to the Editor at e-mail: prenhall@singnet.com.sg or Simon & Schuster (Asia) Pte Ltd, 317 Alexandra Road, #04-01 IKEA Building, Singapore 159965.

NANYANG BUSINESS REPORT SERIES

Business Opportunities in The Philippines

Edited by

Tan Teck Meng (Dean)
Low Aik Meng (Vice Dean and Director of MBA Programme)
John J. Williams (Chief Coordinator, Business Study Mission)
Luis Ma. R. Calingo (Head, Human Resource and Quality Management)

Nanyang Technological University
Singapore

Prentice Hall
Singapore New York London Toronto Sydney Tokyo

First published 1996 by
Prentice Hall
Simon & Schuster (Asia) Pte Ltd
317 Alexandra Road
#04-01 IKEA Building
Singapore 159965

Printed in Singapore

1 2 3 4 5 00 99 98 97 96

ISBN 0-13-713307-3
ISBN 0-13-267915-9 (pbk)

Prentice Hall International (UK) Limited, *London*
Prentice Hall of Australia Pty. Limited, *Sydney*
Prentice Hall Canada Inc., *Toronto*
Prentice Hall Hispanoamericana, *S.A., Mexico*
Prentice Hall of India Private Limited, *New Delhi*
Prentice Hall of Japan, Inc., *Tokyo*
Editora Prentice Hall do Brasil, Ltda., *Rio de Janeiro*
Prentice Hall, Inc., *Upper Saddle River, New Jersey*

CONTENTS

ABOUT THE EDITORS

TAN TECK MENG is Professor and Dean at the Nanyang Business School of Singapore. Since joining the academia in the early 1970s, Professor Tan has combined his university responsibilities with extensive consultancy work, largely in the field of accountancy. He holds senior positions on a number of institutional boards and committees in Singapore including the Accounting and Auditing Services Working Group of the Economic Committee, the Public Accountants Board, the Board of Directors of Singapore Reinsurance Corporation Limited, the Institute of Certified Public Accountants of Singapore (ICPAS) Annual Report Award Competition Committee and the Income Tax Board of Review. Professor Tan is founding Director of the Entrepreneurship Development Centre (ENDEC) and in 1992 was elected to the Board of Governors of the MIT Sloan School of Management Society for Senior Executives. He is a council member of the ICPAS.

LOW AIK MENG is Associate Professor and Director of the MBA programme at the Nanyang Business School. He worked for five years as an accountant and an internal auditor before joining the academia in 1975. He was Vice-Dean of the Faculty of Accountancy and Business Administration at the National University of Singapore until he joined the Nanyang Technological University in 1987. He is currently Vice-Dean at the Nanyang Business School and the Director of its very successful MBA programme since its inception in 1991. Under his leadership, the MBA programme built a network of contacts with businesses and government bodies in Singapore and overseas. He spearheads the thrice-yearly Business Study Missions which are an integral part of the MBA programme. Associate Professor Low continues to be active in the accountancy profession and serves on several committees in the Institute of Certified Public Accountants of Singapore.

JOHN J. WILLIAMS is Associate Professor at the Nanyang Business School and Chief Coordinator of the MBA Business Study Mission programme. He has taught and carried out research projects in several countries including Canada, the United States, Kenya and Singapore. Throughout the latter part of the 1980s, Associate Professor Williams served as Vice-Chairman and Chairman of the Final Accreditation Examination Board for the Society of Management Accountants of Canada, which admitted him as a Fellow in the Society in 1992. Although active in consulting for government agencies in the United States and Canada during this period, he has published extensively in leading academic and professional journals and he continues to pursue the study of emerging regional economies in the ASEAN region.

LUIS MA. R. CALINGO was the Chairman of the MBA Business Study Mission to the Philippines. He is Programme Director for MBA (International Business) and Head of the Division of Human Resource and Quality Management at Nanyang Technological University. Prior to his joining the Nanyang Business School, Dr. Calingo worked for ten years at the California State University in Fresno, where he last served as Dean of the Sid Craig School of Business. He also held visiting appointments at the University of the Philippines, as a Fellow of the United Nations Development Programme. Dr. Calingo has been acting as a consultant/trainer in strategic planning, total quality management and managing cultural differences, to several business and not-for-profit organisations in the United States and South-east Asia. He actively contributed to the formulation and implementation of Singapore's National Quality Strategy, and currently serves on the Board of Assessors for the 1996 Singapore Quality Award. Dr. Calingo has been certified by the American Society for Quality Control as a quality auditor and is author of *The Corporate Guide to the Singapore Quality Award*.

PREFACE

The Master of Business Administration (MBA) programme of the Nanyang Business School at Nanyang Technological University requires participants to complete a Business Study Mission (BSM) before graduation. The purpose of these visits to other countries is to expose MBA participants to business opportunities and the realities of doing business in cultural environments different from that of Singapore.

Singapore and the Philippines are at the crossroads of cultivating a new economic partnership. This partnership assumed a higher level with the launch of the Philippines–Singapore Business Council in October 1994 in Singapore which was attended by President Fidel V. Ramos of the Philippines and Prime Minister Goh Chok Tong of Singapore. In February 1995, Singapore President, Ong Teng Cheong, visited the Philippines shortly after the highly successful trip of a Singaporean delegation headed by the Minister of Trade, Yeo Cheow Tong. Fittingly, the Nanyang Business School organised a BSM to the Philippines from 27 February to 5 March 1995. The BSM enabled our delegates to take advantage of the economic partnership forged by the respective leaders of the two countries.

The Philippines was chosen because the 1986 People Power Revolution elevated the country to a new level of economic aspirations and potential development. The major impetus to move forward as an emerging industrialised economy is manifested in the "Philippines 2000 Vision" which foresees large reductions in poverty, increased employment and industrial production, controlled inflation rate of 4% annually and a doubling of the gross domestic product to 10% annually, all before the end of the century. To facilitate this dramatic turnaround, the Ramos government has introduced full foreign ownership in most areas of business activity, added flexibility to investment structures such as build-operate-transfer schemes and pledged full government support to tax relief export-processing zones such as Cavite and Subic Bay

Freeport, among other business incentives. It is clear that the opportunities for trade, commerce and investment have never been more positive.

Comprising 67 faculty members and MBA participants, the delegation evaluated emerging investment opportunities through corporate visits, academic and business seminars, interaction with leading pro-business government officials and visits to two export-processing zones: Cavite and Subic Bay. In Manila, small groups were formed to conduct visits and interviews at Integrated Microelectronics Inc., the Center for Research and Communication Library, the School of Labor and Industrial Relations at the University of the Philippines, Ayala Land Inc., Globe Telecom, China Banking Corporation, Megalink Inc., Asian Institute of Management, Board of Investments One-Stop Action Center, the Philippine Stock Exchange and SGV & Co. Manila was also the venue for two symposia. The first was on 'Business Opportunities in the Philippines' while the theme of the second was on 'Doing Business in the Philippines'.

In Subic Bay, we were privileged to be hosted by the Chairman of the Subic Bay Metropolitan Authority. A guided tour of the massive infrastructure facilities inherited from the U.S. Navy, together with an on-site seminar featuring investment developments in the export zone, generated a vast amount of information. Equally impressive was our visit to the Cavite Export Processing Zone in Rosario, Cavite, where we were hosted by the Chief Administrator of the Cavite Export Procession Zone Authority. Finally, our delegation visited Tagaytay City, Cavite, overlooking the picturesque Taal lake and volcano, for a seminar on investment opportunities in the Philippine Tourism Industry hosted by the Department of Tourism.

The above programme contributed enormous insights into investment opportunities and exciting areas of economic development in the Philippines, and the contents of this book are a distillation of the total experience by our delegation. While there are many linkages suggested between Singapore and the Philippines, the editors believe that the real scope of the contents is borderless. We hope, therefore, that it will appeal to merchant buyers both in and out of the Philippines, to entrepreneurs contemplating setting up businesses in the Philippines, to external evaluators of marketing strategy and sales distribution whether directly or through the setting up of subsidiaries in the Philippines, to educational researchers, and to executives and managers anticipating employment in the government or industry in the Philippines.

Editors:
TAN Teck Meng
LOW Aik Meng
John J. WILLIAMS
Luis Ma R. CALINGO

ACKNOWLEDGEMENTS

The efforts of many individuals, organisations and institutions are responsible for the success of this Business Study Mission to the Philippines. Thanks to Mr. Hoe Eng Hock, President of Keppel Philippines Holdings for his briefing on a Singaporean perspective of doing business in the Philippines immediately after our landing in Manila. Without the many site visits in Manila, our visit would have been more ordinary and, thus, many thanks to Ms. Gloria L. Tan Climaco, Chairwoman, and Mr. Gerard B. Sanvictores, Partner, of SGV & Co. and to Mr. Jose P. Leviste, Jr., Chairman of Pacific Rim Innovation and Management Exponents, Inc., for organising our corporate visits. In particular, thanks to Mr. Edgardo A. Paynor, Vice-President for Business Development, Integrated Microelectronics, Inc.; Ms. Liew Hui Ping, Economist, Center for Research and Communication Library; Professor Marie E. Aganon, Dean, School of Labor and Industrial Relations at the University of the Philippines; Ms. Helen Lazo, Ayala Land, Inc.; Mr. Filemon T. Berba, Jr., President, Globe Telecom; Mr. Alexander C. Escucha, Vice-President for Strategic Planning, China Banking Corporation; Ms. Carol E. Carreon, Senior Vice-President and General Manager, Megalink, Inc.; Professors Borromeo, de Guzman, and Lopez, Asian Institute of Management; Eloisa Atienza-Lim, Director, Board of Investments One-Stop Action Center; Mr. Jaime del Rosario, Managing Director, Andersen Consulting; Mr. Eduardo de los Angeles, President, Philippine Stock Exchange; and Mr. Orlando Zorilla, Partner, SGV & Co., for hosting our MBA participants in hours of brainstorming.

We are extremely grateful for the in-depth knowledge and experience brought to the symposia by the speakers and we thank The Honourable Dr. Dante B. Canlas, Under-secretary of Socio-economic Planning and Deputy Director General, National Economic and Development Authority; The Honourable Melito S. Salazar, Governor, Board of Investments; Mr. Efren V. Leano, Director of Investment

Marketing Department, Board of Investments; Mr. Gerard B. Sanvictores, Partner, SGV & Co.; Dr. Jerome F. Sison, Vice-President for Operations, Pacific Rim Innovation and Management Exponents, Inc.; and Mr. Alberto V. Reyes, Managing Director, Bangko Sentral ng Pilipinas. Thanks also to Dr. Neo Boon Siong, Director of NTU's Information Management Research Centre, for presenting Singapore's experience in IT policy analysis.

Indeed, we were very fortunate to have among our speakers and hosts four of the most dynamic, pro-business political leaders and administrators in the Philippines. Special thanks to The Honourable Jose C. de Venecia, Jr., Speaker of the House of Representatives, for his opening banquet address; to The Honourable Cesar B. Bautista, Undersecretary, Department of Trade and Commerce, for his welcoming speech at the symposium series; to The Honourable Richard J. Gordon, Chairman of the Subic Bay Metropolitan Authority, for hosting our Subic Bay visit; and to Rear Admiral (Retired) Tagumpay R. Jardiniano, Administrator of the Cavite Export Processing Zone Authority, for guiding our delegation around the many garment and electronics factories, and responding to countless questions on investment potential in the zone.

For serving as our resource persons in Singapore and facilitating our contacts with the Philippine government, thanks to Ambassador Alicia C. Ramos, to the Commercial Attaches, Mr. Eugene Reyes and Mr. Salvador Quiniquini, and to the Tourism Attache, Ms. Janet Blancaflor. Thanks also to the many speakers who gave their time and knowledge at the pre-trip seminars. Of course, we enriched our cultural understanding of the Philippines through visits to historic sites and we appreciate the hospitable greetings from the people at the Malacanang Palace, Intramuros, Fort Santiago and Chinatown, among others.

Finally, we extend many thanks to Grace Cheng and Adelene Ang for their tireless administrative efforts before and during the trip, to the MBA Office, to the MBA participants for their enthusiasm, to Prentice Hall for their guidance, and to Alison Soo for her patience and diligence in bringing this book to completion.

BUSINESS ENVIRONMENT

Chapter 1

Investment Potential in the Philippines: An Overview

BY
TAN Teck Meng
LOW Aik Meng
John J. WILLIAMS
Luis Ma. R. CALINGO

INTRODUCTION

ON 13 OCTOBER 1994, Philippine President Fidel V. Ramos and Singapore Prime Minister Goh Chok Tong were the guests-of-honour at the launching of the Philippines–Singapore Business Council. The Council was formed to encourage Singapore businessmen and their Filipino counterparts to cooperate and take advantage of the business opportunities in the Philippines, Singapore and the Asia-Pacific region. The launch of the Council was a testimony to the Philippines's commitment to achieve its objective of becoming a newly industrialised economy (NIE) by the year 2000.

The earliest recorded trade between the Philippines and its East Asian neighbours was in the ninth century when indigenous Filipinos started trading with the Chinese and the Indonesians. The colonisation of the Philippine islands by Spain via Mexico brought about the galleon trade between Manila and Acapulco, the first recorded trans-Pacific trade between Asia and North America. However, four centuries of Spanish rule did not stop the Philippines's trade with East Asia. By the early 17th century, immigrant Chinese traders, predominantly from the Fujian province, had economically surpassed the Spanish. Therefore, it is not surprising that when the Philippines recently shifted from an inward-oriented trade policy to an outward-oriented, free-market approach, one of the country's earliest moves was the strengthening of trade ties with Singapore and other ASEAN countries.

Currently, Singapore ranks as the sixth largest foreign investor in the Philippines. The Philippine Board of Investments (BOI) projected that Singaporean firms pumped at least P1.2 billion worth of investments into the Philippines during the first seven months of 1994. Singapore's trade with the Philippines has also been healthy. Singapore was the Philippines's third largest trading partner in 1994. The total Philippine trade for 1994 was registered at US$1.4 billion worth of imports from Singapore and US$706.7 million worth of exports to Singapore. The new economic partnership forged between Singapore and the Philippines was augmented further through recent visits to the Philippines by leading businessmen and top government officials from Singapore. To add perspective to the contents of this book, we deem it important to understand the Philippines's developmental setting and to provide an overall market assessment of the Philippines.

THE PHILIPPINE DEVELOPMENT CHALLENGE

The period from 1986 to 1994 witnessed lasting gains in the restoration of the Philippines's democratic political institutions, a process that has come to be symbolised by the 1986 People Power Revolution. The Philippine government has outlined the task of Filipinos of this generation as building on these democratic foundations and transforming the country into a newly industrialised economy (NIE). These aspirations and plans are articulated in the Medium-Term Philippines Development Plan 1993 to 1998, more popularly known as the "Philippines 2000 Vision".

The Philippines 2000 Vision seeks to achieve the following overall development targets:

1. Reduce poverty incidence from 39.2% of Filipino households in 1991 to about 30% by 1998.
2. Generate an average of 1.1 million jobs per year from 1994 to 1998,

thereby reducing the unemployment rate from 9.1% in 1994 to 6.6% in 1998.

3. Achieve growth in gross national product (GNP), in real terms, at an average of 5.7 to 7.4% over the period 1994 to 1998, with growth accelerating from 3.5 to 4.5% in 1994, to 8.5 to 10.0% by 1998. The major source of growth will be investments and exports which are targeted to grow at a double-digit rate.
4. Achieve growth in gross domestic product (GDP) from a rate of 3.4 to 4.4% in 1994, to 8.1 to 9.8% in 1998. Industrial production outside the Metropolitan Manila area will increase from 70% of GDP in 1994 to 72% of GDP in 1998.
5. Reduce inflation from 9 to 10% in 1994 to 4% in 1998.
6. Increase investment's share of GNP from 24.5% in 1994 to 29.5% by 1998 with the private sector providing the bulk. To finance these investments, domestic savings will increase from 19.8% of GNP in 1994 to 27.8% by 1998.
7. Reduce the population growth rate from 2.36% in 1990 to less than 2% by 1998, simultaneously with efforts to reduce population density.

The magnitude of effort called for can be seen by comparing the Philippines's current position with those of other ASEAN member-countries. In 1990, the Philippines's per capita GNP was US$730, exceeding only Indonesia's. The Philippines had the lowest annual growth rate in per capita GNP for the period 1965 to 1992. Growing annually at this rate (1.3%), it would take 53 years for the country's per capita output to double. With production and GDP growing slowly, and at times even declining, a large number of Filipino households continue to live in poverty. Although poverty incidence had declined from 44.2% in 1985 to 39.2% in 1991, the absolute number of poor Filipino families continues to increase.

Rapid population growth continues to be a constraint to raising per capita income. The 1990 census of Philippine households placed the population at 60.7 million, growing at an annual rate of 2.4%. With this growth rate, the population would double in 30 years. A large family cannot accumulate enough savings and bequeath adequate amounts of capital to their children. Population pressure also weakens the capacity of the government to provide enough investment in human capital. Further, high population density contributes to the degradation of the environment, making it exceedingly difficult to provide for future generations.

Another factor that has worked against sustained growth has been the periodic recurrence of serious balance-of-payment crises. Except for the last few years, regulatory policies and incentives have prevented domestic industries from developing along the lines of comparative advantage. Industrialisation has been frustrated by inadequate foreign exchange earnings and heavy reliance on imported inputs. During the 1980s, the Philippine economy became more vulnerable to crisis because of heavy debt repayments to creditors and poor investment inflows.

The most recent crisis began in 1990. In response to an externally induced serious macroeconomic imbalance, the Philippine government adopted a stabilisation programme and momentarily set aside its growth objectives. To reduce inflation, tight fiscal and monetary policies were instituted. To address the widening current account and budgetary deficits, taxes and spending cuts were imposed. A succession of natural disasters (such as the Mt. Pinatubo eruption) and the pressures from the external payments deficit, all contributed to the 1991 contraction of the economy.

There have been signs that the most recent decline in output has bottomed out and that the urgent reasons for stabilisation have diminished. Nominal interest rates have fallen and inflation has remained at single-digit levels. The Philippine economy finally took off in 1994 as the supply of electricity stabilised and foreign investor confidence improved. Real GDP grew by 4.3% in 1994, driven by strong growth in exports and overall recovery by the industrial sector. Foreign exchange reserves climbed to a record level; receipts from privatised government assets exceeded expectations; and a medium-term deal with the International Monetary Fund was sealed. In the meantime, the momentum of reforms has been sustained, the latest being the liberalisation of foreign exchange rules. A continuation of these trends is a signal to the rest of the world that a revival of growth on a healthier level is imminent, and that the Philippines is ready to explore its economic potential in an open and competitive world market-place.

MARKET ASSESSMENT

Historically, the Philippines has followed an essentially protectionist foreign trade policy aimed at promoting input substitution. In 1991, towards the end of President Corazon C. Aquino's term, this inward-oriented policy was supplanted by an outward-oriented policy that future political administrations will find difficult to reverse. Trade liberalisation has continued under President Ramos, and even some areas that have had strong domestic–producer lobbies (such as sugar, corn, poultry, livestock and other key agricultural commodities), have been programmed for trade regulation.

Admittedly, doing business in the Philippines has drawbacks. The main ones are: (a) the high cost of nationwide distribution, owing to the Philippines's archipelagic geography and poor transport infrastructure; (b) local consumers' relatively limited purchasing power, with more than one-half of the country's total income flowing to the richest 20% of the population; and (c) a relatively high degree of wage control. However, Keppel Corporation, Singapore Telecom, and a growing number of other Singaporean businesses, have overcome these obstacles and have reaped first-mover advantages in the Philippines.

The Philippines definitely offers several advantages. First, it has a relatively stable administration committed to further reforms in the economy. President Ramos's programme of negotiations has eased the internal security threat from the Philippines's three main rebel factions (Muslim secessionists, communist insurgents and military rebels). Improved executive–legislative relations have resulted in the passage of policy reforms being smoother and less argumentative.

A second advantage is a generally positive attitude towards foreign investment. The Ramos administration espouses an inviting policy towards foreign investments. The Foreign Investments Act (FIA) of 1991, Republic Act (RA) 7042, allows full foreign ownership in any business activity, except in sectors limited by the Philippine Constitution or other existing laws. Among the recent liberalisation moves are RA 7721, which eases restrictions on the entry and operation of foreign banks, and amendments to the Build–Operate–Transfer (BOT) Law (RA 7718) which increases the opportunity for wholly foreign-owned corporations to undertake projects. Although there are no official figures available on the overall performance of Singaporean investments in the Philippines, the U.S. Department of Commerce data indicate an average return on

U.S. investment of 23.8% in 1993. The return on U.S. manufacturing investments is 25.7%.

A third advantage arises from the emerging special economic zones that make the Philippines an attractive base for manufacturing export products. The export processing zones (EPZs) accounted for US$2.7 billion, or about 20.1% of the Philippines's total exports, in 1994. The Master of Business Administration (MBA) Business Study Mission (BSM) visited two of these EPZs: the Cavite EPZ, located immediately south of Metropolitan Manila, and the Subic Bay Freeport which was created from the former Subic Naval Base of the U.S. Navy's Seventh Fleet.

An additional advantage comes from the increasing receptiveness of family-owned corporations to joint ventures with foreign firms. Many family-owned Filipino corporations have been shifting to professional management under second-generation ownership. This paves the way for large investment projects in which significant local participation is required (such as the setting up of a finance company or acquisition of land) or desirable (such as when local companies can contribute marketing expertise).

A fifth advantage relates to the decline in tariffs and other import barriers. The Philippines participates in the Common Effective Preferential Tariff (CEPT) scheme which calls for a reduction of tariffs on intra-ASEAN trade. Tariff rates will be cut to a range of 0% to 20% by 2003, five years ahead of the previously planned reduction by 2008. Current tariff rates below 20% will be cut to between 0% and 20%, and those above 20% will be cut to 20%.

The last significant advantage results from an English-speaking, highly trainable labour force. Expected investment inflows are inadequate to absorb the annual growth in the labour force which is estimated at an average of 850,000 entrants per year. Filipino workers are well regarded, particularly overseas, because of their high literacy rate, good grasp of English and readiness to learn. Overseas contract workers (OCWs) from the Philippines contributed substantially to the Philippine economy through remittances of their earnings – some 641,500 OCWs remitted about US$2.1 billion during the period January to November 1994.

SELECTION OF PERSPECTIVES FOR STUDY

In selecting programmes of study for the BSM and ultimately, this book, it was patently evident at the outset that all aspects of the Philippine economy were viable alternatives. But of course, it was not possible to examine every aspect under the given constraints. Therefore, our research was directed to sectors of the economy which had been impacted significantly by major policy reforms.

We were privileged to have two distinguished individuals who were keenly aware of emerging developments on the Philippine economic front address our delegation, first in Singapore and then in the Philippines. In Singapore, Her Excellency, Alicia C. Ramos, Ambassador of the Republic of the Philippines, spoke to our delegation and the substance of her presentation is set forth in Chapter 2. Her Excellency provided answers to two questions: 1) Why is the Philippines described as having the most upside potential among South-east Asian countries?; and 2) What are the conditions that will propel the Philippines towards achieving substantial long-term growth?

In the Philippines, Dante B. Canlas, Deputy Director General of the National Economic and Development Authority, spoke on economic policy reforms and the vision of Philippines 2000, which forms the substance of Chapter 3. Canlas provided a rich synopsis of the long-term development objectives under Philippines 2000. He described the government's basic policy reform programme and the recent achievements under the programme.

With these chapters providing a framework of the current business environment in the Philippines, the following study programmes were chosen as the focus of this book: 1) financial markets and banking; 2) foreign investment, accounting and taxation; 3) industry analyses; and 4) regional growth centres. Each of these areas builds upon, and extends, various investment perspectives supplemented by information gleaned from site visits and seminars while in the Philippines.

FINANCIAL MARKETS AND BANKING

This section comprised five chapters. Two papers deal with the Philippine Stock Exchange (PSE). In Chapter 4, Ong *et al.* discuss the historical development of the PSE including the merger of the Manila and Makati exchanges in August 1992. After a discussion of new reforms impacting the governance of the PSE, attention is focused on market regulation of the exchange. The latter part of the chapter examines the recent performance of the PSE, and includes data for 1993, 1994 and the early part of 1995. It then assesses potential opportunities in eight different market sectors before concluding with some environmental factors that might limit investor confidence in the PSE.

Chapter 5 also deals with the PSE but provides some insight into the operational efficiency of the exchange arising from the computerised linking of the Manila and Makati trading floors. Ng *et al.* then survey the benefits and downside problems of converting to scripless trading, a strategy that the PSE is considering implementing to become more competitive with global markets. The authors comment on the inevitability of this decision if the PSE is to compete with other Asian exchanges in the future.

The Philippine banking system is discussed in two study programmes. One is macro and descriptive. In Chapter 6, Ng and Yong provide a comprehensive overview of the structural characteristics of the Philippine banking system. After presenting an historical account of the evolution of the central bank and its structure, the authors portray the characteristics of commercial banks, thrift banks, specialised government banks and rural banks. In particular, a detailed review of banking regulations which covers capital fund requirements, capital adequacy ratio, liquidity requirements and bank supervision is presented. The chapter concludes with the observation that potential investors can be assured of confidence in the Philippine banking system and enumerates four strategies to improve on this confidence level in a deregulated environment.

The second paper dealing with banking is more micro and empirical. Chapter 7 assesses the performance of Philippine commercial banks using a strategic response quotient indicator to analyse a sample of 14 local banks and contrasts this measure with more traditional measures of bank performance. The authors conclude that commercial banks appear to be responding adequately to the changing business environment in the Philippines. This is good news for the investing community because it reduces one more risk factor in the potential investment decision.

Chapter 8, the last in this section, summarises several monetary reforms enacted by the Ramos government and sets forth the functions of the new Central Monetary Authority (CMA) which oversees policy changes in the areas of money, banking and credit. In particular, attention is focused on the foreign exchange market, the money market and the newly emerging derivatives market. The chapter concludes with a brief overview of the liberalisation policy relating to foreign bank entry.

FOREIGN DIRECT INVESTMENT, ACCOUNTING AND TAXATION

There are three study programmes in this section and they largely pertain to institutional aspects which overarch investment opportunities in the Philippines. Chapter 9 is concerned with the legal foundation behind different forms of direct foreign investment (FDI). Laure *et al.* summarise the main features contained in the FIA of 1991. Next, they offer advantages and disadvantages associated with five types of FDI including joint ventures, 100% foreign-owned enterprises and built-operate-transfer (BOT) schemes. The authors conclude their analyses of FDIs with three specific examples to illustrate the different investment types.

Chapter 10 gives attention to accounting standards in the Philippines. Because of the vast domain of generally accepted accounting principles, Chan *et al.* choose six specialised areas in which to contrast the similarities and differences between the Philippines and Singapore and, in turn, to identify their congruence with international accounting standards. The six areas discussed are prudent because they complement the forms of FDI presented in Chapter 9.

Chapter 11 focuses specifically on the tax system in the Philippines as it relates to FDIs. Like Chapter 10, it is comparative, and draws out the unique differences between the tax systems of Singapore and the Philippines. In pursuing this comparative analysis, Loo *et al.* concentrate on the corporate and joint venture forms of FDI that were elaborated upon in Chapter 9. The authors differentiate, among other issues, incentives available to registered enterprises, to registered enterprises in less developed areas of the Philippines and to enterprises located in EPZs. They conclude the chapter with three practical tax incentive suggestions for potential investors.

INDUSTRY ANALYSES

Five chapters comprise this section of the book and they deal with different sectors of the economy ranging from tourism and hotels to electronics and telecommunications. These sectors were chosen as study programmes because they are on the leading edge of high-profile industries in the Philippines's expansionary plans. Chapter 12 adopts a particularly unique approach to the impacts of tourism on the Philippines. Ng *et al.* identify five factors, such as volume of visitor arrivals and socio-cultural characteristics, which lead to economic, environmental, social and cultural consequences for the Philippines. The authors argue that these impacts are often overlooked by potential investors, but that cultivating an awareness of them can enhance positive host-country reactions and, thus, stimulate successful investment opportunities.

In Chapter 13, Chan *et al.* initially review the hotel industry's strengths and weaknesses within Porter's diamond framework. This framework looks at factor industries, demand conditions, related and supporting industries, and the context for competition. After this assessment, the authors examine several current issues facing the industry which include owners, market potential, human resources and investment incentives, among others. The chapter closes with a discussion that underscores the vital importance of securing trained human resources in this industry.

The supply of labour and its integration into the workforce is an essential feature of sustained economic growth. Of particular interest to investors is the quality of the workforce and the quality of management resources. Chapter 14 assesses the former by providing data on sources of employment, educational profile, training, labour–management relations and unions. The authors discuss quality of management in terms of internal and external sources, identify extant examples of organisations in the Philippines with excellent management practices and synthesise reports of studies that have ranked Philippine management practices with other countries. Gan *et al.* conclude that the Filipino workforce has highly desirable characteristics which contribute to a national competitive advantage *vis-à-vis* other countries in the region.

Chapter 15 turns its attention to the telecommunications sector in the Philippines. Too *et al.* first examine the government's framework for deregulation of the industry before discussing future needs of the country. Specifically, the estimated size of the telephone market, current operators, tentative government solutions, and potential risks are considered. Finally, the authors examine a telecommunications joint venture company with partners from the Philippines and Singapore. Chapter 16 pursues more high-technology industries with a special focus on the electronics industry. In this chapter, Gouw *et al.* deal with the potential of supporting industries and the structure of the export markets in order to give investors a sense of the magnitude of opportunities. The authors also mention opportunities in a variety of export processing zones (EPZs) across the country. The authors conclude their analyses with primary data on two firms in the industry and suggest that electronics is a lucrative alternative for investors in the Philippines.

REGIONAL GROWTH CENTRES

The final section of this book is devoted to two study programmes related to site visits by research teams. In Chapter 17, Ong and Chong analyse the advantages of Cebu as a locational centre for investment opportunities. They discuss a number of competitive advantages including markets, labour availability, infrastructure conditions and so forth. The Mactan EPZ is highlighted, given its close proximity to Cebu. The authors also provide an interesting list of priority areas for investment currently endorsed by the government.

Finally, in Chapter 18, Chua *et al.* assess one of the future investment gems in the Asia-Pacific region, namely Subic Bay. They begin with a background of the U.S. Navy's withdrawal and the assets remaining with this re-positioning. However, despite these attractions and the special export zone status, there are numerous conversion problems which need to be overcome. Nonetheless, the authors document the success of Subic Bay to date and recommend several rich areas for investment. They conclude on a positive note that Subic Bay has all the ingredients for future economic success.

Chapter 2

Back in Business in the Heart of Asia: Business Opportunities and Investment Climate in the Philippines

BY
Alicia C. RAMOS[1]

FIRST OF ALL, I would like to thank Dr. Luis Calingo for the invitation to participate as one of the resource persons for this seminar. I also wish to congratulate the Nanyang Technological University (NTU), School of Accountancy and Business, for organising the Business Study Mission to Manila for 60 of its participants in the MBA Programme. It is said that the Philippines is Asia's best-kept secret. For one, its good points are not easily discernible, while its bad news is always touted loudly. But those who have lived there, or even visited, come to know and feel the real values of the country. Foreign investors have realised this, as well as retirees from other countries.

Your trip is indeed timely, for the year 1994 marks a year of economic recovery, record

[1] Excerpts of paper read at the Business Study Mission Seminar held in Singapore, 26 November 1994.
Her Excellency Alicia C. Ramos, Ambassador of the Republic of the Philippines.

capital inflows, improved public finances and political stability in the Philippines. As President Ramos has said, "We are back in business in the heart of Asia." I would also like to quote an assessment from Salomon Brothers Inc.: "We believe that the Philippine economy is in its strongest position in the past decade and that the conditions are now firmly in place for achieving sustainable growth."

Why is the Philippines suddenly being described as the country in South-east Asia with the most upside potential with respect to sovereign ratings? What are the conditions which are now existing that will allow the Philippines to achieve sustainable long-term growth?

PERFORMANCE OF THE ECONOMY

Based on the preliminary estimates of the National Statistical Coordination Board (NSCB), gross national product (GNP), adjusted for inflation, grew by 5.4% in the third quarter of 1994, an improvement over the 4.3% growth rate in the same quarter in 1993. This outpaces the 4.7% growth of the first quarter of 1994. Real gross domestic production (GDP) meanwhile, surged with a growth rate of 4.5% in the second quarter as compared to 2.6% last year.

Agriculture joined the recovery in the second quarter with a growth rate of 5.2% as compared to 4.5% in the same period last year. Industry, meanwhile, posted a growth rate of 5.1%, better than the 2.1% growth posted in the second quarter of 1993. Services came in with a 3.7% growth rate which improved from last year's 1.9%.

On the expenditure side, investments and gross exports continued to fuel the economic expansion. The continued build-up in inventories enabled gross domestic capital formation to grow by 16.4% in the second quarter as compared to only 5.2% in the same period last year. Gross exports accelerated by 20.5%, a substantial improvement over the 9.2% growth recorded last year.

The recovery is clearly gaining momentum, buoyed by the continued rebound of domestic production and sustained inflows of net factor income from abroad. As a result, GNP and GDP expanded by 5.1% and 4.1%, respectively, for the first semester of 1994. The strong comeback of the agriculture sector in the second quarter, continuing recovery of the world economy, and rising consumer and investor confidence, all contributed to the impressive economic performance during the semester.

On the production side, industry grew by 6.1% in the first semester, reversing the decline in the same semester in 1993. For the different sub-sectors of industry, only mining and quarrying remained sluggish as coal production continued to decline while copper exports remained soft, partly due to a slack in demand by the country's traditional trading partners.

Following the growth in industry, services expanded by 3.6% in the first semester as compared to 1.8% in 1993. The financial sector and private services, particularly tourism-related services, posted the highest growth rates of 5.2% and 4.2%, respectively.

Among the major production sectors, only the agriculture, fishery and forestry sector slowed down, posting a growth rate of 2.2% as compared to 3.2% recorded during the same period last year. The strong recovery of the sector in the second quarter was dampened by the decline in the first quarter. Palay, corn, livestock, and other agricultural activities and services, posted higher production growth rates during the semester, offsetting the decline/slowdown in the production of coconut, sugarcane, banana, fishery, forestry and poultry products.

On the expenditure side, the improved performance of the economy during the first semester was led by the private sector. Private-consumption expenditures, capital investment and exports posted much higher growth rates as compared to the same period last year.

Gross capital formation increased by 16.6% as compared to last year's 5.2%. This was on account of the continued build-up in inventories during the semester and strong fixed capital investments. The latter posted a slower growth of 10.1% *vis-à-vis* last year's 12.1%, but its contribution to GNP rose to 24% from 22.9% during the first semester of 1993.

Consumer spending grew by 3.7%, against last year's spending of 2.7%. The continuous improvement in the power situation raised household incomes and bolstered consumer confidence. The lower unemployment rate in April and the increase in rural incomes brought about by the second-quarter recovery of agriculture also contributed to the rise in consumer expenditures during the period.

Government spending recovered slightly at 0.7%, reversing the 9.7% contraction last year. The growth of public construction slowed down to 13.6% in the first semester as compared to the 18% growth for the first half of 1993, as private construction began to take a stronger role in construction growth. Private construction grew at 13.5% in the first semester, an acceleration over last year's growth of 9.4%.

Based on the above aggregate of sectoral performance, it is reasonable to conclude that private-sector production is responding positively to the public investments in power and other infrastructure, and to the public policy measures designed for macroeconomic stability, deregulation and heightened competition in the private sector.

Debt service is estimated at a manageable 18 to 19%, despite an overall rise in foreign debt. Negotiations with the International Monetary Fund (IMF) on a three-year extended fund facility were successfully concluded. This could produce commitments of further economic assistance from the international community in the order of P2 billion annually. It also implies a "good housekeeping seal of approval" for the Philippines's economic management and another positive signal to potential foreign investors. The following is a recapitulation:

1. US$684 million, three-year programme with IMF (to serve an "exist" facility).
2. Completed a modified Paris Club bilateral rescheduling of approximately 20% of the Republic of Philippines's bilateral debt due between July 1994 and December 1995.
3. Pledge from donors – total of P2.8 billion (P1.5 billion from Japan).

POLITICAL FACTORS

President Ramos has stated that democracy's advantages – predictability, transparency and continuity – enhance the business climate because these factors can reduce uncertainty. The President held an "economic summit" of the executive and legislative branches of government in August, and a multi-sectoral people's economic summit in September. The latter led to a "social pact for empowered economic development".

The President belongs to the Lakas (people power) NUCD–UMDP party. It is a coalition of the National Union of Christian Democrats (NUCD) and the United Muslim Democrats of the Philippines (UMDP). The principles of this coalition are:

1. People empowerment – political, social and economic.
2. Devolution and decentralisation (contained in encyclicals of Pope Leo XIII – 19th Century). President Aquino added deregulation; and

President Ramos added democratisation.

3. Sustainable development – to protect the environment, to safeguard resources, and to train people so that the next generation will enjoy an even higher standard of living.

President Ramos looks to the political opposition as a most helpful ally to ensure checks and balances. Moreover, President Ramos consolidated his position with a recent alliance forged in congress between Lakas–NUCD and the opposition Laban Ng Demokratikong Pilipino. The President has a high approval rating, exceeding 60%, and it is predicted that he is likely to make further gains in the May 1995 congressional and local elections.

With his political skills, the President has been able to push through his administration's critical legislative agenda. Some of the bills which have been passed are the following:

(a) Repeal of the Anti-Subversion Law.
(b) Electric Power Crisis Act of 1993.
(c) Creation of the Central Monetary Authority.
(d) Setting elections for ARM (autonomous region of Muslim Mindanao).
(e) Creation of the Subic Bay Metropolitan Authority.
(f) Bank Liberalisation Law.
(g) Expanded value-added tax (VAT).
(h) Amendments to Build-Operate-Transfer (BOT) Law.
(i) Deregulation of various aspects of telecommunications, foreign exchange regime, banking sector, trade, investments, finance and industry.
(j) Senate ratified accession to multilateral investment guarantee agreement.
(k) Introduction of tax and non-tax incentives and duty-free importation of capital for enterprises engaged in preferred areas and registered with BOI.

The creation of the National Unification Commission set the groundwork for a comprehensive peace process with the Moro National Liberation Front (MNLF), the military rebels and the National Democratic Front. These insurgent, rebel and secessionist groups have dwindled in size as the world political situation changed and as they become co-opted into the peace negotiations. A presidential anticrime commission was also formed to wage an all-out war against criminality, particularly the "kidnap for ransom" syndicates.

Of course, we recognise that the country has many problems to overcome and to solve, and that certain critical factors are necessary to sustain economic growth. Although the Philippines's rate of growth may be low when compared with the "Asian Tigers", it compares favourably with certain countries in South America. Our low growth rates in the early 1990s can be attributed to natural disasters (in 1993 alone, the Philippines was battered by 32 typhoons), power shortages and the Gulf war.

Let me cite some of these problems and critical factors:

1. Major new investments in plant, equipment and other productive assets are needed.
2. Lagging perception about political stability and security.
3. Infrastructure deficiencies and regulatory bottlenecks. It is crucial to overhaul the transport sector and the road system. There is a need for better land/sea links to weld together a country composed of more than 7,000 islands in a land mass of 600,000 square kilometres.
4. Restructuring and reforms in the financial sector to support mobilising capital resources. Rates of saving and investment are still low.
5. Continuation of government's programme to liberalise the financial sector.
6. Constraints on funds available for investment. Augment domestic savings with foreign savings or direct foreign investment funds.
7. Legal structure is an impediment for domestic and foreign investment and seems to favour incumbent firms. The perception is that the Philippines is a litigious society. The courts have sometimes issued decisions that are detrimental to foreign investment.
8. Investment ratios remain low.
9. Servicing foreign and domestic debt consumes much of the government's revenue and little is left over for capital spending on roads and other infrastructure. The budget deficit has been 3% of GDP for the past three years.
10. Population growth rate is 2.5%.
11. Natural resources – trees, fish, soil, fresh water – are being consumed or damaged at an alarming pace by 66 million inhabitants.

12. Rural poverty is driving the population to congested urban areas.
13. Natural disasters are unpredictable.
14. Social reforms are needed: Agrarian reform, equity in revenue collection, environmental management, crackdown on crime and corruption, public health and population control, all require change.

With the political will and the quality of development administration which characterises the Philippines today, we are very confident that these problems and challenges can be overcome. We are optimistic that, as a nation, we can push forward and thus realise our vision of Philippines 2000. I look forward to a constructive exchange with you on these issues.

Thank you and good day to all of you.

Chapter 3

Economic Policy Reforms and Philippines 2000

BY
Dante B.
CANLAS[1]

IT IS A pleasure to be one of the resource persons in this panel discussion on "Business Opportunities in the Philippines". The topic that has been assigned to me is "Philippines's Economic Development: Strategies and Thrusts". I will start with the long-range development objectives under Philippines 2000, President Ramos's vision of development. Next, I will move on to discuss the economic policy reform programme of the government which is spelled out in the Medium-Term Philippines Development Plan for 1993 to 1998. I will then present briefly the recent performance of the economy to illustrate the gains that have been achieved under this programme and the additional economic policy reforms that are in the pipeline.

Paper read at the Symposium on Business Opportunities in the Philippines, Nanyang Technological University, MBA Business Study Mission to the Philippines, 1 March 1995.

1 Dr. Dante B. Canlas, Deputy Director General, National Economic and Development Authority, Philippines.

AN OVERVIEW

Upon assuming office in 1992, President Ramos rallied the country around the vision of Philippines 2000 which seeks to transform an economy that is still largely agricultural into an industrialising one. At this stage, about 45% of the workforce is still in agriculture as either unpaid family workers, self-employed workers or hired workers. The rest of the workforce is distributed almost evenly between industry and services. The task at hand involves shifting workers away from low-paying agricultural pursuits into high-wage, high-skilled jobs in industry and services.

To bring about the desired economic transformation, an important first step being taken is to raise agricultural productivity. As productivity goes up, real earnings rise. But productivity improvements also mean that fewer workers are needed to produce the same agricultural output level. Hence, as part of the overall strategy, industry and services must grow at a sufficiently rapid pace so that excess workers in agriculture will be gainfully employed. For the non-agricultural sector to grow fast, savings and investments must increase, and labour and capital productivity must be enhanced.

Industrialisation has many requirements. Fundamental changes are called for economically, politically and socially. Knowing that political stability, peace and order, and industrial harmony are preconditions for sustained economic growth, the Administration made sure at the very start that the economic programme took this into consideration. Moreover, the development plan stressed two main themes or objectives: international competitiveness and people empowerment. These two goals call for a workforce that is motivated to work hard and inclined to save. This requires enterprises that are prepared to advance in a competitive setting and managers that can instil teamwork and quality consciousness. Equally important is a bureaucracy that is honest and competent as well as a legal and judicial framework that is conducive to contractual performance and adjudication of contractual disputes. And to make sure that market agents are able to plan with minimum uncertainty and become engaged in mutually beneficial trade, the government tries to ensure macroeconomic stability while making adequate investments in the economic and social infrastructure.

These are all emphasised in the Medium-Term Philippines Development Plan for 1993 to 1998, with the following as priority areas:

macroeconomic stability, human resource development and effective governance.

MACROECONOMIC POLICY REFORMS

The guiding principle of the government's economic policy reform programme is increased reliance on the coordination ability of private markets guided by a decentralised price system. Government intervention is selective and one important area is in the conduct of macroeconomic policy. In the 1970s, excessive government spending led to large public-sector deficits. Financing these deficits brought high interest rates and high inflation rates. The latter were largely responsible for the economic stagnation and decline ushered in during the early 1980s.

Thus the starting point of the government's efforts for macroeconomic stability is sound fiscal policy. The public-sector deficit is programmed for reduction, to be balanced eventually over the medium term. To achieve this goal, the government has put in place a programme of reforms for both revenues and expenditures.

On the revenue side, the tax system is moving in the direction of lower average tax rates but applied to a wider and more comprehensive base. The value-added tax, which replaces a variety of sales taxes, is one example. At the same time, since tax administration is tax policy, administrative reforms in the Bureau of Internal Revenue are taking place to improve the tax collection machinery of the government. The bureau, for instance, is being computerised. Similar reforms have been proposed for personal and business income taxes, and these have been submitted to Congress. All of these changes are designed for simplicity and efficiency.

Meanwhile, privatisation of some government enterprises continues to be pursued. This serves not only to raise revenues for the government but, over the long term, the entire economy benefits from the increased output and additional jobs that result from the more efficient running of these enterprises by the private sector.

On the expenditure side, the government has a streamlining programme for the bureaucracy. This puts a lid on spending for personnel services while enabling the government to pursue the objective of the Salary Standardisation Law which is to match productivity gains of public-sector employees with real salary increases. At the same time, careful evaluation of public investments significantly raises the returns from the capital outlay portion of the government's budget. Moreover, the privatisation programme has profoundly reduced subsidies and net lending to government corporations. And as interest rates go down, as a result of successful macroeconomic stabilisation, government interest payments on its outstanding debt decrease.

An integral component of macroeconomic stabilisation, along with fiscal policy, is monetary and exchange rate policy. Monetary policy is guided by the pursuit of price stability. The Bangko Sentral ng Pilipinas (BSP) ensures the money supply is consistent with the demand for it. The exchange rate system in place is a flexible one. The BSP has liberalised foreign exchange transactions aimed at full convertibility of the peso at a market-determined rate. Coordination of fiscal, monetary and exchange rate policy has led to a decline in interest and inflation rates, and has served to reduce fluctuations in the nominal exchange value of the peso, with salutary effects on the overall balance of payments.

TRADE AND INDUSTRIAL POLICY

To bring about long-term industrial restructuring, the government has put in place a package of trade and industrial policy reforms. The industrialisation strategy in place is outward-oriented. It is aimed at making domestic enterprises internationally competitive. In line with this goal, the policy measures involve strengthening the country's links with the rest of the world through trade in goods, services and securities. To achieve this end, the government has been implementing an import liberalisation and tariff reduction programme.

This clearly represents a break from the import substitution policy that was put in place after World War II, a strategy that led to a highly protectionist trade regime, which included import restrictions, and high and widely spread tariff rates. Under that protectionist trade regime, however, serious balance-of-payments crises emerged and endured.

And, so, a policy reform process towards import liberalisation, and a low and narrowly dispersed, preferably uniform, tariff rate structure, were put in place recently. Such a policy environment removes the bias against exports. Import liberalisation enables local entrepreneurs to acquire lower-cost raw materials, capital equipment and technology available worldwide. Inventive activity is encouraged. Resources, including labour and credit, enjoy greater mobility – free to move to sectors where they are most productive.

Executive Order (EO) No. 470, issued on 20 July 1991, governs the tariff rate reduction for the period 1991 to 1995. A minimum tariff rate of 3% and a maximum rate of 30% were established, with some exceptions. By the end of 1995, a four-tiered tariff rate structure ranging from 3 to 30% was in place. For the period 1996 to 2004, the 1995 tariff structure will be narrowed down further. The rates will be phased down to 3 to 10% by the year 2003, and be collapsed into a uniform rate of 5% in year 2004.

Implementation of the tariff phase-down towards a uniform rate has been undertaken. EO 172, issued in April 1994, raised zero-rated items to 3%. EO 189, released in July 1994, reduced tariff rates on capital equipment under Chapters 84 and 85 of the Tariff and Customs Code to either 3 or 10%. EO 204, issued in September, further reduced the tariff rates on textiles and chemicals used by the industry. The next EO will cover Chapters 25 to 97 and was released in the second quarter of 1995 following consultations with the private sector.

Meanwhile, the Philippine Senate has ratified accession to the World Trade Organisation (WTO). Commitments under WTO include replacement of remaining quantitative import restrictions by tariffs, except for rice.

The Philippines is also committed to a free-trade area in the Association of South-east Asian Nations (ASEAN) region. Under AFTA–CEPT, tariff rates will range from 0 to 5% by the year 2003 in ASEAN. The Philippines is also a member of the Asia-Pacific Economic Cooperation (APEC), which envisions a free-trade area by the year 2020 among the member economies.

OTHER LIBERALISATION MEASURES

The Foreign Investments Act (FIA) of 1991 expands the areas where foreign investors can come in with 100% equity participation. The only industry areas where some ownership limits still exists are in the negative lists.

To raise savings and to improve financial intermediation, the government has also started a capital market development programme based on liberalisation and deregulation. Interest rates are market-determined and are permitted to seek positive levels amid changing inflation rates. The commercial banking sector was further liberalised recently with the entry of foreign commercial banks. The new entrants are expected to raise competition in commercial banking, thereby reducing the cost of financial intermediation. The quality of investments is also expected to go up as heightened competition leads to improved risk assessments of projects proposed for loan financing.

In infrastructure development, the government encourages private participation as a matter of policy. The amended BOT Law (RA 7718) was passed recently and it expands the range of infrastructure activities that the private sector can undertake under a BOT scheme or some variation of it.

In the telecommunications industry, EO 59 and EO 109 make possible the entry of new firms by mandating interconnection along with the provision of local exchange service. Long-distance telephone charges have gone down as a result while the local exchange service has greatly expanded with the entry of firms providing cellular mobile telephone systems. In the maritime industry, EO 212 provides for competition in cargo handling and port services.

HUMAN RESOURCE DEVELOPMENT

The Philippines has a large pool of skilled human resources. To ensure that this continues well into the future, the government has a continuing human resource development programme. Basic quality education is emphasised. This is complemented by vocational and technical education and training programmes. The development of scientific personnel is a main thrust of the science and technology plan.

Tertiary education, including the training of business managers, is largely a private-sector undertaking; there are some state colleges and universities that are being streamlined and transformed into centres of excellence. The Department of Education was restructured into three agencies with separate administrative jurisdiction over basic education, technical and vocational training, and higher education.

RECENT ECONOMIC PERFORMANCE

The economy has responded positively to the economic policy reform programme of the government. In 1994, the economic recovery gained strength with a real GNP growth rate of 5.1%, a vast improvement over the 2.6% growth rate in 1993.

All sectors of the economy – agriculture, industry and services – were part of the economic expansion. Industry led all sectors with a growth rate of 6.1%, followed by services with 3.8% and agriculture with 2.4%. With the power shortage resolved, all the industry subsectors, namely utilities, construction and manufacturing, recovered strongly with growth rates of 13.9%, 10.9% and 5.1%, respectively.

The outward-oriented strategy of the government is paying off. Gross exports grew at the rate of 19.5%, a big jump over the 6.2% growth in 1993. The top merchandise exports were non-traditional: semiconductors, electrical equipment and machinery.

Investments, given the success of stabilisation and opening up of the economy to new entrants, grew at 10.1%, about the same growth rate as last year's. In construction, the private sector at 10.8% outpaced the public sector which grew at 10.1%.

The inflation rate, based on the consumer price index, decelerated from an average of 9% in January to 7.1% in December. This can be traced to the success of the stabilisation policies. The national government was able to post a budget surplus, but because of the deficits of some government corporations, the public-sector deficit registered an increase of about 0.1% of GNP. Financing this deficit posed no difficulties judging from the behaviour of interest and inflation rates, which resumed their downward movements.

The overall balance of payments remained in a surplus. The current-account deficit was financed by normal inflows into the capital account. The government's efforts at liberalising capital flows enabled the economy to tap foreign savings and private foreign capital to support its growth and inflation targets.

FURTHER REFORMS

To sustain the economic recovery, the government is committed to continuing with its policy reform programme based on stability, liberalisation, privatisation and deregulation.

The tax and tariff reform programme is proceeding with proposed reforms for personal income, business and corporate taxes. The bill to streamline the bureaucracy is in Congress, and it is expected to be enacted before the end of Ramos's term in 1998. Monetary policy will continue to be prudent, with a 6.5% inflation rate as a target.

More opportunities for private-sector investments are envisioned given the recent enactment of the Mining Code and the expected liberalisation of retail trade. Privatisation of government corporations will continue. Lined up are the Philippine national banks, Philphos and the Manila Hotel.

Meanwhile, the infrastructure programmes of the government received a boost from the strong performance of the economy in 1995, which raised government revenues from tax and non-tax sources. Under the flagship infrastructure programmes, the extension of Circumferential 5 (C5) will be carried out, while new lines for the light railway transit and the Subic expressway, among other projects, have already commenced.

Lastly, there have been surprises from deregulation, such as in telecommunications. This pertains to the pricing of telecommunications services and the cross-subsidies for various types of services. In general, the government seeks to refine its regulatory framework so that private investments in various sectors of the economy will continue to increase.

Before I end, let me thank the School of Accountancy and Business at Nanyang Technological University for inviting me to this symposium and for organising this Business Study Mission in the first place. I now look forward to a frank, but constructive, exchange of views with all of you. Thank you.

FINANCIAL MARKETS AND BANKING

Chapter 4

Investment Opportunities in the Philippine Stock Exchange

BY
ONG Joo Hua
Jeffrey WU
Maureen NG
Daniel TAN T. S.

INTRODUCTION

THIS CHAPTER PROVIDES investors with information about investment opportunities in the Philippine Stock Exchange (PSE). Typical concerns of investors are addressed via a brief description of the historical development of the PSE and the market regulations governing it. The performance of the exchange, both historical and prospective, is further elaborated upon. Attention is focused on individual sectors and pitfalls that an investor should consider.

In May 1992, President Fidel V. Ramos of the Lakas–National Union of the Christian Democrats, was voted in as the twelfth President of the Philippines. In the short time that he has been in office, President Ramos has succeeded in putting in place most of the elements that are required for national development (see Appendix 4–1). Furthermore, he has brought political stability (see Appendix 4–2) to the country, a crucial factor in attracting foreign investment. President Ramos's vision of "Philippines 2000" seeks to transform a largely agricultural economy into an industrial one by the year 2000.

The Philippine economy stagnated in 1991 and barely recovered in 1992. In 1993, growth was driven more by the local economy than by earnings from abroad. However, in 1994, the economy's performance improved significantly. Its GNP grew by 5.6% and its GDP by 5.2% (see Table 4–1).

TABLE 4–1
Selected Economic Data Relating to the Philippines for the Period 1991 to 1996

	1991	1992	1993	1994F*	1995F*	1996F*
GNP Growth	0.2	1.9	2.4	5.6	7.0	7.5
GDP Growth	–0.7	0.9	2.0	5.2	6.3	7.0
Inflation (%)	17.7	8.9	7.6	9.8	8.6	8.0
Merchandise Exports (US$bn)	8.8	9.8	11.4	13.5	16.2	19.6
Merchandise Imports (US$bn)	12.0	14.5	17.6	21.1	25.1	30.1
Trade Surplus/(Deficit) (US$bn)	(3.2)	(4.7)	(6.2)	(7.6)	(8.9)	(10.5)
Net Foreign Debt (US$bn)	30.0	30.9	34.4	35.0	37.0	39.0

F* = forecast
Source: Baring Securities, September 1994.

The 5.6% GNP growth was the highest experienced by the country over the past decade. The key factor fuelling the strong recovery is a more stable power supply, with the industrial sector leading the growth (see Appendix 4–3). Demand came chiefly from exports and domestic demand. The Philippine government is optimistic that GNP will grow by 7.0 and 7.5% in 1995 and 1996, respectively.

The economy performed well in 1995. Government-backed structural reforms aimed at maintaining sustainable growth, deregulation of highly protected sectors and the privatisation of inefficient state-run businesses were government priorities. In addition, the economy received a boost from congressional elections in May 1995. Private consumption and public construction activities in 1995 benefited from election spending and a higher disbursement rate of government funds.

Private investment was buoyant, reflected by the large number of initial public offer (IPO) listings as well as the high level of approved BOI projects. Against the background of an improved investment outlook for the country, capital inflows are likely to remain strong, thus exerting upward pressure on the peso. This may widen the trade deficit and underscore the fragility of the economy's recent growth. However, the country's balance of payments position may experience a surplus in 1996 because of strong capital inflows resulting from relaxation of foreign exchange restrictions in 1995.

The Philippines now stands at a crucial point in its path towards continuing economic growth. Poised to assume its place as a priority investment area in the heart of Asia, the country has an investment climate that is more conducive than ever before to foreign investments. As early as 1991, significant structural reforms were implemented that shifted national policies towards an outward-oriented and free-market policy. With a liberalised policy towards foreign investment, and a firm belief in the vital contributions of foreign investment to national growth and development, the Philippines presents tremendous opportunities to foreign investors. The country's highly skilled, productive and English-speaking workforce, strategic location and abundant natural resources also make the Philippines an attractive place to do business (see Appendix 4–4). In their pursuit of growth, local companies have turned to the PSE as one avenue for generating new funds for new investments.

THE PHILIPPINE STOCK EXCHANGE

The Merger

Prior to the incorporation of the PSE in August 1992, stocks were traded at the two main exchanges, namely, the Manila Stock Exchange and the Makati Stock Exchange. The rationale for the merger of these two fiercely independent exchanges was mainly due to price discrepancies for the same stocks quoted at the two exchanges. This arose because both exchanges have different computerised trading systems (American/Japanese) and locations. Since each exchange has a different membership, it was possible for one broker to call another broker in the other exchange to buy/sell stocks at a lower/higher price. This was a major deterrent to investors. President Ramos, therefore, mandated the unification of the exchanges which ended years of bitter squabbling (Davies, 1993).

The impetus to merge was also encouraged by the provision of a US$13.5 million grant by the U.S. Agency for International Development (USAID) to help improve the capital markets in the Philippines. One of the conditions of the grant was the unification of the exchanges.

The grant was aimed at:

1. Enhancing the efficiency of the Philippine securities market by improving the quality and transparency of investor information available to its participants.
2. Increasing the operational capacity of the capital markets so that increased numbers and types of equity and debt securities become available to investors and thereby attract additional investments.

The project addressed the immediate need to transform the share market into a more efficient mechanism for capital formation and investment. This was done by focusing on the critical problems that appeared to impede market expansion, which included the following:

1. Segmented and inefficient market operations.
2. Inadequate supply of high-quality equity issues.
3. Limited demand for shares. This could be due to the lack of timely and accurate market information (i.e., the same factors that inhibit investor confidence and market credibility).

The unification, however, was not perfect. Two exchanges with different personalities and trading systems were forced to marry overnight. Thus, a situation arose where there was one stock exchange (PSE), two trading floors/systems (Makati and Manila) and, hence, two order books. The mechanics will be addressed more fully in Chapter 5.

Policy Developments

The stock exchanges of the Philippines used to be the largest in Asia in the 1960s. Owing to the country's economic slowdown over the past two decades, they are now the smallest bourses in the region in terms of market capitalisation and listed issues. Policies have been developed with the intention of stimulating the growth of the capital markets.

1. ***Financial Market Liberalisation:*** In 1948, a banking act was passed preventing foreign banks from opening up new branches. In order to make the banking industry more competitive, a law was passed on 19 May 1994 (Bank Liberalisation Law) which allowed the entry of foreign banks into the country. This liberalisation of the financial markets has allowed the entry of at least ten foreign banks

during the first quarter of 1995. The foreign banks are targeting niche markets, such as international and trade finance, investment banking services, and so forth. They do not compete with existing banks for the retail markets. The gradual lifting of foreign exchange restrictions also contributes to a large inflow of remittances from abroad. These actions are expected to act as catalysts in the growth of the capital markets.

2. ***Capital Market Development:*** Every deal transacted at the PSE requires a transfer certificate to be issued. Hence, if a particular lot is transacted five times during the same day, five transfer certificates have to be raised and cancelled by the transfer agents. The stock market boom in 1993 led to a backlog on these transfers. This is a major hindrance to investors as dividends and capital gains cannot be accounted for on time. A solution is currently being discussed. It involves establishing a fully computerised clearing depository and settlements system to be owned and operated by a privately held entity called the Philippine Clearing Depository (PCD). The PCD will act as custodian for handling securities centrally, thus allowing settlement of securities without physical delivery. However, no concrete steps have yet been taken.

   Another project in the pipeline involves strengthening the role of the Securities and Exchange Commission (SEC). Traditionally, the SEC had been very regulatory-minded in order to protect the investor. In so doing, many rules had been introduced which also made it difficult for new foreign investors to enter the capital markets. This is elaborated upon in a subsequent section. New policies and projects have recently been implemented in a bid to improve market efficiency and liquidity and, thus, to attract foreign investments.

3. ***Other Macroeconomic Adjustment Reforms:*** The Import Liberalisation Act passed after prolonged debate significantly lowers import tariffs and opens up the economy to foreign investors (e.g., Subic Bay). Industries which had previously kept foreign investors at bay are now opening up. The capital markets, therefore, will provide an avenue for investors to raise the required funds.

Some Vital Data

The PSE offers equities that are categorised into eight sectors (i.e., banking, cement/construction, consumer, hotel, mining, property, telecommunications and utilities). There were 191 companies (see Figure 4–1) as at the end of 1994, with 292 issues. The market capitalisation and market turnover of the PSE from 1985 to 1994 are depicted in Figures 4–2 and 4–3 respectively.

The PSE composite index is the key indicator of share price movement in the stock market. It comprised 30 composite index stocks, 31 commercial–industrial stocks, seven mining stocks, ten oil stocks and ten property stocks. This is dramatically different from the stock index of the 1960s which comprised largely of oil and mining stocks.

FIGURE 4–1
Number of Companies and Composite Index of Selected Stock Exchange Data: 1980 to 1994

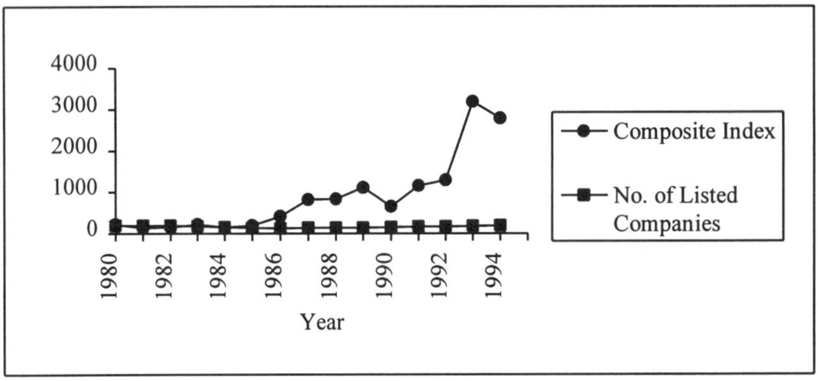

MARKET REGULATION OF PSE

Securities and Exchange Commission

Under the Revised Securities Act 1994, the SEC is responsible for regulating the securities market. It is a quasi-judicial government agency under the administrative supervision of the Office of the President of the Philippines. The SEC is responsible for:

FIGURE 4–2
Market Capitalisation of PSE from 1985 to 1994

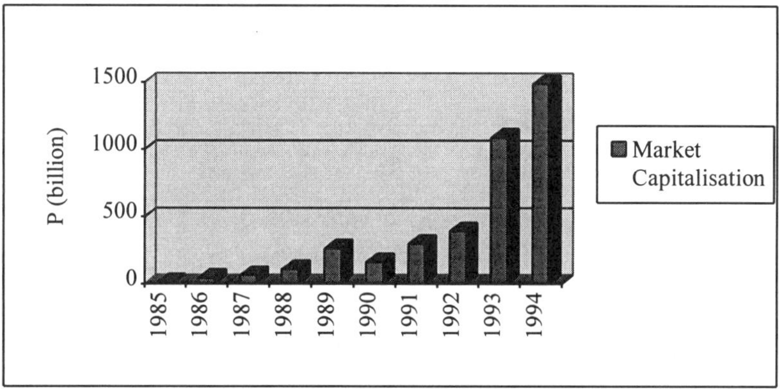

FIGURE 4–3
Market Turnover of PSE from 1985 to 1994

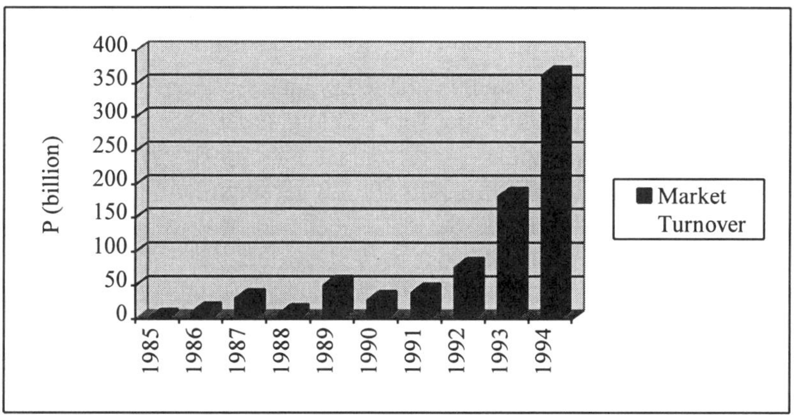

(a) registration and regulation of the exchanges;
(b) regulation of the securities markets;
(c) licensing of securities brokers and dealers;
(d) promulgation of rules and regulations on securities trading; and
(e) the issuance of opinions and rulings pertaining to the proper application of the corporation code, the Revised Securities Act and certain other statutes.

Big and Small Boards

The shares in the PSE are traded either on the big or small board. The difference between the two is that the small board is a second-tier market established to enable applicants that do not yet meet all the requirements for a big-board listing to raise funds from the stock market. The creation of the small board also increases the supply of securities in the Philippines.

Listing Requirements for the Big and Small Boards

The Revised Securities Act provides for the registration of securities (except for certain exempt securities and exempt transactions) and for the periodic submission of corporate information and financial statements. In conjunction with the Exchanges, the SEC screens all potential candidates for listing and sets specific requirements for the listing of securities on the exchanges. A brief outline of the listing requirements of the two boards is given in Table 4–2.

Reporting Requirements

The PSE requires all listed companies to submit a semi-annual financial report, which may be audited or unaudited, within 60 days from the end of the one-half year period and an audited annual financial report within 105 days after the end of the fiscal year of the company.

Whenever the price of a listed stock moves up by 50% or moves down by 40%, when calculated from the last closing price or last posted bid price, whichever is higher, the price of the security is automatically frozen by the exchange. This occurs unless there is an official announcement from the company or proper government agency justifying such a price fluctuation, or approval granted by the SEC under certain specified circumstances. The affected shares can still be traded, but only at the frozen price.

Trading and Settlement Procedures

Trading is conducted by posting bidding and asking prices on a board on the exchange floor. Payment for stock must be made by the buying customer on or before the fourth business day after the trade date (the "settlement date").

TABLE 4–2
A Brief Comparison of Listing Requirements Between Big and Small Boards

Listing Requirements	Big Board	Small Board
Minimum Capital Requirements:		
• a minimum authorised capital stock	P 400 million	P 100 million
• a minimum paid-in capital	P 100 million	P 25 million
• or 25% of authorised capital stock, whichever is higher	Yes	Yes
Track Record:		
• continuous profitable operation	3 years	2 years
• accumulative consolidated pre-tax profit	> P 50 million	-
• minimum pre-tax profit for this period	P 10 million	-
• under substantially the same management	3 years	2 years
• minimum number of stockholders required	300	300

Note: ***Exception for Small Board.*** For a new corporation with no track record, an applicant may be considered for listing if it shows that it requires funds to finance a project or the development of a new product, the feasibility of which must be fully researched and costed (6).

Source: PSE Manual, 1994.

The exchange has two clearing houses (which are commercial banks) through which all transactions are settled. Brokers must comply with all requirements for the transfer of shares and must deliver the corresponding stock certificates and all requisite documents to the relevant clearing house on or before the settlement date. The clearing house delivers the stock certificates and documents to the stock transfer agent of the relevant company. The agent will make the necessary transfers in the company's books and return the new certificates to the clearing house.

Trading is done in board lots ranging from 10 to 5,000,000 shares, depending on the price range and nature of the issue. Odd-sized lots are traded by brokers on boards specifically designated for odd-lot trading.

Commissions charged by members of the PSE are regulated by the SEC. Stockbrokers may charge a maximum commission of 1.5% on both buying and selling transactions. For transactions amounting to P3000 or less, a minimum charge of P45 is levied.

Trading on the PSE starts at 9.30 a.m. and ends at 12.00 noon, with a 10-minute extension during which time transactions can still be conducted provided they are executed at the last traded price and only for the purpose of completing unfinished orders. Trading takes place on Monday through Friday, except for public holidays.

PERFORMANCE OF THE PSE

Data for 1993

The year 1993 was a year of tremendous growth for bourses around the world. The Philippine bourse topped the region in terms of percentage change in the market index. The index value rose from 1,295.25 in January to 3,287.64 in December 1993. Table 4–3 shows the performance of bourses in the region for the year 1993.

TABLE 4–3
Performance of Regional Bourses in 1993
(Index Value)

Market	Jan	Dec	% Change
Philippines	1,295.25	3,287.64	154%
Hong Kong	5,437.80	11,888.39	119%
Jakarta	273.58	588.77	115%
Kuala Lumpur	632.83	1,275.32	102%
Bangkok	887.17	1,682.85	90%
Singapore	1,531.11	2,425.68	58%

Source : *Investamatic*, 1994.

The performance of the Philippine bourse in 1993 won much-needed confidence for its investors. Continued growth and the ability to raise capital hinges to a large extent on its ability to attract foreign participation.

In the past, the Philippines was a market ignored by many fund managers. Foreign participation was limited because there was a general misconception that only a few stocks were worth owning and that the market was over-valued. However, this misconception is no longer true today, given the improved economic indicators and growing interest worldwide in the Philippines stock market.

Data for 1994

The phenomenal growth of the PSE in 1993 was tantamount to compressing three years of growth into one. Since then, it has been recovering. Following the 154% rise in 1993, the index has tested the 2,500 level three times and rebounded on high volumes. These corrections were essentially driven by global negative sentiment towards equities due to consecutive rises in the U.S. Fed rates. The index ended 1994 at 2,785.81, down 12.8 % on the year (see Table 4–4).

TABLE 4–4
Performance of Regional Bourses from 1993 to 1994 (Index Value)

Market	1994	1993	% Change
Philippines	2,785.81	3,196.08	–12.84
Hong Kong	8,191.04	11,888.39	–31.10
Jakarta	469.64	588.77	–20.23
Kuala Lumpur	971.21	1,275.32	–23.85
Bangkok	1,360.09	1,682.85	–19.18
Singapore	2,239.56	2,425.68	–7.67

Source : *Singapore Business Times*, 30 December 1994.

The year 1994 witnessed the merger of the two exchanges, thus reducing dramatically pricing discrepancies and practices. The stock market operations were revamped, enhancing market liquidity and efficiency. Liquidity improved with daily turnover averaging approximately US$50 million. Fund managers who used to monitor only four counters (i.e., PLDT, Meralco, San Miguel and PNB) realised that there was a breadth of stocks from which to select.

The number of liquid blue chips qualifying for foreign institutional interest increased significantly. There were 27 stocks with a market capitalisation above US$250 million and 13 stocks with a market capitalisation above US$1 billion. The listing of companies such as

Benpres Holdings, Universal Robina Corporation and SM Prime Holdings created attractive new vehicles for participating in fast-growth sectors of the economy at reasonable valuations.

Data for 1995

The economic outlook for 1995 and beyond is promising. The economy is recovering, forecasts of corporate earnings are positive and business sentiment is optimistic. However, this optimism has not been reflected in the equity market as the first quarter of 1995 heralded more bad news than good news for equity markets worldwide. The Philippine stock market has not been spared. The falling Mexican peso, rising U.S. interest rate in late 1994, and the Barings debacle, took their toll on world bourses in the first few weeks of the year.

This was followed by the Kobe earthquake. The concern was over the magnitude of the repair cost required to restore the city which, in turn, would cause Japanese investment withdrawal from the various world bourses. This added to the negative sentiments already present in the market.

The effects of the devaluing Mexican peso cascaded to the shores of emerging economies such as Thailand and the Philippines. Philippine pesos were divested during Asian forex trading sessions. This resulted in an erosion of foreign investment confidence in the Philippine stock market causing a slight dip in performance. The outcome of world events will affect the performance of the Philippine stock market in the years ahead.

A REVIEW OF SECTORS

In this section, we review the major industries so as to give potential investors an overview of the Philippine stock market. It is not intended to provide buying "tips", or to promote the buying of any stocks. The analyses of certain counters merely serve as illustrations.

The Banking Sector

The Philippine commercial banking industry is competitive. There are currently 32 commercial banks in operation: 26 private domestic banks, four private foreign banks and two government banks. No one single bank, or group of banks, controls the entire banking system. However, five banks dominate the industry (accounting for 47% of total assets, 46% of total loans and 51% of total deposits). The dominance of these banks is the result of mergers that took place after the monetary authorities decided to increase the levels of bank capitalisation. Another indication of the industry's competitiveness is that banks do not control interest rate movements. Domestic interest rates in the country are market-driven.

There exists a large spread between interest rates on loans and deposits. The reason for this stems from several factors:

1. The interest that banks pay on their loanable funds and the operating costs that banks incur in deposit generating and lending activities (about 11.2%).
2. The regulatory costs (i.e., 25% agri-agra requirement and the 5% gross receipts tax – about 2.5%).
3. The margin for risks (about 2% in loan loss reserves).
4. The return for entrepreneurial initiatives (about 8%).

The recent Bank Liberalisation Law (RA 7721, signed on 18 May 1994) which allows the entry of foreign banks into the country enhances competition. Apart from establishing its own branches in the country, a foreign bank may also enter the market by buying into an existing local bank. Under the new law, foreigners may own up to 60% of the voting stock in a domestic bank or new banking subsidiary. These changes will create a number of positive factors. Some of these are the following:

1. The new law will result in a more dynamic and efficient banking system. Domestic banks will be forced to innovate and to offer better quality services while lowering interest rates. Foreign banks are expected to bring in new technology which local banks can acquire to improve their services. With greater efficiency in the intermediation process, interest rates will fall eventually, resulting in Philippine industries becoming more competitive internationally.
2. Foreign banks will inspire greater confidence for foreign investors and commit them to a long-term relationship with Filipino partners.
3. Philippine companies will have better access to international capital markets. An international credit window would give companies the opportunity to tap larger and cheaper sources of funds.

4. Domestic savings will be stimulated with greater confidence in the Philippine commercial banking system and the visibility of highly reputable foreign loans. There will be increased domestic resource mobilisation with more linkages between domestic financial institutions and global capital centres.

However, negative factors may emerge including the following:

1. The entry of foreign banks may bring about a short-term increase in domestic liquidity which may fuel inflationary pressures.
2. Medium-sized banks may merge and consolidate into bigger banks for competitive reasons.
3. Government banks that do not privatise, or link up with foreign banks, may find it difficult to compete with private banks.

The implication of the reforms is that banks will undergo some structural changes to fit into the monetary system. Deregulation in foreign exchange flows also will lead to stiffer competition. With more funds available through the equity markets, companies will rely less on debt in their capital structures. Hence, banks' earnings may be constrained by lower margins as lending rates fall.

The Cement/Construction Sector

The government, through the BOT scheme, has been attracting substantial infrastructure investments from the private sector. There are 19 cement manufacturers divided into three major groups:

(a) the Phinma group (BCC, Central, Hi Cement, DUCC, Rizal and Solid);
(b) the Alcantara group (Alsons and Iligan); and
(c) the Araneta group (Titan, FR Cement, and Lloyds Richfield).

In 1989, cement manufacturing was included in the BOI Priorities Plan which allows cement plant projects to take advantage of tax incentives such as a four-year income tax holiday, tax and duty-free imports of equipment and tax credit on locally purchased equipment. Several positive factors emerged from these actions:

1. The outlook for the construction and cement sector is very optimistic considering the sizeable number of infrastructure projects, development of industrial centres and the active property sector. Major projects, such as Ayala Land's 1,300-hectare Canlubang development and the Fort Bonifacio redevelopment, create a rich and sustainable market over the medium term.
2. For construction companies such as EEI and AGP Industries, the continued build-up of new power plants also provides a profitable client base.
3. Cement prices are expected to rise as construction activity accelerates. In 1995 and 1996, Philcemcor, an association of cement companies, projects a shortage of cement bags.
4. The government budgeted P49.5 billion for infrastructure development in 1995 which should grow at least 20% per annum over the next three years. From 1995 to 1998, the government and the private sector are expected to spend as much as US$70 billion on infrastructure projects.

However, there are also several negative factors:

1. Cement plants in the country are old, with 17 out of the 19 plants over 20 years old.
2. There will be a cement surplus by 1997 of 12 million 40-kilogram bags, given the expected 174.3 million additional capacity which represents 267 million 40-kilogram bags. Of the total additional capacity, some 111.8 million bags are intended for Cebu. This surplus should put some downward pressure on prices by 1997 and intensify the competition between players.

Thus, the cement and construction industry will continue to benefit from economic expansion, and foreign contracts will remain another large market. In the long run, companies that have a diversified contract base are expected to excel in the industry.

The Consumer Sector

Since consumer spending accounts for approximately 74% of GDP, this sector should benefit from an acceleration in GDP growth that grew by over 6.3% in 1995 and which is forecast to grow 7.3% in 1996. With increasing disposable income, fuelled by rising amounts of overseas workers' remittances, counters in this sector look poised to benefit from the strong consumer demand.

Dominant players in this industry include San Miguel Corporation, Universal Robina Corporation, RFM Corporation, SM Prime, Jollibee and Selecta. San Miguel Corporation remains the favoured stock as its market capitalisation of US$6 billion is the largest in the sector. However, because it is trading at a premium now, it offers only long-term upside potential. Earnings should grow by at least 25% in the next three years. Another player, SM Prime, a leading mall operator, offers quality play on the domestic consumer retail sector since 87% of its revenues are linked to sales by tenants.

The Hotel Sector

The tourism industry is well on its way to recovery after nearly three years of economic and political instability, and natural calamities. After the 1992 elections, the industry was expected to pick up, but it was curtailed by negative news concerning kidnappings and power outages. However, the Department of Tourism's promotion efforts have gradually brought back interest in the country as an investment area and have renewed tourist confidence. New deluxe hotels, especially in Metropolitan Manila, have boosted the country's image as they are partly owned by international chains while the existing ones have been refurbished to keep up with competition.

On the positive side, tourist arrivals were over two million in 1995 as compared to 1.4 million in 1994. This growth can be attributed to the government's effort to make tourism a priority sector. The average length of stay for each tourist is approximately 12 days, one of the highest in Asia. In May 1993, the Miss Universe Pageant held in Manila was a resounding success as it highlighted the country's tourist spots, Philippine culture and famous beach resorts.

Subic Bay continues to attract more domestic and foreign tourists due to its unique combination of beach resorts, virgin forest, golf courses and casinos. Moreover, investors have shown confidence in the former American base. Indicative of this confidence is the amount of total investments approved so far of some US$480 million. However, poor tourism-related infrastructure, such as roads and airport facilities, remain a bane to the sector.

The addition of new hotel rooms signals optimism towards the tourism sector. Also, further development of tourism spots in Cebu and Davao City are underway. Kuok Philippines Properties remains the favoured stock as it offers the best play, albeit indirectly, on the hotel sector via its investment in three Shangri-La hotels which are all doing well.

The Mining Sector

There are 36 listed companies accounting for only 3.4% of the total market capitalisation. Manila Mining has the biggest market capitalisation and is also the most lucrative. It has kept operating costs at an enviable level of US$150 per ounce. The group has begun investing P150 million in 1995 to boost mining capacity to 8,000 tonnes per day.

On the positive side, the signing of the Mining Code into law should provide some relief to mining companies. In particular, generous tax breaks should lure badly needed investments by highly leveraged mining companies. The lowering of excise taxes which took effect in the second half of 1994 will enhance the profitability of mining companies.

But several negative factors are apparent. Earnings of mining companies are sensitive, not only to fluctuations in gold prices, but also to foreign exchange. Moreover, substantial capital expenditure is needed to revitalise the industry. Mining firms may have to compete with manufacturing, telecommunications and energy firms to attract capital.

The long-term prospects appear positive with the development and expansion of mines, such as the 12 million-tonne Bulawan project of Philex and Manila Minings' P150 million expansion programme. The outlook for gold and copper prices remains positive.

The Property Sector

There are now 15 listed stocks with a combined market capitalisation of approximately 13% of the total market. Ayala Land remains the largest listed property company in the sector, despite the entry of new large developers such as SM Prime and Filinvest Land. There are currently three major business districts in the country, namely, Makati, Ortigas and Manila. There are also close to 50 commercial centres in Metropolitan Manila with high-end spaces also found in Makati and Ortigas.

Land use in Metropolitan Manila is predominantly residential and accounts for two-thirds of the total area (67,000 hectare) based on the

1991 survey made by the government. However, commercial and industrial uses have accelerated in the past three years such that their combined use may have increased by about 7 to 10%. Nonetheless, four positive factors are apparent:

1. Stronger demand for properties is rapidly emerging in an environment with low interest rates, growing personal income and accelerating GDP growth.
2. Interest rates, which have hit a seven-year low, have made house financing more attractive and accessible. This is expected to fuel demand. The lower cost of money also gives developers access to cheaper funds.
3. The privatisation of Fort Bonifacio has created a rich development potential as it is the largest tract of undeveloped land within Metropolitan Manila. Its privatisation has attracted the best developers in the country.
4. A housing backlog of 3.8 million units highlights the demand already in place. At a household formation rate of 355,000 per annum, and housing production of only 150,000 per annum, the backlog is likely to grow larger.

But the negative factors are that the 10% VAT, while initially accelerating demand (to avoid the added cost), will have a limiting impact on demand. The net effect, however, is a 5 to 7% increase in property prices so that the developers can charge the input VAT paid against the output VAT. Moreover, based on 1994 household income, only 60% of the population can afford a P150,000 (low-cost) housing unit, and less than 3% in total can afford a P1 million housing unit.

In summary, rising per capita income, growing consumer confidence and lower interest rates, along with accelerating foreign investments, will create massive demand for properties. Housing backlog remains a potent market base for residential developers.

The Telecommunications Sector

The heavyweight of the industry is the Philippine Long Distance Telephone Company (PLDT). However, other heavyweights with foreign strategic partners may emerge as serious competitors to PLDT. They include ICC Telecommunications of the Lopez family and Globe

Telecommunications of the Ayalas in joint venture with Singapore Telecommunications.

The telecommunications sector is subdivided into various business segments. They include land lines, international gateway, mobile/pager, national backbone and others. Companies like PLDT are undertaking a major capital expenditure programme to install 2 million phones by the year 1996 and 4 million by the year 2001.

On the positive side, the industry is still at an early stage of development and is undertaking massive expansion programmes at reduced investment costs, while new technology provides new revenue streams. Installation costs per line have fallen to US$800 from US$2500 five years ago due to the stiff competition among suppliers. As a result of the liberalisation of the industry and the improved perception of the economy, global telecommunications players are committing substantial capital into joint ventures with local groups. As the country achieves a critical mass in installed capacity and in GDP per capita, demand for telecommunications services should grow. The economic acceleration, and rising foreign investment and exports, should also expand the market size.

However, there are some negative factors. Telecommunications firms need massive capital at a time when revenue streams are being threatened by growing competition and rate cuts. Thus, while long-term earnings will be strong, the sector faces a choice between diminishing returns on equity and taking a leveraged position, and becoming vulnerable to rising international interest rates.

In summary, PLDT's weight has declined to only 9% of the new composite index from 32% previously, reducing its appeal as a convenient play on the market. The latest information revealed that PLDT suffered a decline in profit of 5.9% for the year ended 1994, but a rebound is expected by the end of 1996 as it will start to realise the impact of its expansion network. Other players, such as Globe and ICC, are potential "winners", but it is difficult to value them because their earnings prospects are uncertain.

The Utilities Sector

Utilities are the best play in the country's accelerating GDP growth. Key players in this industry include ICTS, Meralco and Petron.

1. ***Power Generation/Distribution:*** Meralco is the best play on power as the other companies, Tegre and IRC, are much smaller and are relatively new power plays. As of 19 August 1994, the generating capacity in Luzon was 3,529 megawatts which was adequate to meet the 3,441 megawatts demand. The generating capacity is expected to reach 4,500 megawatts. About 31% of the existing plants are gas turbine, 28% are hydro-based, 21% are thermal, 13% are geothermal and 7% are coal-fired.
2. ***Oil Refiners:*** There are three oil refiners in the country: Petron, Philippine Shell (a subsidiary of Royal Dutch Shell) and Caltex Phils. Petron is the only listed company of the three and has the largest crude distillation capacity. The country imports about 96% of its oil requirement.
3. ***Container Handling:*** ICTS handles about 70% of total throughput in Manila's ports. The capacity of the north and south harbours are currently being expanded.

Four positive factors are apparent in this sector:

1. The threat of power supply shortage is minimal now that adequate and reliable power has been achieved. The government is now concentrating on building up the country's base-load capacity.
2. Natural gas will be available in the country soon. It will come from the Camago–Malampaya field where several oil field operators are set to connect it to power plants.
3. In anticipation of increasing oil demand of approximately 8% per annum, refiners are expanding their capacities.
4. Container volume is expected to grow at an average of 15% per annum over the medium term.

However, there are three factors on the down side:

1. Generating capacity needs to be built and the country's ageing plants need to be rehabilitated.
2. Oil prices are highly regulated and politically sensitive, given the strong consumer groups. The oil refinery sector carries high external risk since it is highly susceptible to global crude oil price fluctuations and foreign exchange swings.
3. Growth of port operators including ICTS will depend heavily on

volume. Rate increases in cargo handling have been deferred indefinitely by the port authorities, despite requests from port operators.

Overall, utilities are the best play on the country's economic growth path since they are basic necessities. There is substantial upside potential for the key players identified earlier.

PITFALLS AND RISKS

Given the background of buoyant business confidence and a strong potential for upward assessment of market performance forecasts, there are other factors that must be taken into consideration. They include:

Forex Risk

Like any investment that goes beyond national boundaries, the foreign exchange risk sets in. The Singapore currency has been strong and appreciating against the major currencies, so potential investors have to be wary of the foreign exchange risk involved when purchasing Philippine equities. This is especially evident after the recent Mexican debacle. Since there is no automatic hedge mechanism available to minimise the forex risk, an investor must incorporate the foreign exchange risk element in the calculation of expected return.

Stock Liquidity

In emerging markets like the Philippines, investors may face the problem of market liquidity. A longer holding period is probably needed. Moreover, up-to-date market information may not be so readily available as it is in an overseas bourse.

Choice of Broker

To invest in a regional bourse, one has to select the services of a reputable and dependable stockbroker. Unless the broker is familiar with the operations of the market, an investor faces the risk of not getting prompt execution of orders. Brokers with up-to-date information will be a boon to investors.

Economic Risks

No investment decision should be made in isolation of economic risks. Despite clear government policy orientation, critical reforms have been delayed by the bureaucratic process, especially those requiring legislative approvals. Politicking and populist concerns may delay or derail reforms.

The economy is still very sensitive to its major partners, especially the U.S. and Japan (which together account for 56% of Philippine exports and 42% of investments), although the risk is now being spread among European and Asian economies. The country is still financing its expansion through debt which will become burdensome if internal resource generation does not improve, and if the dollar interest rate continues to climb.

THE NEXT LEAP

With the dynamic growth experienced in the ASEAN region, there undoubtedly will be very keen competition among regional exchanges to improve their market infrastructure and to attract foreign capital in order to sustain growth. What, then, are some of the future directions of the PSE?

Strengthening of the SEC/PSE

The PSE, with the SEC's assistance, is starting to develop and implement an efficient trading and settlement infrastructure, with constant vigilance and attention given to improving corporate regulation and investor protection. The PSE has commissioned a company to develop a market surveillance system similar to that of the New York Stock Exchange. Currently, any unusual factors or movements in the market will be investigated by the PSE for insider trading or fraudulent activities. If, however, the case becomes too complex, then it will be passed on to the SEC to handle. All these factors will ensure that the PSE will eventually become an efficient and self-regulatory market.

There are plans to change the protectionist attitude of the SEC. Currently, the SEC adopts a merit disclosure policy whereby information on quoted stocks is made known only to the SEC, which then gives a stamp of approval. The SEC hopes to make the public responsible for its own investment decisions by making full information available to the public.

Expansion of Capital Markets Beyond Manila

The PSE plans to expand its operations nationwide through the establishment of computer trading terminals in provinces outside Metropolitan Manila, such as Davao City and Cebu. This is to tap into the booming economic activity that is occurring outside Manila. The expansion is being undertaken with the objectives of sustaining economic growth, funding corporate expansion and providing investment opportunities to the public.

Trading terminals will be set up in the other provinces and they are expected to be operational by the end of 1996. This is another positive step forwards in developing the PSE as an efficient market.

Education of the Public

The PSE intends to divide all listed issues into five boards ranging from the blue-chip stocks to speculative counters. The objective is to classify the counters based on the risk–return profile so as to educate the less informed investors. The PSE is using various means to educate the public on equity, bonds and even derivatives investing.

Uniform Trading System

The PSE has installed a uniform trading system in both exchanges. This now eliminates the arbitrage opportunities that used to exist. However, differences between the two exchanges must be sorted out to ensure a smooth transition is maintained.

CONCLUSION

The PSE has come a long way since its inception. Many improvements have been implemented in the past two years and excellent directions have been charted for its future. The PSE might wish to learn from the experiences of other bourses in the region in order to maximise its potential. It can implement measures to become a more efficient market. Various instruments, such as electronic share application, scripless trading, authorised trading centres, automated transaction matching system and tender price system, have enabled exchanges such as the

Stock Exchange of Singapore to become an efficient regional market in a short time span. The PSE may wish to introduce some of these instruments to enhance and improve its market efficiency.

APPENDIX 4–1
Initiatives Taken by President Ramos Since 1992

1. ***July 1992: Ramos Succeeds Aquino – First on His Agenda:***
   (a) Make political opponents promise not to create trouble.
   (b) Have all politicians concentrate on the economy.
   (c) Get legislative support to pass bills quickly.
   (d) Privatise functions and assets to raise money.
   (e) Fix customs and tax collection.
   (f) Reorganise the Central Bank.
2. ***Open up the Economy:***
   (a) Decontrol forex flows.
   (b) Promote exports and tourism.
   (c) Lower tariffs (AFTA/GATT); counter the protest of non-competitive industries.
   (d) Approve the 75-year land lease for foreigners.
   (e) Invite investment and bilateral relations. (In 1993, Ramos visited Malaysia, Singapore, Japan, China, Korea, Indonesia and the United States).
   (f) Break up monopolies that harm public interest; starting with telecommunications and power generation.
3. ***Get Stock Exchanges to Merge:***
   (a) After ten years of bitter squabbling, the Manila and Makati Stock Exchanges are to merge into the PSE.
4. ***Reduce Budget Deficit:***
   (a) Sell government assets such as the national oil company, Petron and the shipyard Philseco (done).
   (b) Either impose oil levy (stop-gap measure) to raise P10 billion, or have Congress pass new tax laws to raise P22 billion.
   (c) Improve tax collection in the care of Vinzons Chato. (Chato is the tough new internal revenue commissioner; she is working on it.)
   (d) Pass new VAT laws to widen tax base (done).

(f) Reduce debt service burden; increase export earnings (making progress).

5. ***Improve Peace and Order:***
   (a) Negotiate with Nur Misuari of the MNLF.
   (b) Reconcile warring tribesmen in Mindanao.
   (c) Reduce countryside banditry.
   (d) Increase salary of soldiers (done).
   (e) Reduce urban street crime (actually diminishing).
6. ***Push for Consistent Investment Policies:***
   (a) Stop changing the guidelines for foreign investors.
   (b) Do not touch regulations on Subic Bay Freeport.
   (c) Make doubly sure that cabinet members do not issue contradictory statements.
   (d) Improve bidding system – allow negotiated contracts (done).
   (e) Terminate the Retail Trade Law which keeps foreigners out from retail trade.
   (f) Invite foreign banks in (done).
   (g) Invite more foreign contractors in, via BOT arrangements.
7. ***Meet Infrastructure Concerns:***
   (a) Triple the amount of road surface.
   (b) Build seaports and airports.
   (c) Support local fishermen/stop overfishing.
   (d) Build railways, canal waterways.
   (e) Let cities issue more municipal bonds.
   (f) Open up telecommunications and transport businesses.
   (g) Fix water supply, provide cheap housing and improve public health.
   (h) Build schools and hospitals.
   (i) Push for the education of women.
8. ***Push for a High GNP Growth Rate:***
   (a) Upgrade capital market.
   (b) Improve agricultural technology.
   (c) Build up steel, petrochemical and defence industries.
   (d) Nurture export winners.
   (e) Help provinces with potential, such as Cebu, Batangas and parts of Mindanao.
9. ***The Judiciary:***
   (a) Rein in meddlesome judiciary.
   (b) Stop corrupt judges.

(c) Install an express lane for adjudicating business crimes.

10 ***The Legislature:***

(a) Get cooperation of both senate and house. Congress normally passes 20 bills a year; Ramos wants them to start passing 100 bills a year.

(b) Keep the opposition senators busy.

11. ***Organised Labour:***

(a) Rein in militant labour (strikes are down; more disputes are being solved via negotiation).

(b) Improve worker training (dual training bill passed on 24 February 1994).

(c) Create new jobs.

12. ***Government:***

(a) Upgrade bureaucracy.

(b) Privatise yet more government functions.

13. ***Anti-smuggling:***

(a) Improve technical ability of customs.

(b) Build up a coast guard.

APPENDIX 4–2
Political Situation

1. ***Politically Less Explosive:*** The country has just brought its political problems down to a level where they do not openly interfere with economic growth. We sense a movement towards a sober understanding of public policy. The public and the legislature are beginning to understand the necessity of trade-offs and hard choices. For instance, taxes need to be paid, even if the payback is long in coming. But the fine-tuning of policies and systems is very difficult.

2. ***Privatisation:*** When all else fails, circumvent the system. This is a favourite approach of President Ramos. Where the government cannot deliver, Ramos invites the private sector to step in. We like the style. We think it is a good idea to admit inadequacy in advance rather than see public welfare prejudiced.

   So now government is perceived to be honestly offering solutions to prime the economy while keeping the peace, forging alliances, and in general working in the public interest. This is a big improvement over the situation five to ten years ago when the government was unpopular and the communists were pushing hard at the gates.

3. ***Spread Money-Making Opportunities:*** What is Ramos trying to do? He is putting together an American-style of political democracy and an economy controlled by a few wealthy and powerful families. He knows that it is a terrible fit that has never worked well. His solution is to liberalise the economy via reforms so as to spread money-making opportunities more democratically.

   This means that the government must dismantle private armies, collect the right taxes, break up harmful cartels and monopolies and open up the economy. It should also clean up the civil service and push private family-run corporations to become more professionally operated. The government's goal is to push and challenge national industry to stand against the best in the world.
4. ***Breakthroughs:*** Quite a few breakthroughs have been made, such as the stabilisation of the economy, greater openness to the outside world, the reorganisation of the Central Bank, private participation in infrastructure projects and renewed access to international credit. Foreign investment inflows have grown rapidly since 1990. And, on the labour front, unions have resorted more often to arbitration than to strikes. It could mean that tensions are simmering down overall. Right now the nation is better prepared to tackle its worst deficiencies, such as infrastructure, social inequalities, and multiple deficits in trade and balance of payments.
5. ***One Massive Educational Effort:*** The message being driven home is that the country has to get more organised; attitudes have to change and everybody has to shoulder their civic responsibility. The people's attitude is one of suspicion of the government and frustration at the many years of no progress. Many business leaders have identified the central problem to be the lack of civic responsibility. They say the biggest challenge is for all Filipinos to act responsibly at the individual level. All too many neglect to think before acting; they typically refuse to face the consequences of their actions. This is a basic problem which is arguably the central issue in running this country. It is the main reason for the legendary "un-governability" of the islands.

DEVELOPMENTS TO WATCH:

1. ***What if Fidel Ramos Dies?*** Too much is at stake for everything to be based on the presence and personality of Fidel Ramos alone. A fatal plane crash involving Ramos could interrupt the momentum of economic growth and throw the future into serious doubt. It might be argued that the momentum of economic growth would continue nevertheless, but we do not know that.
2. ***The Legislature:*** Ramos has to pass numerous bills through the legislature. The lawmakers have to cooperate or else the reform programme gets derailed. On the few occasions they have worked together, there had been a lot of opposition.
3. ***The Judiciary:*** The courts have to fulfil their function. The Supreme Court has to stay out of the economic policy. The courts have to clear their backlogs.
4. ***Law and Order:*** The government has fought policemen and rebellions only to be swamped by street crime. It is not surprising that policemen were involved. The current approach is to clean up the police force and hire new trainees. In 1993, the police dismissed or fired 700 officers and destroyed 33,876 loose guns. As a result, the volume of crimes declined by 8%.

   There will never be a crimeless time but somehow a higher level of economic development will refine the style. There may be an inevitable shift from petty blue-collar crime to high-stakes white-collar crime.
5. ***Regions Outside Manila:*** Regions outside Manila will be providing most of the growth via construction and investment. Manila is too congested.

   (a) The Cebu economy is growing faster than Manila's.
   (b) Subic Bay is attracting light industry and service firms such as Federal Express. The plan for Subic is to use it as an alternative container terminal for outbound cargo from shippers located in northern Luzon.
   (c) Mindanao holds great potential for agriculture and industry.

APPENDIX 4–3
Positive Economic Indicators

1. ***Heavy Investment Spending:*** Fixed capital investment will be the main GNP driver, having risen by 14% in 1994 and more than 16% in 1995. The following factors are important:

   (a) The implementation of large-scale, high-impact infrastructure projects is accelerating. We are seeing this in the mad scramble by the private sector to participate in telecommunications, power, transport and road construction projects.
   (b) More private firms are building up their capacities in anticipation of stronger demand.
   (c) The 24.6% surge in imports in the first quarter of 1994 was propelled by purchases of capital goods and raw materials which accounted for over 90% of total merchandise imports. Acquisition of equipment and machinery went up by 47% during the first quarter.
   (d) Applications to the BOI already reached P229.8 billion as at May 1994, even surpassing 1993's full-year capital inflow of P95 billion. Still, the figure already exceeded the BOI's target of P115 billion for 1994.
2. ***Export Recovery:*** Exports are expected to put in a modest performance, with 15.5% growth in 1994 and 16% expected in 1995. Greater reliability in delivery of goods with a more stable power supply will make Philippine exports more competitive this year. A key factor is the recovery of the U.S. market which takes up 36% of the total exports. Increased trade with other Asian economies is expected to offset flat trade with Japan which accounts for about 17% of Philippine exports. The opening of world markets following the GATT–Uruguay round should benefit Philippine exports in the long term.
3. ***Robust Private Spending:*** Private consumption is likely to firm up along with rising household incomes. Rising inflationary expectations and higher taxes, however, may slightly dampen spending. At the same time, the prospect of higher prices may tick off the Filipinos' strong propensity to hoard, thus boosting demand in the short term.

4. ***Sectoral Growth:***
   (a) The engine of growth should be the industrial sector (mainly in manufacturing and private construction) which grew by 6.5% in 1994 and is expected to be 7.5% in 1995.
   (b) Manufacturing output grew by just under 7% and is expected to be 8.0% in 1995 on the back of strong domestic consumption and export recovery.
   (c) Private construction activities are expected to pick up significantly as the implementation of large-scale infrastructure projects speeds up. The increased receptiveness of the private sector towards the government's BOT programme is a key factor.
   (d) The government's grains production enhancement programme boosted agricultural production by 2.4% in 1994 and it is expected to reach 3.5% in 1995 and 1996.
   (e) Stable growth is expected in the service sector.
5. ***Surge in Direct Foreign Investments:*** Direct foreign investments in the Philippines have been weak and rather flighty. The shaky political situation and weak infrastructure have turned off huge capital inflows entering the country. Moreover, external factors such as the weak economies of the United States and Japan, the country's major investors, have come into play.

   However, the foreign investment picture should start turning around this year as investor confidence is regained. The political situation has stabilised. The necessary infrastructure is slowly being provided. Investment locations are more focused. The so-called regional industrial centres (Cebu, Davao, Batangas, Cavite, Cagayan de Oro) are starting to take shape. The former U.S. bases, Subic and Clark, now industrial freeport zones, are attracting attention. Finally, the wave of deregulation in telecommunications, power generation and banking is inspiring investment blitzes from local taipans in teamwork with foreign investors.

   The initial push is coming from the government's privatisation programme. The BOT programme is another key venue for investments. Foreign companies, through joint ventures with locals, have been quite active in the power, transport, telecommunications and oil drilling projects. This is likely to happen in the banking and mining sectors as well, as foreign entry is further deregulated. With the basic infrastructure in place, investments in the manufacturing sector and core industries should start pouring in.

6. ***Government's Financial Health Still Shaky but Improving:*** High fiscal deficit remains a critical issue due to its dire consequences on the Philippine economy. To address the deficit, the government has done the following:

   (a) ***It has acted to curb expenditure level:*** While the government is trying to control its domestic debt borrowings, it is unrelenting in its commitment to pay up debt-servicing obligations despite enormous pressure from the senate and the public to do otherwise. As a result, for the past three years, there has been a negative growth in real government consumption which culminated in a 6% decline in 1992. A positive note is that the spending behaviour of government has improved. Although it has been cutting its expenditure levels in 1993, it did not do so at the expense of its capital outlay account.

   (b) ***It has increased taxes and improved tax collection efficiency:*** Out of the 19 laws enacted in 1993, ten were revenue-related and appropriations measures. The government expects to generate P32.8 billion out of the new tax measures. It is anticipated that tax revenues will rise modestly in the near term. With the economy on its recovery cycle, the government should benefit from a larger tax base. The new tax laws should provide the government with more muscle to plug tax evasion. In fact, signs of better fiscal performance are emerging. At the end of April, revenue collections reached P113.8 billion, slightly exceeding the P112.5 billion target due to the higher-than-expected collections of the Bureau of Customs.

   (c) ***It has placed greater reliance on the private sector:*** The long-avowed government goal of a private-sector-led industrialisation is beginning to be realised. The two main vehicles are the sale of government assets and the BOT scheme for infrastructure projects.

APPENDIX 4–4
Investment Policies

The Philippines encourages private investments, both domestic and foreign, in industry, agriculture, mining and other sectors of the economy. In general, anyone, regardless of nationality, is welcome to invest in the Philippines. No less than the Philippine Constitution safeguards foreign investments by guaranteeing:

(a) protection from expropriation without just compensation;
(b) remittance of profits, capital gains and dividends;
(c) repatriation of investments; and
(d) the ability to obtain foreign exchange to repay foreign obligations.

1. ***Foreign Investments Act:***
   (a) simplified foreign investments by eliminating multiple registrations that used to make investments into the country a difficult process;
   (b) removed protectionism.
2. ***Liberalisation:*** A law has been passed further liberalising the entry of foreign investments in areas such as import and wholesale trading, insurance, travel agencies, convention and conference organising. Another proposed law would bring the minimum paid-in capital requirement to US$150,000.
3. ***Omnibus Investments Code of 1987:*** Among the major benefits available under the Code are income tax holidays of six years for pioneer projects and four years for non-pioneer projects, and tax-and duty-free importation of capital equipment up to 31 December 1994. Many investors find these incentives necessary and useful to improve the viability of their projects and the government is willing to grant these to qualified projects.

BUSINESS REFORMS

Apart from the FIA, dramatic efforts have been made by the government in the last few years to liberalise business in the Philippines.

1. ***Foreign Exchange Liberalisation:*** Foreign exchange may be freely sold and purchased outside the banking system. Foreign exchange receipts, acquisitions or earnings may also be deposited in foreign currency accounts, whether in the Philippines or abroad, or brought out of the Philippines.
2. ***Import Liberalisation:*** The Philippine government is also imple-

menting an aggressive programme to liberalise the country's foreign trade. Export of commodities that generate foreign exchange earnings is encouraged. With the liberalised policies on foreign exchange, all commodity exporters may retain their foreign exchange earnings and freely use these for any purpose.

The Philippines actively supports the ASEAN free trade area (AFTA) which seeks to transform the regional grouping into a common market by the early part of the next century. The country is also a participant in the global trading arrangements brought about by the General Agreement on Tariffs and Trade (GATT).

3. ***Extension of Period for Lease of Land:*** Under the Philippine Constitution, foreign ownership of land is not allowed. Realising that this restriction deters many foreign investors, the government has recently increased the maximum lease period. From the previous 50 years, commercial land may be leased for an initial period of 50 years plus an additional 25 years, or a total of 75 years.
4. ***Banking Liberalisation:*** The Government has also recently liberalised the banking sector. RA No. 7221 widens the scope of operations of foreign banks to establish branches in the Philippines. The Act allows ten new banks to establish branches in the country and permits an unlimited number of new entrants to set up subsidiaries or buy into existing banks.
5. ***BOT Law:*** The government has likewise opened the door to companies wishing to participate in infrastructure development. Through the BOT law, the private sector may finance, construct, operate and maintain necessary infrastructure projects that support economic development. Recent refinements to the BOT law provide for such variants as build, operate and own and build, maintain and operate, and now make it possible for proponents to earn a reasonable return on investments and maintenance costs.
6. ***Reforms to Come:*** Other key sectors of the economy are being opened up. There are now more players in the telecommunications industry due to the government's drive to encourage competition in the sector. Major shipping routes are now open to more than one operator and land transportation is also being deregulated. Major efforts are expected during the next few years to liberalise the oil industry.

REFERENCES

Davies Ben, "One and One Makes Three Philippine Stock Exchanges", *Asia Money*, No. 16, pp. 48–50, 1993.

Gelston Sally, "Makati Stock Exchange to Automate", *East Asian Executive Reports*, Vol. 15, No. 1, p. 7, 1993.

"Manual of Rules Governing the Listing of Securities", Philippine Stock Exchange, 1994.

"Philippines: Exchanging Vows", *Asian Business,* Vol. 29, No. 5, p. 9, 1993.

Tierney Robin, "Global Exchanges: Stock in Trade", *World Trade,* Vol. 6, No. 9, pp. 26–8, 1993.

Tiglao Rigoberto, "Soap and Bubbles: Manila's Bourses May Merge by Early 1993", *Far Eastern Economic Review,* Vol. 155, No. 50, p. 66, 1992.

Chapter 5

Upgrading the Philippine Stock Exchange

BY
Ronald NG Kok Tiong
LOW Chin Wui
David HO Weng Cheong

INTRODUCTION

RIDING ON THE strong economic growth of the country, the PSE is bracing for competition with regional exchanges. This chapter looks at the computerisation programme of the PSE. It also makes recommendations for successful implementation of scripless trading in the Philippines.

The Philippines was the first country in ASEAN to have a stock exchange. The Manila Stock Exchange was incorporated on 10 August 1927 as a voluntary, non-profit-making organisation patterned after the New York Stock Exchange. The SEC was established in 1936 to regulate securities transactions. Subsequently, a group of stockbrokers broke away from the Manila exchange to form the Makati Stock Exchange in 1963.

Until the 1960s, the Manila and Makati stock exchanges together formed a larger and more active market than that of Hong Kong. However, during the Marcos' era there was a substantial flight of capital out of the country

---

The authors wish to acknowledge Ms. Elizabeth C. Pasion, Manuel L. Lopez, Ms. Judy Tan and Dr. Luis Ma. R. Calingo for their assistance.

leading to the decline of the two exchanges.

After the ousting of President Marcos in February 1986, investors' confidence in the Philippines was slowly restored. By 1989, substantial foreign investments were flowing into the country at a rate of US$3.2 billion a year. The smooth transition of power from President Aquino to President Ramos in 1992 further boosted confidence in the Philippines. Consequently, trading activities at the two exchanges have recovered so much that the Philippine equities market was one of the best-performing stock markets in the world in 1993.

Although listing on one of the Philippine exchanges guarantees listing on the other, price differentials between the two exchanges created arbitrage opportunities as well as confusion among investors. Operating costs were high, making it difficult for Manila to compete successfully with other Asian stock markets. Recognising that a unified exchange is vital in developing a strong capital market that is imperative to sustained economic growth, President Ramos appealed to the two feuding exchanges to put aside some 30 years of rivalry and merge. Consequently, the PSE was formally incorporated on 12 October 1993.

The unification of the Manila and Makati bourses was effectively only a paper merger. The bitter battle between the two exchanges' landlords, namely, Philippine Realty and Holding Corporation (PRHC) and Ayala Land Inc., for the right to house the new PSE prevented a physical unification. As the principal site, PSE Tekite (owned by PRHC) hosts the PSE's board room and the offices of the chair, president, treasurer, secretariat, and the training and education centre. PSE Plaza (owned by Ayala Land), on the other hand, is the venue of the central depository and clearing house.

Since the unification of the two exchanges, significant changes in the following aspects were implemented over the last few years:

1. Market capitalisation was improved to US$49 billion.
2. Liquidity and the range of stock offerings was increased.
3. The Philippines's stock index was revised to make it more responsive.
4. A more equitable distribution of IPOs was implemented (e.g., 25% of IPOs can go to retail investors through banks).

The PSE has planned the establishment of four trading boards. The first board will be for companies with a track record of at least three years. The second board is for venture capital funds. The third board will allow trading of bonds and futures. Finally, the fourth board will cater to the funding needs of small businesses.

Derivatives trading on the PSE is slated for 1995. Operations will be set up to tap funds from booming provinces, such as Cebu and Baguio. The PSE will also continue with the computerisation programme originally initiated by the two exchanges that will see scripless securities trading. Due to the important role of information technology in the PSE's modernisation plan, we will look at the computerisation initiatives of the PSE in the following section.

THE MOVE TO COMPUTERISATION

Initial Computerisation

The Manila Stock Exchange went electronic on 4 January 1993, ending 65 years of blackboards, chalk and the "open-outcry" system. The automated trading system was acquired from Intelligent Ware. Two months later, in March 1993, the Makati Stock Exchange announced its own system, MakTrade. MakTrade was developed by the Chicago Stock Exchange and went "live" in June of the same year. Table 5–1 compares the two trading systems.

TABLE 5–1
Comparison of Trading Systems at Manila and Makati Stock Exchanges

	Manila Stock Exchange	**Makati Stock Exchange**
System	Automated Trading System	MakTrade
Vendor	Intelligent Ware	Chicago Stock Exchange
Platform	Stratus	DEC VAX
Terminal Type	Dumb terminals running on emulation	Intelligent terminals running on Windows-based software
Response Time	3–7 seconds	0.5 second

Unification Challenges

Despite the agreement to merge, existing property commitments and investments render a physical unification impossible in the short term. The challenge for the exchanges, therefore, is to link up the two trading floors through a computer system in order to create a one-price market for all the listed issues. The short-term solution involves the building of an interface to effect a functional unification.

The Interface Programme

With the interface in place, each system will have its own pre-open market from 9:00 a.m. to 9:30 a.m. Brokers from the two exchanges can enter whatever price they want without regard to what is happening at the other exchange. When the markets open at 9:30 a.m., only one price is published and used as the official pre-opening price.

During regular trading hours from 9:30 a.m. to 12:00 noon, orders are matched based on the price, time and location priority rule. To illustrate the workings of the rule, consider the following three examples using orders for San Miguel Corporation 'A' shares. Note that location refers to where the order was entered; i.e., either the Manila or the Makati Stock Exchange.

Example 1: The first criterion for matching is price. Even though both order 1 and order 2 were entered at the same time, order 1 will be matched with order 3 since its offered price matches the seller's price.

Order 1	**Order 2**	**Order 3**
Type: *Buy*	Type: *Buy*	Type: *Sell*
Price: *P92.0*	Price: *P91.5*	Price: *P92.0*
Time: *9:45 a.m.*	Time: *9:45 a.m.*	Time: *9:48 a.m.*
Location: *Manila SE*	Location: *Makati SE*	Location: *Makati SE*

Example 2: Since both order 1 and order 2 offered to buy at P92.0, the system will try to match the orders by time. Order 2 was entered earlier than order 1. Therefore, order 2 will be matched with order 3.

Order 1	**Order 2**	**Order 3**
Type: *Buy*	Type: *Buy*	Type: *Sell*
Price: *P92.0*	Price: *P92.0*	Price: *P92.0*
Time: *9:45 a.m.*	Time: *9:41 a.m.*	Time: *9:50 a.m.*
Location: *Manila SE*	Location: *Makati SE*	Location: *Makati SE*

Example 3: Since both order 1 and order 2 offered to buy at P92.0

and both were entered at the same time, the system cannot do a match based on either price or time. The last criterion of location will be used. Order 2 will be matched with order 3 since they were both entered from the Makati Stock Exchange.

Order 1	**Order 2**	**Order 3**
Type: *Buy*	Type: *Buy*	Type: *Sell*
Price: *P92.0*	Price: *P92.0*	Price: *P92.0*
Time: *9:45 a.m.*	Time: *9:45 a.m.*	Time: *9:47 a.m.*
Location: *Manila SE*	Location: *Makati SE*	Location: *Makati SE*

At any time, only the best three bid and offer prices will be shown on the screen of both systems regardless of where the orders were placed. The locations of the orders are not displayed. The closing price is based on the last trade at 12:00 noon.

Towards One Trading System

Although the physical union of the two exchanges will not be possible for years to come, the PSE had decided that there should be only one trading system. The Manila Stock Exchange has replaced its existing system with "MakTrade".

MakTrade

MakTrade was developed by the Chicago Stock Exchange. The US$4 million automated order matching system is a customised version of the system "Midwest" installed for the Stock Exchange of Thailand in 1991. It employs a client–server architecture.

At the Makati Stock Exchange, the system runs on two digital equipment VAX 810 servers (one to serve as backup in the event of failure) and Market Works, which is a new trading workstation using Microsoft Windows software. The system offers an average response time of 0.5 second and can process most transactions within one minute. Currently, MakTrade handles some 3000 transactions a day at the Makati Stock Exchange. The maximum capacity is expected to be 20,000 transactions per day. When the Manila Stock Exchange switches to the MakTrade system, it will be linked to the Makati Stock Exchange with three leased lines.

Apart from the move towards a single trading system, the plan to go scripless poses an even greater challenge to the new PSE. As a result of the 1993 bull run, there was a substantial backlog which resulted in investors not getting their dividends. It was not until the latter half of 1994 that all of the backlog was cleared. Therefore, in order to improve backroom efficiency, the PSE has chosen to introduce scripless trading in the Philippines. We will look at scripless trading and its implication for the PSE in the following section.

SCRIPLESS TRADING

The Nature of Scripless Trading

In the race to be more competitive and attractive to investors, the PSE is only one of many stock markets around the world rushing to convert to scripless trading. Scripless trading has brought efficiency and convenience to stock markets everywhere. The benefits also include better protection against fraud and share forgeries. Table 5–2 lists some of the exchanges that have introduced scripless trading.

Scripless trading involves the trading of financial securities without the physical transfer of share certificates. Under such a system, all share certificates are deposited with a central depository which keeps the securities under its name. Share transfers between investors are recorded electronically at the depository. Consequently, scripless trading requires all investors to open a securities account with the central depository to trade on the exchanges.

Benefits of Scripless Trading

Going scripless will result in wide-ranging changes for the investing community at large, from stockbrokers and investors, to companies and company registrars. Scripless trading will permit a substantial reduction in paper work, increased efficiency and improved share settlements.

In countries where trading has already gone scripless, stockbroking firms have been able to cut down their backroom manpower by as much as 10%. On a scrip-based system, investors who sell their shares have to hand in their share certificates to brokers, who then send them to the clearing house. When investors buy, brokers also have to deliver the certificates. Consequently, broking houses spend a lot of time tracking the movement of the scrips. Under a scripless system, the buying and selling of shares is reflected by crediting and debiting the investors' accounts electronically.

TABLE 5–2
Implementation of Scripless Trading

Country	Established	Implementation
Immobilisation:		
Australia	NA	1994
Canada	1970	1981
Germany	1989	1990
Japan	1984	1991
Hong Kong	1992	1992
Malaysia	NA	1992
Netherlands	1977	1977
Shanghai	1990	1990
Shenzhen	1991	1991
Singapore	1987	1987
Switzerland	1970	1970
Taiwan	1989	1990
United States	1973	1973
Dematerialisation:		
Denmark	1980	1983
France	1949	1984
Norway	1985	1985
Sweden	1971	1990
United Kingdom	NA	1993

Note: NA = not available.

Prior to going scripless, a listed company must appoint a registrar to keep track of its shareholder list. With scripless trading, the central depository effectively acts as the registrar for all listed companies. It is the function of the central depository to pay out dividends, and to issue bonus shares and rights. Scripless trading, therefore, will make the duties of share registrars obsolete. Much of the administrative work that was previously handled by the registrars will be taken over by the central depository.

For the investors, scripless trading is convenient since it is no longer necessary for them to pick up or deliver scrips. Investors need not send in scrips to register for dividend, bonus or rights entitlements. The advantage of scripless trading is that the management of the securities accounts lies with an independent body, namely, the central depository, and not with the brokers. The risk of manipulation is minimised. Thus scripless trading will offer better protection against forged scrips.

Downside of Scripless Trading

When companies go scripless, they tend to lose control of their share registers to a certain extent. Previously, the company's registrar could advise its clients on the movement of certain shareholders' accounts. This is most useful when the company is vulnerable to take-over attempts. Under the central depository system, the central depository will be acting as the registrar of many more companies. There is also a need to maintain a high degree of confidentiality to protect investors' interests. Companies are required to provide justification for urgently needed information. Therefore, companies lose their ability to know their shareholding status at any point in time on short notice.

Scripless trading is a taboo for investors who want to maintain complete secrecy over their shareholdings for whatever reasons. Under the former system, share scrips could have changed hands several times, and it would be almost impossible to trace the current owners unless they send in their scrips for registration. Scripless trading, on the other hand, makes share transactions more transparent, so that it is always possible to trace the shareholders even if they choose to maintain a securities subaccount with a depository agent such as a bank. Thus, it is likely that scripless trading may drive some investors to other regional bourses where they can maintain their anonymity. One solution to the problem of confidentiality is for the central depository to ensure that stockbrokers have access to client accounts to execute orders only, but have no access to the contents of the accounts.

Shares are transferred in and out of the shareholders' central depository account based on instructions from any person claiming to be the shareholder's broker. No written instruction is required from the owner. Normally, shareholders will receive only a statement of account on a quarterly basis. Unless owners were to challenge the statement within a certain time period, it is deemed conclusive. It is important that the PSE consider additional safeguards. For example, investors in Singapore are notified four times of any trade: via a contract note, and a settlement note, and monthly and quarterly statements. The PSE may also want to look into facilities for investors to make electronic confirmation of their orders and to block their accounts to stop illegal sales.

Scripless trading provides many benefits which enhance the exchange's attractiveness to investors. However, if not properly implemented, scripless trading can result in much confusion and many loopholes. The PSE must address all of these problems in its plan to go scripless.

CONCLUSION

With the integration to a single-trading system, new opportunities are opening up for the PSE. For example, the PSE can now set up remote trading facilities in branches of local banks to extend the reach of the exchange. By providing more trading centres at provinces such as Cebu and Subic, the PSE will be able to benefit from the growth of these provinces.

The last few years have been an exciting time for the PSE. The PSE's modernisation programme is an obvious indication of the exchange's commitment to greater efficiency and, thus, attractiveness to investors. Clearly, the PSE is gearing itself to get back into business to compete with other Asian exchanges.

REFERENCES

George Robert Lloyd, "The Philippines: A Guide to Asian Stock Markets", Longman Publisher, 1991.

"Monthly Report", Philippine Stock Exchange, January 1995.

"Perfecting CDP's Scrip", *The Straits Times,* 29 September 1992.

"Philippines", *Asia Money*, March 1994.

"Philippine Bourses Agree to Merge Under New Exchange", *The Straits Times*, 24 December 1992.

"SES Journal Discusses Safety of Scripless Trading System", *The Business Times*, 16 October 1992.

"The Pros and Cons of Scripless Stock Trading", *The Straits Times*, 28 March 1993.

Chapter 6

The Philippine Banking System

BY
Jimmy NG
Alex YONG

INTRODUCTION

THIS CHAPTER DESCRIBES the Philippine banking system. Four different types of banks are examined first, followed by a detailed analysis of capital fund requirements, the capital adequacy ratio and liquidity requirements. Next, the monitoring of bank activities is analysed including the role and powers of the Central Bank. The chapter concludes with four critical safeguard measures that should be initiated to strengthen the Philippine banking system in a deregulated environment.

High economic growth in the Asia-Pacific region has fuelled investment opportunities. This has spawned a dynamic market for institutions, corporations and private investors hungry for more complex and sophisticated financial products to manage their increased risk profiles. Governments are reforming their financial sectors to foster a conducive environment supportive of economic growth. As new opportunities arise, existing financial service providers will see the emergence of new players and increased international competition.

The Philippines looks set to follow the path of high growth, like other Asia-Pacific emerging economies. The GNP growth rate reached a record high of 5.07% in 1994, and it was over

5.30% in 1995. To foster economic growth and encourage foreign investments, the government under President Ramos has lifted foreign exchange restrictions to allow repatriation of funds, and liberalised the terms of entry and participation of foreign banks in providing more credit, banking services and products. Up to ten foreign banks may set up operations in the next five years (see Appendix 6–1). The new deregulation subjects the local banks to increased competition.

The introduction of new services and products such as derivatives will increase the systemic risk of the banking industry. Are the Philippine banking regulations and supervision adequate to provide for a sound banking environment, and to foster confidence in the banks?

There are four key elements which are essential in ensuring the soundness of financial institutions and which, collectively, determine the strength of the banking industry. One is the minimum capital required. The level of capitalisation of a bank is a measure of its operating power. Capitalisation has a bearing on profit margins and the bank's ability to compete. The higher the capital, the more it is able to expand its business without compromising depositors' risk level. Another element is the risk-based capital requirements. This is a measure of how much of the bank's capital is put at risk based on the different classes of assets. A third element is the liquidity ratio. This measures the amount of funds available at any moment to meet cash requirements. Finally, there is the process of supervision. This determines the effectiveness in the enforcement of bank regulations. In addition, the Central Bank should be vested with sufficient power to enforce the banking regulations.

We examine these four key elements in the Philippines's banking regulations *vis-à-vis* the Singapore model. The latter is highly regarded as affording a sound system of control in the international banking community.

This chapter provides a brief history and describes the structure of the Central Bank of the Philippines, Bangko Sentral ng Pilipinas (BSP). Next, it provides an overview of the banking system and the different types of banks operating in the Philippines. Finally, the report concludes with a summary of the findings.

HISTORY OF THE CENTRAL BANK

The history of banking services in the Philippines started with the founding in 1594 of credit institutions organised by a Spanish priest. They were known as *Obras Pias* (pious works) which were religious foundations that accumulated large funds donated by wealthy individuals. The funds were invested in real estate and in financing foreign trade.

The first commercial bank, Banco Espanol-Filipino de Isabel II, was established in 1851. It is now known as Bank of the Philippine Islands and it is one of the largest domestic commercial banks in the Philippines. Most of the funds originally came from the *Obras Pias* and from the government. It was founded by Junta de Autoridadas (Board of Authority) which gave it the functions of a Central Bank, and it was responsible for the money supply and issuance of the Spanish colony's first paper money.

In 1873, the Chartered Bank of India, Australia and China (now known as the Standard Chartered Bank) opened its first Philippine branch. This was followed by the Hong Kong and Shanghai Banking Corporation in 1883 with a bank in Manila. Both banks were set up to finance the rapidly expanding sugar industry. These commercial banks were primarily involved in buying and selling drafts and bills of exchange, and banking operations such as acceptance of deposits and loans.

In 1882, the first savings bank started operations. It now exists as the Monte de Piedad Savings Bank and it is under the exclusive authority of the Roman Catholic Archbishop of Manila.

In 1910, the Bank of the Philippine Islands had its first note-issuing function severely curtailed and the notes in issue were gradually withdrawn over a period of years. The Postal Savings Bank was established in 1906 in an attempt to bring banking services to the rural areas. This was abolished in 1976 and its assets and liabilities were transferred to the Philippine National Bank (PNB).

The PNB was founded in 1916 by the government to take over the note-issuing duties of the privately owned banks of the Philippines and to act as the sole depository of government funds. It has expanded into commercial activities. PNB still functions as the government's principal commercial bank.

With the Japanese invasion in 1941, all foreign banks, other than those of the Chinese and Japanese, were expropriated. The first to commence operations after the war were the foreign banks, followed by the four main domestic banks. In 1949, the Central Bank of the Philippines was established to administer the monetary, banking and credit system of the Philippines, and it took over the note-issuing function from PNB.

RA 337 (General Banking Act) enacted in July 1948, vested the Monetary Board of the Central Bank with the authority to regulate the establishment, operations or liquidation of banking and credit institutions of the Philippines, including branches and agencies. The banking reforms of 1972 and 1980 introduced many changes into the country's banking system, and in the powers and authority of the Central Bank in maintaining monetary authority.

STRUCTURE OF THE BANGKO SENTRAL NG OF THE PHILIPPINES

The Central Bank of the Philippines is an incorporated body owned by the State, whose powers and duties are laid down by the Central Bank Act (RA 265, as amended) and General Banking Act (RA 337, as amended). The powers granted to the Central Bank are exercised by the Monetary Board (MB). The latter consists of the following:

(a) Secretary of Finance;
(b) Director-General of the National Economic and Development Authority;
(c) Chairman of the Board of Investors; and
(d) three part-time members from the private sector appointed by the President.

The main duties of the Central Bank are to maintain monetary stability in the Philippines, preserve the international value of the peso and the convertibility of the peso into other freely convertible currencies, and to foster monetary, credit and exchange conditions conducive to a balanced and sustained growth of the economy. The Central Bank has jurisdiction over all banking institutions, non-banking financial intermediaries and non-banking thrift institutions.

THE BANKING SYSTEM IN THE PHILIPPINES

There are different types of banks operating in the Philippines, namely, commercial banks, thrift banks, specialised government banks and rural banks. The commercial banks contribute the bulk of the assets in the banking environment.

Commercial Banks

A commercial bank is a corporation that carries on the business of commercial banking, including the acceptance of current accounts, demand and time deposits, accepting drafts, issuing letters of credit, discounting and negotiating promissory notes, drafts, bills of exchange and other evidences of debt, buying and selling foreign exchange and lending money (see Appendix 6–2).

Expanded commercial activities may be defined as the combination of commercial banking (domestic and international) with the powers of an investment house (underwriting, securities dealership, equity investing). The latter may be achieved either by an in-house department or through a separate subsidiary.

The Monetary Board requires all commercial banks with expanded banking activities to have capital accounts of at least P1 billion each or, in the case of investment houses, either by the conversion to or by merger/consolidation with commercial banks. As of March 1995, there were 33 commercial banks of which 11 were engaged in expanded commercial banking operations and 14 were Philippine branches of foreign banks while the rest were domestic banks with branches nationwide.

Thrift Banks

Three types of thrift banks exist, namely, the savings and mortgage banks, the stock savings and loan associations and the private development banks. A savings and mortgage bank is defined as "any corporation organised for the purpose of accumulating the savings of depositors and investing them". The General Banking Act limits their lending activities to certain types of financing. They may also invest in high-grade bonds, drafts, bullion and equities of allied undertaking as approved by the MB.

The Savings and Loan Associations Act was enacted to regulate and supervise the activities of existing savings and loan associations. Their importance in the Philippine banking sector is small, and their activities are limited to the acceptance of small deposits from their members or stockbrokers and the granting of small personal loans.

The Private Development Banks Act was enacted to control the activities of the private development banks. These banks provide medium- and long-term loans to meet the needs of industry and agriculture. They are allowed to invest up to 25% of their net worth in approved equities and 75% of their loanable funds must be in medium- and long-term loans for economic development purposes. A ceiling of 25% of loanable funds is imposed on investment funds in short-term loans or securities other than real estate mortgages.

Rural Banks

Rural banks provide credit facilities to small farmers and merchants. Ownership of rural banks is restricted to Filipino citizens. They are closely supervised by the Monetary Board of the Central Bank. The Monetary Board has the power to place limits on the maximum credits allowed to any individual borrower and to take over the management of any rural bank in certain circumstances. With the permission of the Central Bank, rural banks may accept savings and time deposits, open current accounts, act as correspondent or collecting agents, or act as a trustee of small farmers' estates or properties. They may also invest in equities of approved undertakings engaged in related activities.

Specialised Government Banks

These are government-owned/controlled banks created by special laws and organised primarily to provide credit facilities necessary for specific projects in order to promote and accelerate socio-economic growth and development, and to expand agriculture and industry.

The following specialised banks are subject to the purview of the Central Bank:

1. The Development Bank of the Philippines was originally known as The Rehabilitation Finance Corporation. Its purpose is the allocation of government funds to all sectors of the economy.
2. The Land Bank of the Philippines charter is contained in the Code of Agrarian Reforms. Its purpose is to provide financial support in the execution of the agrarian reforms which were put into effect shortly after the declaration of martial law in 1972.
3. The Philippines's Amanah Bank was created by Presidential decree in 1973 with the purpose of providing a wide range of banking fa-

cilities to the primarily Muslim provinces on the island of Mindanao. Its head office is located in Marawi City.

Offshore Banking Unit

An offshore banking unit may be a branch, subsidiary or affiliate of a banking corporation, which is duly authorised by the Central Bank as a separate accounting unit to transact offshore banking business in the Philippines. This involves the receipt of foreign currencies of funds principally from external sources and the utilisation of such funds. The unit may transact in any currency other than the Philippine peso. The offshore banking system was established by Presidential Decree No. 1034 in September 1976.

BANKING REGULATIONS

Regulations refer to the issuance of rules of conduct or the establishment of modes or standards of operations for uniform application to all financial institutions or functions covered. In determining such coverage, the distinctive character of the financial institution and the substantive similarities of specific functions to which such rules, modes or standards apply are taken into consideration.

The Manual of Regulations on the Supervision of Financial Intermediaries is a systematic guide used by the Central Bank in the discharge of its examination and supervisory functions. The laws and regulations relevant to the operations of banks are as follows:

(a) the Central Bank Act (RA 265, as amended);
(b) the General Banking Act (RA 337, as amended);
(c) the Philippines Deposit Insurance Corporation Act (RA 3591, as amended);
(d) the Foreign Currency Deposit Act (RA 6426, as amended); and
(e) Authorising Banks to Invest in the Equity of Venture Capital Corporations (RA 1688, as amended).

CAPITAL FUNDS REQUIREMENTS

The minimum capital requirement for commercial banks is P1.25 billion (S$78 million) and for commercial banks with an expanded banking licence (EKB) it is P2.5 billion (S$156 million). For comparison, the minimum capital fund is S$800 million capitalisation for local banks in Singapore (see Appendix 6–3).

In addition, foreign banks under IMF agreement may come in as owners (up to a maximum of 60%) of new or existing banks or full-service banks and be allowed up to six branches, with a minimum capital of P210 million (S$13 million) for the first three branches and P35 million (S$2.2 million) for each of the others. This is above the S$10 million required for foreign banks in Singapore. The high capitalisation and stringent conditions for the entry of foreign banks is to protect the depositors (see Appendix 6–4). However, the level of capitalisation for the local banks differs with that required of foreign banks. This has implications on the ability of the local banks, with their lower capitalisation, to compete with foreign banks.

To compete effectively with foreign banks, local banks need to increase their minimum capitalisation to a level comparable to that of the foreign banks. This may necessitate smaller banks merging with other smaller banks in order to operate as viable commercial banks with expanded licences.

CAPITAL ADEQUACY RATIO

The combined capital account for each commercial bank has to be maintained at 10% of its risk assets which is defined as total assets minus cash on hand, amounts due from the Central Bank and loans or acceptances under letters of credit. While it is higher than the Bank for International Settlement recommendation of 8%, the calculation of risk assets does not include off-balance-sheet items such as derivatives which are becoming a substantial portion of the banks' assets. This capital adequacy ratio is lower than that in Singapore where the Monetary Authority of Singapore (MAS) prescribed a ratio of 12% which takes into account off-balance-sheet assets.

With economic growth and capital inflows into the Philippines, investors are increasingly exposed to the strength of the peso. Various types of derivative instruments are used to hedge against peso depreciation or appreciation as well as interest rate increases. Local banks are increasingly engaged in derivatives trading which are left largely unregulated by the Central Bank. Thus, the 10% capital adequacy ratio which might appear higher than the Bank of International Settlements (BIS) recommendation may not be adequate if off-balance-sheet assets are taken into account. In the future, BIS will require banks to provide capital not only for credit risks but also for market risks. In this respect, the capital adequacy ratio calculation should be maintained at least at the BIS-recommended level of 8% (and maybe even more with the anticipation of the capital requirements for market risks) and should take into account off-balance-sheet assets.

LIQUIDITY REQUIREMENTS

The required reserve requirements against liabilities in the local currency of commercial banks against demand, time and saving deposits varies from 17 to 25% for each type of deposit liability, of which 25% of the required reserves is deposited with the Central Bank (see Appendix 6–5). The remaining portion of the required reserves may be held by a bank in the form of cash or in government securities. The different reserve requirements are imposed by the IMF programme which obliges the government to pursue sound monetary and fiscal policies to promote economic growth. In this regard, the reserve requirement is one of the monetary policy instruments used by the Central Bank to control the money supply (M3) in the economy. This ratio of 17 to 25% is slightly lower than in Singapore where the banking regulation prescribes a minimum 24%. (In adverse situations, banks may be required to hold a reserve requirement of up to 35% on a case-by-case basis.) The 25% of required reserves deposited with the Philippine Central Bank is much higher than the 6% minimum cash balance required by the Monetary Authority of Singapore.

Since the reserve requirement is used basically as a monetary tool to control the money supply rather than to ensure the solvency of banks, it may not be an effective tool for ensuring that banks maintain sufficient liquidity to meet any eventualities. The higher percentage of reserve requirements deposited at the Central Bank would also translate into a higher net cost of funds for the banks in the Philippines as compared to banks in Singapore. Perhaps, an alternative is to adopt a more flexible approach by requiring each bank to formulate its liquidity policy subject to the approval of the Central Bank. This will allow the banks to tailor their policy requirements and at the same time reduce the percentage of funds held by the Central Bank, thus optimising the liquidity/cost of funds ratio.

BANK SUPERVISION

The activities of financial institutions are closely monitored by the Central Bank. There are two ways by which the Central Bank monitors financial institutions: supervision and regulation. Supervision includes not only the issuance of rules and regulations but, also, the overseeing of operations of financial institutions. This is to ascertain that such rules and regulations are complied with. It also includes an investigation to determine whether the financial institution is conducting its business on a sound financial basis (i.e., whether the institution is liquid and solvent). Supervision is broader in scope than regulation because the former seeks to look into the details of operations, activities and performance of a particular institution as it affects both private and public interests.

OBJECTIVES OF BANK SUPERVISION

Supervision is undertaken by the Central Bank for the following purposes:

(a) to ensure full compliance with the laws, rules and regulations affecting the operations and activities of the financial institution;
(b) to ensure that the financial institutions being supervised and regulated are operating on a sound financial basis, so that stockholders are assured of a fair return on their investments;
(c) to act as a guardian of depositors and money market investors in order to ensure that they receive their interest payments and also their deposits and placements;
(d) to protect the investment interest of the government;

(e) to protect the interest of other creditors of financial institutions; and

(f) to ensure the stability, solvency and security of the financial system.

MECHANICS OF BANK SUPERVISION

A supervision and examination sector within the Central Bank is responsible for the prudent supervision and periodic examination of banking institutions operating in the Philippines. Its responsibilities are discharged in accordance with instructions from the Monetary Board.

Supervision is basically undertaken through the review and analysis of reports submitted by a financial institution to a government agency. Upon receipt of the reports, an employee of the government agency examines their contents and, if such reports are financial statements, the employee checks the mathematical accuracy and determines the changes and causes of such changes. The checking process also seeks to determine the compliance of the financial institution with the existing rules and regulations being enforced by the government agency. Should a representative of a regulating office visit the financial institution, it is to secure reports which the former may not have received, or to seek some explanations on certain specific matters not clear to the government agency.

TYPES OF EXAMINATIONS

The Central Bank uses three types of examinations in supervising the banks:

1. ***General or Regular Examination:*** This is undertaken once a year. The examination covers the verification of assets, liabilities and capital accounts to determine the stability and solvency of the bank. It also reviews the income and expenses of the bank to determine the probable profit that stockholders can expect from their investments.
2. ***Special or Interim Examination:*** This is conducted as often as is necessary. It includes a review of special accounts or groups of ac-

counts such as loans or deposits. The examination is usually of short duration since its purpose is limited to a specific area of activity or investigation. It follows up findings from a previous examination to determine whether the bank has implemented the recommendations of the Central Bank, or whether the errors had been corrected as suggested by the examiners.

3. ***Special Investigations:*** Although these are not examinations, the procedures sometimes involve some steps performed during a regular or special examination. Investigations are carried out when a complaint is received by the Central Bank from a borrower, stockholder, depositor, employee, or anyone else regarding the operations of a financial institution. If there is non-compliance, then remedial actions are taken to correct the erroneous or illegal practice of the institution, its officers or employees.

The Central Bank examines banks at least once every 12 months and each examination encompasses at least 85% of the bank's total resources. The approach to bank supervision by the BSP is different from the MAS approach which relies mainly on external auditors. The BSP approach provides a more independent assessment of the bank's financial statements and operations. While it can be argued that external auditors are independent, they operate, nevertheless, as profit-making organisations. The coverage also appears to be more thorough compared to reviews by external auditors.

POWERS OF THE CENTRAL BANK

To assist the examiners in conducting the inspection, the Central Bank has the following powers:

1. Examination of books, documents and records of the bank.
2. The department heads and examiners of supervising departments are authorised to administer oaths to any directors, officers or employees of the bank.
3. Compel the presentation of all books, documents, papers or records necessary to ascertain all the facts relative to the true conditions of the bank, as well as the books and records of persons and entities in

connection with the operations, activities or transactions of the concerned bank.

4. No restraining order or injunction is to be issued by the court enjoining the Central Bank from any examining institution subject to the supervision and/or examination by the Central Bank, unless there is convincing proof that the action of the Central Bank is arbitrary and has been made in bad faith.
5. Department heads and examiners are authorised to examine, inquire or look into all the deposits, including investments in debt instruments issued by the national government, its political subdivisions, and its instrumentalities, after being satisfied that there is reasonable grounds to believe that a bank fraud or serious irregularity has been committed and that it is necessary to look into the deposits to establish such fraud or irregularity.

The Central Bank is further empowered with the following new powers for effective supervision:

1. In addition to the penalties provided by the law, the Central Bank is empowered to impose administrative penalties or sanctions on supervised institutions, and their directors and officers, for any specific offences committed by them.
2. To maintain the quality of bank management and afford better protection to depositors and the public, the Central Bank has the authority to consider and review the qualifications of persons who are elected or appointed bank directors and officers not only before incorporation but, also, during the entire existence of the bank and to disqualify those who are found unfit.
3. The Central Bank also has discretionary authority to appoint a conservator, not connected to the Central Bank, to take over the management and assets of a bank in distress as a step short of liquidation. The conservator is responsible to the Central Bank for the discharge of his duties. The conservator has the power to take charge of all the assets, liabilities and management of the depressed bank, collect all monies and debts due to the bank and exercise all powers necessary to preserve the assets of the bank. He also can reorganise the management of the bank, restore its viability and overrule or revoke the actions of the previous management and Board of Directors, any provision of law to the contrary notwithstanding, and

such other powers granted by the Central Bank which are deemed necessary.

4. To facilitate timely detection of irregularities or practices that may adversely affect the financial condition of a bank, the Central Bank may require the bank to engage the services of an independent auditor who is responsible not only to the bank's Board of Directors but, also, to the Central Bank.

As these points illustrate, the Central Bank is vested with wide-ranging powers to effectively supervise the banks as deemed necessary.

SUMMARY OF FINDINGS

The Philippine banking system, which has been protected from foreign competition for the last four decades, has finally been deregulated. While the deregulation falls short of full liberalisation, the opening of markets to foreign competition on a limited basis, nevertheless, should force an improvement in banking services. However, for local banks accustomed to a protected environment, competition with foreign banks may compel the banks to provide new services such as derivative instruments. These are not only new in the market, but they are also notoriously known to be the cause of huge losses for companies like Proctor and Gamble, and Gibsons. Derivative trading has also caused the downfall of some of the more established banks like Barings. This introduces a new dimension of higher risk taking.

The Philippine banking regulations essentially have all of the elements to ensure confidence in the banking system in an environment where traditional banking services prevail. However, there needs to be improvement in four critical measures to further strengthen the banking system under a deregulated environment. First, the minimum capitalisation of banks should be substantially increased to allow banks to compete and expand their operations, especially in the area of derivative trading. This may cause some smaller banks to merge and consolidate into a handful of highly capitalised banks. Second, the capital adequacy ratio should be amended to take into account off-balance sheet items. It should move towards the BIS recommendations and ideally provide allowance for market risks as well. However, a move towards BIS recommendations requires the banks to either lower their risk assets or increase their capital, which will achieve the same effect as raising the minimum capital level. Third, banks should establish their own liquidity policy and not rely on Central Bank directions, as the liquidity ratio is used by the latter as a monetary tool. While the liquidity ratio moves according to IMF policy to control money supply in the economy, the underlying liquidity need not move with the money supply change. Fourth, the supervision of the banks should cover critical business areas such as derivative trading as well. In summary, it will take substantial resources of the Central Bank to further strengthen the banking environment and allow the local banks to compete with foreign banks, without compromising confidence in the banking system.

APENDIX 6–1
List of Foreign Banks

Approved

1. Deutsche Bank.
2. Chemical Bank.
3. Bangkok Bank.
4. Fuji Bank.
5. Bank of Tokyo.
6. International Commercial Bank of China.
7. Development Bank of Singapore.
8. ING Bank.
9. ANZ Banking Group Ltd.
10. Korea Exchange Bank.

Applications

1. Chase Manhattan.
2. Bankers Trust.
3. Bank of Nova Scotia.
4. Toronto-Dominion Bank.
5. ABN Bank N.V.
6. Banco Santander.
7. Keppel Bank of Singapore.
8. Bank International Indonesia.
9. Overseas-Chinese Banking Corporation.

10. Overseas Union Bank Ltd.
11. Bank Dagang Nacional.

APPENDIX 6–2
Products and Services Offered by Banks

1. Deposits and Related Services:
    (a) demand deposits;
    (b) regular savings deposits;
    (c) time deposits;
    (d) commercial papers;
    (e) manager's checks;
    (f) gift checks;
    (g) domestic collections;
    (h) automated teller machines.
2. International and Export Financing:
    (a) import and export financing;
    (b) foreign and domestic commercial letters of credit;
    (c) standby letters of credit;
    (d) collection of clean and documentary bills;
    (e) bank guarantees;
    (f) foreign and domestic remittances;
    (g) travel funds;
    (h) servicing of foreign loans and investments;
    (i) trade inquiry.
3. Foreign Currency Deposit Unit (FCDU):
    (a) foreign currency savings and time deposits;
    (b) foreign currency loans.
4. Loans and Credit Facilities:
    (a) agricultural, commercial and industrial loans;
    (b) personal loans;
    (c) pre-export financing;
    (d) special lending programmes;
    (e) guarantee programmes;
    (f) consumer lending programmes.
5. Trust and Investment Services:
    (a) investment services;
    (b) corporate trusts;

   (c) estate planning;
   (d) employee benefit planning retirement plans;
   (e) other fiduciary services;
   (f) common trust funds.
6. Others:
   (a) safety deposit boxes;
   (b) payroll services;
   (c) pickup services.

APPENDIX 6–3
Minimum Capital Funds Requirements for Different Types of Banks

1. Commercial banks for FCDU authority – net worth not less than P150 million.
2. Thrift banks located:
   (a) within Metropolitan Manila – P150 million;
   (b) outside Metropolitan Manila – P50 million.
3. Foreign banks with an offshore banking unit (OBU) in the Philippines must hold, at all times, at least US$1 million of its net head office funds either in deposits with the Central Bank, or in investments in primary issues of foreign-currency denominated securities of the Philippine government. Alternatively, it may hold other assets that the Central Bank may approve of from time to time.
4. Rural Banks – P500,000.

The combined capital accounts of each bank should not be less than an amount equal to 10% of its risky assets (which are generally assets other than cash), and the direct and indirect liabilities of the Republic of the Philippines and cash collateral loans.

APPENDIX 6–4
Liberalisation of Foreign Bank Entry

1. The liberalisation law allows ten new foreign banks to open branches in the country within the five-year period, of which four of

the ten shall be chosen by the President upon recommendation by the Monetary Board.

2. A foreign bank must have a permanent assigned capital of not less than P210 million for the first three branches and P35 million for the additional three branches.
3. Only foreign banks belonging to the top 150 in the world, or which are among the top five banks in their country of origin as of the date of application, shall be allowed to operate here.

Guidelines set by the Monetary Board in the selection of the ten new banks:

(a) geographic region;
(b) the volume and trade between the Philippines and the country that the foreign bank represent;
(c) size in terms of the bank's total assets;
(d) banking expertise and international orientation;
(e) global reputation for financial innovations and stability;
(f) reciprocity rights enjoyed by the Philippines's banks in the applicant's country;
(g) willingness to share its technology.

APPENDIX 6–5
Detailed Reserve Requirements

The required reserves against all foreign currency deposit liabilities are as follows:

1. ***Circular No. 343***: Banks authorised to accept foreign currency deposits must maintain at all times 100% foreign currency cover for their deposit liabilities where at least 15% is in the form of foreign currency deposits with the Central Bank. The remaining portion of the required reserves may be in the form of foreign currency deposits with foreign banks, foreign currency short-term loans, readily marketable securities, foreign currency notes and coins. It may also be foreign currency swapped with the Central Bank as represented by the peso amounts arising therefrom.
2. ***Foreign Deposits Liabilities Outside Circular No. 343:*** All foreign

currency deposit liabilities incurred prior to the approval of Circular No. 343, regardless of whether such deposits are classified as demand, time or saving deposits, are 10% of the total amount of such liabilities.

3. ***Presidential Decree No. 1035*:** FCDUs authorised to accept foreign currency deposits must maintain at all times a 100% eligible foreign currency cover. FCDUs are exempt from the requirements of maintaining 15% of the cover in the form of foreign currency deposits with the Central Bank.

Whenever the reserve position of any bank is below the required minimum, it is liable to pay the Central Bank one-tenth of 1% per day on the amount of deficiency occurring one or more days in a week against excess reserves which it may hold on other days of the same week. The penalty to be paid is based on the average daily net deficiency during the week.

REFERENCES

"Asia/Pacific Capital Markets – A Vision of Change", Arthur Anderson, January 1993.

"Banking and Finance in ASEAN", KPMG, September 1991.

"Doing Business in the Philippines", Ernst and Young, December 1992.

Nolledo Jose N., "Banking Laws of the Philippines", 1994.

"Philippines", Moody's Investors Service, January 1994.

Chapter 7

Performance of Local Commercial Banks in the Philippines

BY
FOO May Li
Wilson LAU Wei Hsien
TAN Suat Pheng

INTRODUCTION

BANKS PERFORM WELL when the economy is bad and perform even better when the economy is good. If this idiom is true, then the economic rebound experienced in the Philippines in 1994 has made the banking industry more optimistic. The economy grew 5.1% in real terms, almost double the 2.6% achieved in 1993. Despite this, inflation continued to decelerate and hit 7.1% in December 1994. The economic progress seen in the Philippines was also enhanced by the substantial monetary inflows represented by foreign investments and remittances of earnings of OCWs. Since the condition of the economy reflects the condition of the banking industry, economic growth means a good year for the banks. Judging by the fact that the banks' total assets hit P1 trillion sometime in the fourth quarter of 1994, the above figures certainly paint a rosy picture of the Philippine banking industry.

We wish to thank Dr. John Vong for his guidance and invaluable contribution.

The commercial banks in the Philippines comprise about 80% of the Philippine banking industry which makes them the largest banking sector. They dominate the Philippine financial landscape with their vast branching and office networks, and they are reported to be at the cutting edge of marketing, technology and financial innovation. These banks are certainly the economic backbone and foundation of the country. With this in mind, it is clearly an opportune moment to take a step back and take an in-depth look at the performance of the top commercial banks in the Philippines.

The objectives of this chapter are two-fold. The first objective is to analyse the performance of banks using the Strategic Response Quotient (SRQ) indicator and to compare the findings with those of traditional approaches to the financial analyses of banks, which use return on assets (ROA) and return on equity (ROE). Any deviations in the set of indicators and ratios would be a prime candidate for in-depth studies and further investigation. Such investigation could yield interesting findings otherwise missed by the traditional approach to financial analysis. This information could highlight commercial banks in the Philippines that offer strong growth potential for investors to consider for business partnerships or equity holding. The second objective is to highlight the usefulness of the SRQ indicator to bank analysts or investors for understanding the pressures borne by banks, and how their responses can be measured.

The major source of data was annual reports published by the various banks. A total of 14 annual reports were collected for the study, of which 11 banks are in the top 15 ranking of commercial banks in the Philippines in terms of total assets. Other sources of information include the results and findings from a financial study of commercial banks in the Philippines by SGV & Co., a local accounting firm, which is also a member firm of Arthur Andersen; newspaper cuttings on the latest update on commercial banks as of the fourth quarter of 1994; and a site visit to the China Banking Corporation.

BACKGROUND

Review of Commercial Banking Performance in the Philippines

For the past five years, the Philippine commercial banking industry's performance has been robust. The banking industry has been growing at a yearly average of more than 20%, with net incomes showing an annual increase of over 25% during the same period. Overall, the banking system seems to have outpaced the rest of the economy. Liberalisation, or deregulation, has been a significant feature of Philippine economic policy for the past three years.

In the financial sector, beginning as early as the 1980s, there have been significant policy reforms including the liberalised entry of foreign banks (1994), dismantling of controls over foreign exchange (1992), liberalised branch banking rules (1991) and abolition of interest rate ceilings (1981). These financial reforms have been designed to help strengthen the financial system and to gradually prepare the local banks for a more open regional market.

The performance for the whole commercial banking sector between 1992 and 1993 in terms of earning assets increased 27.1%, from P404,256.6 million to P513,797.3 million (SGV & Co., 1993). Total deposits increased 23.4%, from P424,742.4 million to P524,326.4 million while total loans increased 35.4%, from P298,819.4 million to P404,472.2 million.

Profile of Commercial Banking System in the Philippines

Presently, there are 32 commercial banks operating in the country, of which 26 are private banks, four are foreign banks and two are government-owned banks. Sixteen of the commercial banks are expanded commercial banks or universal banks[1]. The four foreign banks operate as branches of their respective head offices in the Philippines. According to BSP figures, the total assets of the commercial banking system rose to P852.6 billion by the end of 1993, up 27% from 1992. The commercial banks and universal banks account for about 66.2% of market share in terms of total assets in the commercial banking system, state-owned banks account for 25%, and foreign banks account for 8.8%.

Entry of New Foreign Competitors

In May 1994, President Ramos signed into law RA 7721 (the act

---

1 Universal banks are allowed to undertake non-allied banking activities and to underwrite securities (investment banking).

liberalising the entry and scope of operations of foreign commercial banks) after more than two years of intense debate on the issue of banking liberalisation. This Act will allow ten new foreign banks to open branches in the country within a five-year period. Six of the ten will be chosen by the Monetary Board (MB) while the remaining four will be chosen by the President upon recommendation of the MB. As of October 1994, 31 foreign banks had applied for the ten foreign bank branching licences to be issued in the first quarter of 1995. The foreign banks that have been granted branching licences are Deutsche Bank (Germany), Chemical Bank (U.S.), Bangkok Bank (Thailand), Fuji Bank (Japan), Bank of Tokyo (Japan), International Commercial Bank of China (China), Development Bank of Singapore (Singapore), ING Bank (Netherlands), ANZ Banking Group Limited (Australia-New Zealand) and Korea Exchange Bank (Korea).

The rationale for the entry of foreign banks is to decrease concentration in the banking industry. The presence of more foreign banks will facilitate the country's access to foreign capital and increase inflow of foreign investments. The liberalisation of foreign bank entries will create a number of benefits for the financial system. These include more credit available to investors, competitive interest rates on loans and deposits, easier access of exporters to foreign markets, introduction of more innovative banking products, possible transfer of technology, enhanced efficiency in the banking sector and encouraging efficient financial intermediation process between sources (savers) and users (investors) of funds.

However, with the liberalisation of foreign bank entry, the Central Bank has to guard against possible risks, such as selecting "poor" quality banks, the possibility of being "over-banked" and the possible domination by foreign banks in the local commercial banking system, which could subject the Philippines's financial system to external manipulation. In addition, foreign banks may repatriate more capital than they put in as well as engage in transfer pricing (e.g., foreign banks may overvalue credits on loans to their head office).

Nature of Foreign Bank Presence

The operations of foreign commercial banks can be classified into three categories: (a) representative or regional offices; (b) offshore banking units or OBUs; and (c) bank branches. Representative offices serve the function of liaisons, soliciting business for the parent bank and its local affiliates. As liaison offices, they require only limited physical presence.

OBUs, in operation since 1976, are allowed to accept deposits from non-Philippine residents and extend loans to foreign countries. However, they are not allowed to transact in pesos, or borrow and accept deposits from local residents. The assets of OBUs are all offshore and, therefore, are not part of the domestic financial system.

Foreign bank branches are much like local commercial banks. They operate under a full commercial bank licence and can perform all the traditional banking functions, such as accepting deposits and extending loans, but they are not allowed to become universal banks or to fully participate in trust activities. The number of branches is also limited to three.

Profile of Foreign Commercial Banks in the Philippines

To date, there are 19 representative offices, 18 OBUs, 19 banks with minority equity participation in commercial banks and thrift banks, and four foreign bank branches. Some prominent OBUs include AMEX Bank, Bank of Tokyo, Banque Indosuez, Banque Nationale de Paris, Chase Manhattan Bank, Credit Lyonnais, Deutsche Bank and Korea Exchange Bank. The foreign banks are Citibank NA, Standard Chartered Bank, Hong Kong and Shanghai Banking Corporation, and Bank of America. These banks have been in existence in the Philippines prior to the passage of the General Banking Act in 1948. There are six local commercial banks with existing tie-ups with foreign banks: Citytrust (Citibank NA, 40%); Far East Bank (Chemical Bank and Sakura Bank, 24%), Philipinas Bank (Bank of Tokyo, 30%); Prudential Bank (Bank of Tokyo, 10%); RCBC (Sanwa Bank, 25%); and Solid Bank (Bank of Nova Scotia, 39%).

CHALLENGES IN THE BANKING ENVIRONMENT

There are three major challenges facing banks today. They are: capital adequacy requirement, bank operating costs and fee-based income. These challenges are described and discussed in the following sections.

Capital Adequacy Requirement

The capital adequacy requirement is mandated by the MB, and it is established to be a minimum ratio between capital- and risk-weighted assets. Managing this ratio is of concern for banks as it affects their core business, that is, making loans and advances. Banks need to maintain an adequate level of capital to provide for any adversity and, at the same time, leverage on different types of loans and advances to maximise their profitability.

According to the Bank for International Settlements (BIS), bank capital is divided into two classes: tier one and two. Tier one (or core) capital comprises items such as paid-up ordinary shares, non-payable share premiums, general reserves, retained earnings, non-cumulative irredeemable preference shares and minority interest in subsidiaries. Tier two (or supplementary) capital comprised items such as general provisions for doubtful debts, asset revaluation reserves, cumulative irredeemable preference shares and mandatory convertible notes.

Risk-weighted assets are financial claims such as loans and advances that are weighted by their levels of risk. Not all loans have the same risk profile. Any increase in loans and advances will need an increase of capital. The risk profile of the additional loans will also determine the level of capital increase. Thus, we can see that the ability to raise capital affects the lending growth and, consequently, the bank's profitability since interest earnings form a major portion of a bank's total income. For the Philippines, the capital adequacy requirement has been reduced from a high of 25 to 17%.

Operating Costs

The second major challenge facing banks is rising costs. The days of booming business expansions and strong economic growths worldwide are in the past. The 1990s is largely a period of uncertain or recessionary growth prospects for many economies. Businesses have had to reorganise and restructure in light of keen competitive pressures. To remain viable, organisations are down-sizing or streamlining their business processes and embarking on cost control measures to respond to the changes in the business environment.

For banks, we can classify operating costs into two broad categories of costs: interest cost (IC) and non-interest cost (NIC). IC, or the cost of funds, is dictated by the forces of supply and demand. Banks normally will lend at a certain percentage above the cost of the funds. The interest rate at which a bank chooses to price its loans is dependent on factors such as credit risk and competition. The differential between the lending rate and the cost of funds is the interest spread which is a chief source of income for banks. The ability to effectively manage the interest spread is of prime concern for the banks. The NIC relates to factors such as staff, technology, property and communications. Both of these cost categories form the broad operating overheads that banks have to deal with.

Fee-based Income

To ensure profitability, banks are constantly faced with the prospect of generating income while addressing the issue of raising additional capital to meet legislative requirements, managing the credit risk involved in lending, as well as capping bank operating overheads. One way to tackle these complicated issues is through activities-generating fee-based income.

Fee-based income consists of items such as fees, commissions, dividends from its investments, brokerage and exchange profit. Collectively, these are known as non-interest revenue (NIR). In an attempt to increase their NIR to boost their earnings, banks have resorted to measures such as risk management products (forwards, options, swaps), financial markets, secondary markets, consumer banking (current account with a savings element and linked to a credit card), trade finance (underwriting and overdraft facilities) and enhanced delivery processes (remote electronic transacting).

TRADITIONAL APPROACHES FOR MEASURING BANK PERFORMANCE

Use of Financial Ratios

Traditionally, the primary concepts of business finance which have been developed for analysing non-financial, profit-oriented corporations have also been used for analysing the performance of commercial banks. Two principal dimensions of bank performance are profitability and risk. The two most commonly used measures of profitability are the return on assets (ROA) and the return on equity (ROE). In addition, other measures considered specific to banks and financial institutions are often calculated. Capturing the essence of the risk concept is more difficult because there are numerous dimensions of risk – credit risk, interest rate risk, liquidity risk, capital risk and fraud risk. Nevertheless, proxies for such measurements have been determined and used. Banks often make adaptations to ratios in order to suit their needs as well as use other supplementary ratios to enhance the evaluation.

A Model for Measuring Bank Performance – The CAMEL Approach

The CAMEL rating system is used by bank regulators to assess the general financial condition of banks. These secret ratings go by the acronym CAMEL which is taken from the key components of the safety and soundness examination process and includes capital adequacy, asset quality, management, earnings and liquidity.

Each of these dimensions is rated on a scale from one to five for its level of supervisory attention at the bank under examination. A low level of supervisory concern receives a one while a high level is a five. Finally, a composite rating based upon the individual components is given to the bank. The possible meanings of the composite rating, as defined by the regulators, are as follows:

1. ***Composite 1:*** Banks in this group are sound institutions in almost every respect.
2. ***Composite 2:*** Banks in this group are also fundamentally sound institutions but may reflect modest weaknesses correctable in the normal course of business.
3. ***Composite 3:*** Banks in this group exhibit a combination of weaknesses ranging from moderately severe to unsatisfactory. Such banks are vulnerable and require more than normal supervision.
4. ***Composite 4:*** Banks in this group have an immoderate volume of asset weaknesses or a combination of other conditions that are less than satisfactory. A potential for failure is present but it is not pronounced.
5. ***Composite 5:*** Banks in this group possess an intensity and nature of weaknesses that require urgent aid from the shareholders or other sources. The probability of failure is high for these banks.

The model has sometimes been used by researchers to study bank performance or predict bank failures. For example, Thomson (1991) used CAMEL-motivated variables to model bank failures of all sizes. Proxy variables based on balance sheet and income data were drawn from an extensive literature on bank failures. The ratio of book equity capital, less bad loans, to total assets was the proxy for capital adequacy. Net charge-offs to total loans, and net loans and leases to total assets, were some of the measures used as proxies for asset quality. Overhead to total assets, and insider loans to total assets, were the proxies for management risk. ROA was the proxy for the earning component, and non-deposit liabilities to cash and investment securities were included to proxy for liquidity risk.

THEORETICAL FRAMEWORK: THE SRQ INDICATOR

In an article published in the *SES Journal* (Vong, 1994), a new indicator was introduced for measuring bank performance – the SRQ. The SRQ indicator is a financial representation of the strategic responses of a bank to challenges in the business environment. It is an indicator of how well a bank is performing in response to challenges such as fulfilling capital adequacy requirements, managing bank operating costs, absorbing competitive pressures, managing credit risks and interest spread and, at the same time, satisfying bank shareholders and institutional investors with a favourable picture of growth and profitability.

The SRQ is made up of four key components of a bank: (a) interest revenue (IR); (b) interest cost (IC); (c) non-interest revenue (NIR); and (d) non-interest cost (NIC). IR refers to items such as interest from loans, investments and deposits with banks. IC refers to items such as interest paid for deposits or borrowings by the banks. NIR refers to items such as trading gains, service charges, commission and foreign exchange profits. NIC refers to items such as compensation, fringe benefits and other operating expenses. The SRQ is derived by dividing net interest income by net non-interest costs, or (IR – IC)/(NIC – NIR).

The quotient is expressed as the number of times coverage of net operating cost by the net interest margin. This is a reflection of the level of responsiveness of a bank to changes in the business environment. It provides an insight into the way banks manage key issues of cost control and revenue generation. Banks with improved quotients would indicate improved levels of responsiveness whereas banks with declining quotients would indicate a reduced ability to respond to the business environment.

With the indicator, one can also analyse the nature and source of the improvement or reduction in responsiveness. For example, the NIC is an indication of whether a bank is effectively managing its operating overhead while the NIR is an indication of the significance of the fee-based income to the bank. The net interest income (IR – IC) is an indication of how well a bank's interest spread is managed. These indicators can enable us to gain valuable insights into the operational and management philosophy of a bank.

ANALYSIS AND IMPLICATIONS

Cost and Expenditure Patterns of Banks

On a net interest margin (i.e., IR–IC) basis, Prudential Bank scored a 48.8% increase, followed by PNB with a 23% increase and Security Bank with a 19% increase (see Table 7–1).

On a net operating cost basis (see Table 7–2), Urban ranked first for lowering net operating costs by 64.2%. This was followed closely by Landbank (50.2%) and Metro Bank (38.1%).

TABLE 7–1
Changes in Net Interest Margin

Name of Bank	Change in Net Interest Margin	Change in IR	Change in IC
Prudential Bank	48.8%	3.1%	−16.9%
PNB	23.0%	1.3%	−11.0%
Security Bank	19.0%	9.7%	−1.8%
Landbank	12.2%	54.2%	121.1%
Chinabank	12.0%	4.5%	−1.3%
RCBC	12.0%	−13.0%	−24.3%

TABLE 7–2
Changes in Net Operating Costs

Name of Bank	Change in Net Operating Cost	Change in NIC	Change in NIR
Urban Bank	–64.2%	7.0%	22.6%
Landbank	–50.2%	33.2%	181.9%
Metro Bank	–38.1%	7.5%	43.3%
Equitable Bank	–7.7%	26.4%	44.7%

In terms of SRQ, eight (57%) banks showed a decline in SRQ. With the exception of RCBC, the declines were marginal (2.5 or less). Two banks maintained their SRQ, and four banks reflected increases in SRQ – an indication that these four banks were able to respond appropriately in their strategic programmes to macroeconomic challenges.

Detailed figures of interest revenue and interest costs can be found in Appendices 7–1, 7–2 and 7–3. A more thorough analysis of changes in the SRQ is discussed next.

Analysis of Changes in SRQ

1. ***Increases in SRQ:*** Those banks which showed increases in SRQ are presented in Table 7–3 (see Appendix 7–4 for details).

   Equitable Bank experienced a decline of 7.6% and 13.3% in IR and IC, respectively. The decline in IR was mainly due to a drop in interest income collected on trading account securities, investment securities and on deposits with banks. The drop in interest expense on deposits, bills payables and other borrowings contributed to the 13.3% decline in IC. NIC and NIR, on the other hand, have increased by 26.4% and 44.7%, respectively. The increase in NIC was due mostly to increased compensation, fringe benefits expenses and other operating expenses incurred. However, a 96.7% increase in foreign exchange profit as well as substantial increases in service charges, fees, commissions collected, trading gains and increased net earnings of subsidiaries, contributed to a 44.7% increase in NIR. Overall, there was a slight increase in SRQ of 0.3%.

TABLE 7–3
Positive Changes in SRQ

	1993	1992	Absolute increase
Equitable Bank	3.8	3.5	0.3
Landbank	4.3	1.9	2.4
Metro Bank	3.1	2.0	1.1
Urban Bank	13.9	5.5	8.4

For Landbank, all four components, namely IR, IC, NIC and NIR, showed substantial increases ranging from 33.2% to 181.9%. A 287% increase in interest earnings in 1993 over 1992, from trading account securities, significantly contributed to a 54.2% increase in IR. IC increased by 121.1% due to a 185% increase in interest paid on deposits brought about by a 43.8% increase in the bank's borrowings in 1993 (an additional borrowing of P3,095,220,000 from 1992). The largest increase of 181.9% was registered for NIR, and was attributed to substantial increases in foreign exchange profits (P487.59 million in 1993 against P76.57 million in 1992) and other non-interest income (P821.02 million in 1993, up from P150.14 million in 1992).

In the case of Metro Bank, while NIC increased by 7.5%, there was a substantial increase in NIR (43.3%) and, hence, a resultant net decline of net operating cost (NIC – NIR) by 38.1%. This accounted for the increase in SRQ from 2.0 times in 1992 to 3.1 times in 1993.

As a result of its prudent and anticipatory positioning strategy, Metro Bank's foreign exchange gain of P356.33 million was among the highest in the industry in 1993, contributing to the 43.3% increase in NIR. More importantly, Metro Bank's performance in servicing client needs was consistent throughout the year, even during the turbulent last quarter of 1993 when the peso sank to a low of P30.55/US$1 and interbank call loan rates soared to a high of 50%.

Metro Bank was able to improve its profitability in foreign currency dealings through intensified bond trading activities and new loan bookings. Trading volumes in U.S. treasuries, investment grade and Philippine bonds reached record levels and yielded substantially improved trading gains. In addition, Metro Bank's fund management arm was named the most outstanding commercial bank under the Industrial Guarantee and Loan Fund (IGLF)

Programme funded by the World Bank and the Asian Development Bank. Also, Metro Bank successfully retained its leading position as an accredited government securities dealer, and held the top spot among all private commercial banks in BSP's rankings for most of the year.

Therefore, the bank's strategy should be to capitalise on its strength in fund management and foreign exchange dealings to further improve its NIR. It will be to the bank's advantage to continue broadening its scope and reaching into non-traditional financial products.

For Urban Bank, IR and IC increased by 4.4 and 29.3%, respectively. Net interest margin was thus dampened by the higher increase in IC as compared to the IR. The 29.3% increase in IC was attributed to a significant increase (285% in 1993) in interest paid on bills payable and other borrowings. However, the bank had a high increase in NIR of 22.6% brought about by a 44.4% increase in service charges, fees and commissions as compared to an increase of NIC of 7.0%. Overall, SRQ increased from 5.5 times in 1992 to 13.9 times in 1993.

2. ***No change in SRQ:*** The two banks which showed no change in SRQ were Far East Bank and PCI Bank. Despite changes in the four components of SRQ, SRQ remained stable because of some offsetting effects (see Appendix 7–4 for details).

   For Far East Bank, IR decreased by 8.1% but this was offset by a larger decrease of 19.4% in IC. This led to a small increase in net interest margin. The improvement in net interest income by 2.3%, moderated somewhat by the overall decline in interest rate levels, was attributed to the expansion in earning assets and the relative decline in funding cost due to the enhancement in the deposit mix. The bank's strategic move towards loan portfolio expansion and diversification protected the earnings base from the eroding impact of low interest on net interest income. The portfolio build-up also afforded the opportunity to derive collateral foreign exchange business and compensating deposit balances.

   Income from foreign exchange operations, as well as other commissions and charges, accounted for 63.5% of total other income, and grew by 32.3% to P1,173 billion during 1993. In addition, equity income from earnings of unconsolidated subsidiaries rose from P8.49 million in 1992 to P89.66 million in

1993 which represented an increase of 956%. The improvement of 40.3% in miscellaneous income came from non-interest fees from the various consumer banking portfolios, gains on the disposal of property and fees derived from other commercial banking operations. However, a 53.97% decline in trading gains on securities holdings moderated the increase in NIR to 22.8%. An increase in NIC by 15.6% led to a moderate increase in net operating costs of 3.6%. Overall, the SRQ remained stable.

3. ***Decreases in SRQ:*** Eight out of the fourteen banks had decreases in SRQ. All the declines were fairly small, with the exception of RCBC which showed a decline in the SRQ of 7.7 (from 12.3 times in 1992 to 4.6 times in 1993). Although RCBC had an increase in net interest earnings of 12%, it was burdened by a substantial rise in net operating costs of 200% which more than offset the gain, thus giving a decline in the SRQ. A closer examination of the income statement of RCBC indicated that the greatest increase for NIC came from the item "compensation and fringe benefits" with a cost increase of P121 billion (or 30.3%) as compared to 1992. To improve its financial performance, RCBC should adopt new strategies to improve its IR (which declined by 13.0%) and NIR (which only improved by a marginal 0.3%) while NIC increased by 14.7%.

COMPARISON OF SRQ WITH TRADITIONAL APPROACHES

Changes in ROA, ROE and SRQ

Table 7–4 depicts comparative figures of the changes in ROA and ROE, that is, the traditional approaches, and SRQ for the 14 banks in our study.

The ROE measure focuses on returns accruing to the residual owners of the firm (i.e., common shareholders). The ROA measure can be interpreted in two different ways. First, it is an indicator of management's operating efficiency, or how well management is using the assets at its disposal to generate profits. Alternatively, it can be viewed as the total return accruing to the providers of capital independent of the source of capital.

TABLE 7–4
Percentage Changes in ROA, ROE and SRQ
(1992 to 1993)

Name of Bank	ROA	ROE	SRQ
Allied Bank	– 1.1	– 8.0	– 1.2
BPI Bank	– 0.2	– 4.3	– 0.3
Chinabank	– 0.4	– 5.0	– 2.5
Equitable Bank	– 0.3	– 3.7	0.3
Far East Bank	0.0	– 2.4	0.0
Landbank	NA	NA	2.4
Metro Bank	0.0	0.2	1.1
PCI Bank	– 0.4	– 3.8	0.0
PNB	– 0.2	– 1.6	– 0.7
Prudential Bank	0.2	– 0.8	– 1.7
RCBC	– 0.5	– 6.6	– 7.7
Security Bank	0.1	– 2.3	– 0.1
Union Bank	– 0.7	– 3.4	– 0.5
Urban Bank	– 1.5	– 3.1	8.4

Note: NA = not available.

Table 7–4 shows that banks generally experienced declines in ROA and ROE in 1993 as the banking industry became increasingly, and fiercely, competitive. It is interesting to note, however, that despite declining ROA and ROE, some banks showed increases in the SRQ which indicates that these banks were responding positively to challenges in the business environment. These banks are Equitable Bank, Landbank, Metro Bank and Urban Bank (see Appendix 7–4).

Ranking by ROA, ROE and SRQ – Cross-Sectional Comparison

In Table 7–5, ranking the 14 banks by ROA, ROE and SRQ showed mixed results. The best performance in terms of SRQ is posted by Urban Bank (ranked number one with a SRQ of 13.9 times). The ranking indicates that it has the best strategic response to the macroeconomic challenges in the business environment. Urban Bank's position is also confirmed by being ranked number one in terms of ROA, but it has a ranking of 13 in terms of ROE.

TABLE 7–5
Ranking of Banks by SRQ, ROA and ROE (1993)
(thousands of pesos)

Name of Bank	SRQ	Rank	ROA	Rank	ROE	Rank
Allied Bank	3.1	8	2.9	2	20.4	9
BPI Bank	2.6	11	2.3	8	25.5	4
Chinabank	3.9	4	2.9	2	21.0	7
Equitable Bank	3.8	5	2.3	8	20.7	8
Far East Bank	2.6	11	2.7	4	21.5	6
Landbank	4.3	3	2.6	6	29.9	1
Metro Bank	3.1	8	2.5	7	26.2	3
PCI Bank	3.2	7	2.7	4	22.6	5
PNB	3.5	6	2.2	10	16.6	10
Prudential Bank	2.0	13	1.8	12	15.4	11
RCBC	4.6	2	2.1	11	27.1	2
Security Bank	1.8	14	1.6	14	14.4	12
Union Bank	2.7	10	1.7	13	11.5	14
Urban Bank	13.9	1	3.4	1	13.7	13

Source: ROA/ROE figures from SGV & Co. Report on "A Study of Commercial Banks in Philippines"

RCBC ranked second in terms of both SRQ (4.6 times) and ROE, but it ranked seventh in terms of ROA. RCBC's performance must take into account the fact that it posted the largest decline in SRQ. In the same context, Chinabank ranked fourth by SRQ (3.9 times), second by ROA, and seventh by ROE, but posted declines in all the three ratios in 1993 as against 1992. Therefore, besides Urban Bank, those that showed strong growth prospects are Landbank (ranked third by SRQ, sixth by ROA and first by ROE) and Equitable Bank (fifth by SRQ, and eighth by both ROA and ROE).

CONCLUSION

With the ROA and ROE analyses, one side of the story is revealed. However, with the application of the SRQ indicator, another perspective into the workings of banks is presented, which includes operating overheads, competitive pressures and non-interest revenue generation. The SRQ indicator is certainly a useful technique, not only to complement existing approaches in examining the financial health of the banks in question, but also to ferret out useful nuggets of information that might otherwise be missed by other approaches. With the SRQ, prospective bank analysts or investors are better equipped with the necessary information to make the appropriate business decisions.

Based on the findings, banks are responding to the business environment in varying degrees. About 50% of the banks studied registered a decline in their responsiveness. This indicates that, despite good financial showings, their degree of responsiveness to increased competition could be a source of concern in the future. However, this is no cause for alarm. With the pace of economic progress lifting the nation out of the doldrums, this insight would enable banks to take decisive steps to rectify and/or improve their responsiveness. There is a clear indication that banks should carefully examine their cost control measures to ensure that they continue to stay competitive. Fee-based income is also widely acknowledged to be an important source of revenue for banks.

The key determinants to long-term success for banks lie in balancing the activities of garnering deposits, lending and controlling expenses. How well banks respond to these challenges is dependent on managements' ability to strategically position themselves in the market. Only then will banks assume a leading role in the economy and be a vital success factor in the Philippines.

APPENDIX 7–1
Bank Interest Revenue and Interest Cost: 1992 and 1993
(Thousands of pesos)

Name of Bank	Interest Revenue (IR)			Interest Cost (IC)		
	1993	1992	Change (%)	1993	1992	Change (%)
Allied Bank	2,182,978	2,186,549	-0.2	1,016,253	1,010,692	0.6
BPI Bank	7,377,887	8,118,308	-9.1	3,908,238	4,630,535	-15.6
Chinabank	2,106,609	2,015,000	4.5	1,114,104	1,128,830	-1.3
Equitable Bank	2,086,499	2,258,434	-7.6	1,141,621	1,316,413	-13.3
Far East Bank	4,146,898	4,512,361	-8.1	1,749,065	2,169,033	-19.4
Landbank	5,471,120	3,548,830	54.2	3,023,640	1,367,270	121.1
Metro Bank	6,335,252	6,506,469	-2.6	3,452,132	3,500,108	-1.4
PCI Bank	3,524,356	3,893,257	-9.5	1,412,116	1,821,173	-22.5
PNB	9,144,475	9,030,779	1.3	5,147,544	5,780,598	-11.0
Prudential Bank	1,432,205	1,389,216	3.1	803,116	966,569	-16.9
RCBC	2,978,645	3,424,865	-13.0	1,784,284	2,358,388	-24.3
Security Bank	1,129,652	1,029,561	9.7	564,980	554,938	1.8
Union Bank	1,294,923	1,040,879	24.4	873,082	624,547	39.8
Urban Bank	287,177	274,987	4.4	133,626	103,364	29.3

Source: Annual reports.

APPENDIX 7–2
Bank Non-interest Cost and Non-interest Revenue: 1992 and 1993
(Thousands of pesos)

Name of Bank	Non-interest Cost (NIC)		Change (%)	Non-interest Revenue (NIR)		Change (%)
	1993	1992		1993	1992	
Allied Bank	1,099,696	862,518	27.5	719,799	587,707	22.5
BPI Bank	3,122,578	2,741,435	13.9	1,785,653	1,543,471	15.7
Chinabank	775,809	644,932	20.3	524,079	507,102	3.3
Equitable Bank	975,160	771,454	26.4	726,799	502,417	44.7
Far East Bank	2,770,800	2,396,438	15.6	1,847,279	1,504,828	22.8
Landbank	2,393,690	1,797,050	33.2	1,819,940	645,510	181.9
Metro Bank	3,621,915	3,369,528	7.5	2,704,446	1,887,875	43.3
PCI Bank	2,363,790	2,065,504	14.4	1,698,423	1,415,802	20.0
PNB	4,307,749	3,662,276	17.6	3,162,853	2,887,421	9.5
Prudential Bank	693,881	514,639	34.8	379,128	399,676	-5.1
RCBC	1,383,279	1,206,109	14.7	1,123,006	1,119,348	0.3
Security Bank	724,971	539,277	34.4	407,932	281,272	45.0
Union Bank	560,687	412,577	35.9	401,561	280,870	43.0
Urban Bank	184,365	172,369	7.0	173,293	141,404	22.6

Source: Annual reports.

APPENDIX 7–3
Strategic Response Quotient: 1992 and 1993
(Thousands of pesos)

Name of Bank	IR less IC		Change (%)	NIC less NIR		Change (%)	SRQ		Change in SRQ
	1993	1992		1993	1992		1993	1992	
Allied Bank	1,166,725	1,175,857	-0.8	379,897	274,811	38.2	3.1	4.3	-1.2
BPI Bank	3,469,649	3,487,773	-0.5	1,336,925	1,197,964	11.6	2.6	2.9	-0.3
Chinabank	992,505	886,170	12.0	251,730	137,830	82.6	3.9	6.4	-2.5
Equitable Bank	944,878	942,021	0.3	248,361	269,037	-7.7	3.8	3.5	0.3
Far East Bank	2,397,833	2,343,328	2.3	923,521	891,610	3.6	2.6	2.6	0.0
Landbank	2,447,480	2,181,560	12.2	573,750	1,151,540	-50.2	4.3	1.9	2.4
Metro Bank	2,883,120	3,006,361	-4.1	917,469	1,481,653	-38.1	3.1	2.0	1.1
PCI Bank	2,112,240	2,072,084	1.9	665,367	649,702	2.4	3.2	3.2	0.0
PNB	3,996,931	3,250,181	23.0	1,144,896	774,855	47.8	3.5	4.2	-0.7
Prudential Bank	629,089	422,647	48.8	314,753	114,963	173.8	2.0	3.7	-1.7
RCBC	1,194,361	1,066,477	12.0	260,273	86,761	200.0	4.6	12.3	-7.7
Security Bank	564,672	474,623	19.0	317,039	258,005	22.9	1.8	1.8	-0.1
Union Bank	421,841	416,332	1.3	159,126	131,707	20.8	2.7	3.2	-0.5
Urban Bank	153,551	171,623	-10.5	11,072	30,965	-64.2	13.9	5.5	8.3

APPENDIX 7–4
SRQ, ROA and ROE: 1992 and 1993
(Thousands of pesos)

Name of Bank	SRQ		Change in SRQ	ROA		Change in ROA	ROE		Change in ROE
	1993	1992		1993	1992		1993	1992	
Allied Bank	3.1	4.3	-1.2	2.9	4.0	-1.1	20.4	28.4	-8.0
BPI Bank	2.6	2.9	-0.3	2.3	2.5	-0.2	25.5	29.8	-4.3
Chinabank	3.9	6.4	-2.5	2.9	3.3	-0.4	21.0	26.0	-5.0
Equitable Bank	3.8	3.5	0.3	2.3	2.6	-0.3	20.7	24.4	-3.7
Far East Bank	2.6	2.6	0.0	2.7	2.7	0.0	21.5	23.9	-2.4
Landbank	4.3	1.9	2.4	2.6	NA	NA	29.9	NA	NA
Metro Bank	3.1	2.0	1.1	2.5	2.5	0.0	26.2	26.0	0.2
PCI Bank	3.2	3.2	0.0	2.7	3.1	-0.4	22.6	26.4	-3.8
PNB	3.5	4.2	-0.7	2.2	2.4	-0.2	16.6	18.2	-1.6
Prudential Bank	2.0	3.7	-1.7	1.8	1.6	0.2	15.4	16.2	-0.8
RCBC	4.6	12.3	-7.7	2.1	2.6	-0.5	27.1	33.7	-6.6
Security Bank	1.8	1.8	-0.1	1.6	1.5	0.1	14.4	16.7	-2.3
Union Bank	2.7	3.2	-0.5	1.7	2.4	-0.7	11.5	14.9	-3.4
Urban Bank	13.9	5.5	8.4	3.4	4.9	-1.5	13.7	16.8	-3.1

Source: ROA and ROE figures from SGV & Co. report on "A Study of Commercial Banks in the Philippines".

REFERENCES

"A Study of Commercial Banks in the Philippines", SGV & Co., 1993.

Annual reports of banks, 1993.

Davies B., "A Shake Up Is Coming", *Asia Money and Finance*, Special Supplement, September 1992, pp. 33–5.

Garcia Paul Joseph M., "Banking on a Better Future: Medium-Term Prospects of Commercial Banking Under a Liberalised Environment", *Financial Forecast*, Vol. 2, No. 11, November 1994.

Lucero Cybele C., "Opening Windows of Opportunity", *Business World,* Special Report on the Commercial Banking System Year End Performance, 15 February 1995, pp. 27–8.

Rigoberto Tiglao, "High Interest: Philippines Prepares to Allow More Foreign Banks", *Far Eastern Economic Review*, 21 April 1994.

Scott David F. Jr., William G. Jens and Spudeck Raymond, "Give Public Access to Taxpayer-Funded Secret Bank Ratings System", *Challenge*, Vol. 34, No. 6, November/December 1991, pp. 58–60.

Site Visit to Chinabank Corporation on 28 February 1995.

Thomson James B., "Predicting Bank Failure in the 1980s", *Economic Review*, Vol. 27, No. 1, 1991, pp. 9–20.

Vong John, "Strategic Response Quotient – A Major Indicator of Bank Performance", *SES Journal*, August 1994, pp. 11–16.

Chapter 8

Monetary Reforms and the Central Monetary Authority

BY
Albert EE
LEE Wai Fai
TAY Lip Guan

INTRODUCTION

THIS CHAPTER INITIALLY describes several monetary reforms enacted by the Philippine government in the post-Marcos era. It then focuses on the objectives of the new Central Monetary Authority and the policy tools available to attain these goals. Next, monetary policy is examined from the perspective of foreign exchange markets, money markets, and the emerging impact of the derivatives market.

During the Marcos regime, martial law gave the President extensive powers to enforce his policies unopposed, especially in fiscal matters. Fiscal prudence was not exercised because the government was able to finance its fiscal matters through foreign loans, borrowing largely from the IMF. The period between 1970 and 1983 was a debt-driven growth period in which external imbalances and the lack of investment were offset by the availability of foreign loans. From 1970 to 1979, the economy grew an average of 6.3% per annum.

After 1979, external financing was reduced and foreign aid was no longer sufficient to meet the country's balance-of-payments deficit. The political uncertainty of Marcos's reign in 1983 exacerbated uncertainty when the country declared a debt moratorium. Massive capital outflows greatly undermined investor confidence in the economy. From 1984 to 1985, the Philippines was faced with negative real growth of 15.7% and an average inflation rate of about 28%, after the relatively peaceful expulsion of President Marcos.

With a balance-of-payment crisis at hand in 1986, the new Aquino government formulated the Medium-Term Philippine Development Plan for the period 1987 to 1992 to resuscitate the economy and sustain economic development. For a short period of time, Aquino's government represented political stability that restored confidence in foreign investors to return to the country. However, the Aquino government was constantly threatened by military coups and one of the coups was almost successful. Fortunately, the timely intervention by the United States, which had a strong military presence at Subic Bay, helped to restore political stability.

The plan called for the implementation of major structural reforms to rejuvenate the private sector and remove market distortions that had deterred consumption and new investments. Liberalisation of foreign investment laws and the foreign exchange market, tariff and tax reforms, and the deregulation of the industry sector, were all instrumental in developing various sectors of the economy. In addition, the government's pump-priming measures to kindle consumption and investment resulted in a real GNP growth rate of 7.2% in 1988. Real GNP from 1986 to 1989 grew at an average rate of 6% per annum. Unfortunately, the momentum of economic growth and development initiated by the plan could not be sustained. During the period 1989 to 1992, growth was severely hampered by inadequate infrastructure facilities, an unstable political environment, deteriorating macro-economic conditions and a succession of natural disasters.

Faced with inflationary pressures that undermined the economy and a balance-of-payments crisis in early 1991, the government had to temporarily suspend the plan's growth objectives in order to implement the economic stabilisation programme (ESP). The ESP was to provide new foreign loans to the country on the condition that the Philippines comply with the IMF's prescribed fiscal and monetary targets on a quarterly basis. Huge macro imbalances in the balance-of-payments and government budget made it very difficult for the Philippines to sustain growth and development. However, in July 1991, the Philippines violated its ESP terms and the IMF was forced to freeze credit lines to the country. Overall, stabilising the economy was done at the expense of growth. Real growth contracted by 0.1% in 1991.

The ESP, which ended in March 1993, was supposed to be followed by an "extended fund facility" to be effective by June. However, talks with the IMF broke off because the Ramos government disagreed with the IMF macroeconomic targets. The government had a growth target of 3.5% for 1993, adjusted downward from the earlier target of 4.5%. The IMF, however, did not agree with a high-growth strategy because it might lead to a higher deficit and inflation in light of the country's power crisis. If the country continues to experience acute power shortages, then business confidence is undermined. This, in turn, curbs new investment that could alleviate the power crisis.

The government has set for itself a medium-term plan that runs from 1993 to 1998. The major macroeconomic objectives contained in the plan include broad-based growth of output and employment, price stability and a sound balance-of-payments position.

Inflation

High inflation has plagued the economy in the past ten years. The inflation rate averaged 15% between 1989 and 1991. After two years of negative growth in the country, inflationary pressures were suppressed in 1992. The adverse impact of inflation during the planning period produced distortions in investment. Investors shifted from much-needed, long-term commitments to short-term projects and rent-type activities. The country's investment attractiveness and export competitiveness were reduced by higher production costs. Average annual inflation rate for 1990/91 was 16.4% as compared to 8% in 1988/89. Because of high imports (about 65% from oil), inflation soared. This made it extremely difficult for the government to draw a balance between managing a competitive exchange rate for much-needed export growth and to ease inflationary pressures.

Existing power facilities were overloaded by the country's energy needs, which frequently resulted in power failures or "brownouts". Business sentiments towards spending and new investment plans were dampened because brownouts became increasingly severe and very costly in terms of production time. The peso's depreciation during 1992 also meant more expensive capital imports for power-generation projects, which translated into higher production costs. Despite the country's low cost of labour, cost-push factors predominated. Over time, it served to diminish the cost competitiveness of the Philippines as compared to neighbouring countries such as Thailand and Indonesia.

The Turnaround

Improvements in the Philippine economy have caught the attention of the international investment community. Nobody seems more pleasantly surprised than the Philippines's Finance Secretary, Roberto de Ocampo, fresh from the World Bank and IMF meeting in Madrid in early October 1994. "At the meeting last year, it was very difficult getting people to meet you, and the few that would, did so condescendingly," Ocampo said. "What I experienced this time was a difference between night and day. In Madrid, it was difficult to juggle my schedule. Everybody wanted to talk about the Philippines." (*Far East Economic Review*, 1994.)

How has this abrupt change in attitude come about? There are several reasons attributable to the push that the Philippines needed. Politically, the Philippines is much more stable since Fidel Ramos took over as President in May 1992. Being a relative of the late President Marcos, he has strong links with previous governments. He is a graduate of the U.S. Military Academy at West Point and is highly experienced in government affairs, having held positions which has included Chief of the Constabulary, Chief of Staff of the Armed Forces and Secretary of National Defence.

Furthermore, there has been a considerable reduction in power failures because of the rapid installation of several small power stations on the island of Luzon. The involvement of a number of independent U.S. power companies in these projects, such as Enron of Texas and California Energy, was a propitious sign. The Philippines has signed agreements on more than 30 private-sector power projects since the early 1990s, which is more than the combined total of all developing countries.

In addition, Filipino workers are better educated compared to workers from Indonesia, China and Vietnam. Traditionally, these four countries are sources of cheap labour. Of the 800,000 Filipinos entering the workforce each year, 250,000 are college-educated and speak English.

The surge in capital inflows has buoyed the Philippine currency. Relative to the U.S. dollar, the peso moved from P27.7 in January 1994 to less than P24 by October 1994. Inflation, which has been the biggest reform obstacle, is also under control. After surging to 9.9% in August, inflation slowed to 7.8% in October 1994, as good weather helped to stabilise the price of food which weighs heavily in the consumer price index. The government has forecast an inflation rate of 7.5% for 1995. In a further move, the Central Bank cut reserve requirements for banks by three percentage points in August, from 22% to 19%, thus pushing interest rates down. Although rates on a bell-wether 91-day treasury bill have climbed to 10.8% from a low of 8.7% in September, they remain far short of the 16% level that prevailed for much of early 1994.

Lower interest rates and a stronger peso could help deliver the first government budget surplus in two decades, mainly by cutting the cost of servicing foreign and domestic loans. At the end of October 1994, with just two months remaining in the fiscal year, the surplus stood at P15.4 billion which was more than three times the government's original projection.

THE CENTRAL MONETARY AUTHORITY

The objectives of the new Central Monetary Authority (CMA) are to maintain price stability conducive to balanced and sustained growth of the economy, to promote and maintain monetary stability, and to enhance convertibility of the peso. In accordance with the new Central Bank Act, the CMA is now required to be independent. Government representation on the new monetary board of seven members has been reduced to just one member from the Cabinet. The new Central Bank will concentrate on monetary policy and will be relieved of its fiscal responsibilities. The CMA is obliged to report to the President and Congress every year to ask for appropriations for the retirement of debts. Consistent with this new independence, the CMA will be more transparent and accountable.

The CMA provides policy directions in the areas of money, banking and credit. It has supervision over the operations of banks and exercises regulatory powers over the operation of finance companies, non-bank financial institutions and other institutions performing quasi-banking functions.

The powers of the CMA will be exercised by the Monetary Board which comprises seven members appointed by the President of the Philippines. The current governor is Gabriel Singson, who is also the chairman of the board. One member will be a cabinet member designated by the President while the other five will come from the private sector, all of whom will serve full-time. Three of them will have a term of six years and the other two, a term of five years. No member of the MB may be re-appointed more than once.

Operating Targets and Policy Tools

The CMA has no official operating target to carry out its anti-inflationary policies. The average 91-day treasury bill (issued by the government) is the barometer of domestic lending rates. The Central Bank will intervene daily to influence local interest rates and siphon off liquidity. Auction of the bills is done every Friday of the week. The market opens at 12.00 noon local time for bids and the results are announced at 4.00 p.m.

The CMA uses traditional monetary tools to influence the market. In its daily open market operations, the CMA issues central banking bills to manage liquidity in the market. There is no set schedule for issuance of the bills but announcements of the CMA's intentions are usually posted in the morning.

Reserve Period and Liquidity Requirements

Reserve week begins on Friday and ends on Thursday of the following week. Banks may offset daily reserve deficiencies against the other days' excesses provided that net deficiencies are avoided for that week. Otherwise, CMA imposes a bank penalty of 0.1% on the average daily net deficiency of reserves. The CMA limits deficiencies to a maximum of three days in a given week for only two consecutive weeks. Beyond that, banks will lose the privilege of offsetting their deficiencies for a minimum of four consecutive weeks. When a bank maintains a net weekly reserve deficiency of four weeks, it will be denied its credit facilities with the CMA as well as other privileges.

All demand deposits, liabilities and deposit substitutes (promissory notes, repurchase agreements and certificates of assignments) are subject to a 19% reserve requirement. There has been a drastic cut in the reserve requirement from 25 to 22% in July 1993, and a further cut in August 1994 to 19%, resulting in cost reduction related to bank intermediation. Interbank deposits booked within five days are subject to a 1% reserve requirement and, beyond that, they are subject to the 19% reserve requirement. Of the reserve requirement, 75% must be held in the form of cash or reserve-eligible securities, with the remaining 25% in the form of deposits with the CMA.

FOREIGN EXCHANGE MARKET

In general, anyone can buy and sell currency. Before a foreign loan is granted, approval has to be secured or registered at the CMA if the investor wishes to source U.S. dollars from the banking system. The currency surpluses and deficits of banks are limited to 25 and 15% of capital, respectively.

Trading hours are from 8.30 a.m. to 5.30 p.m. local time. Automated foreign exchange trading may be done through the Philippines dealing system. All banks have access to the system which maps out all interbank trades, thus providing the market with real trades and quotes. Settlement is for value of the next business trade, unless otherwise stated. Daily turnover ranges from US$5 million to US$30 million. Banks in the Philippines also deal in the forward foreign exchange and swaps up to 90 days. Beyond that, there is no local interbank market. A brief summary of the exchange rate of pesos to U.S. dollars is shown in Table 8–1.

TABLE 8–1
Historical Trend of Exchange Rate

Year	Exchange Rate
1946	Bell Trade Act – peso was pegged to US dollar.
1962	FX trading pit created by Bankers Association of the Philippines. Official rate US$/P = 2.00.
1965	Official rate US$/P = 3.90

TABLE 8–1 (cont'd)

Year	Exchange Rate
1970	Floating rate adopted on 20 February. 24 February: first interbank guiding rate determined. US$/P slipped from 3.90 to 5.282.
1983	23 June: peso devaluation from US$/P = 9.00 to 11.00.
1983	5 October: peso devaluation from US$/P = 11.00 to 14.00.
1984	6 June: peso devaluation from US$/P = 14.00 to 18.00.
1990	31 October: peso devaluation from US$/P = 25.75 to 28.00.
1994	January: US$/P = 27.70.
1994	October: US$/P = 24.00.

Exchange Rate in 1993

The appreciating trend of the peso exchange rate against the U.S. dollar during much of 1992 was reversed with the slight weakening of the exchange rate to P25.51 per one U.S. dollar by the end of the first quarter of 1993. Strategic BSP participation in the foreign exchange market through the Philippine Dealing System, to the extent of US$655 million in total net purchases during the first quarter, smoothed daily movements in the rates. Thereafter, the narrowing of the differentials between domestic and foreign interest rates, coupled with stronger import demand and non-trade payments, influenced the successive depreciation of the exchange rate over the next six months. Towards the end of the third quarter, inordinate speculative pressure arising from fears of a major devaluation, accelerated the further weakening of the peso and introduced some volatility into the market. Consequently, the exchange rate fell 16.9% from the end of March to P29.81 per one U.S. dollar at the end of September. This occurred despite the strong selling position maintained by the BSP (which reached 41.6% of the total volume of transactions) in the market.

By October, however, the increase in interest rates on peso-denominated assets, together with the seasonally induced lower import requirements, weakened the demand for foreign exchange which continued for the remainder of the fourth quarter. On the supply side, large inflows of foreign exchange from overseas Filipino contract workers, as well as from portfolio investments, further contributed to the strengthening of the exchange rate. It appreciated to P27.7 per one U.S. dollar at the end of December from P28.8 in October.

Exchange Rate in 1994

The surge in capital inflows buoyed the peso in 1994. It breached P24 to the U.S. dollar in October 1994, up from P27.7 in January, despite Central Bank efforts to cool its rise. The Central Bank continued to wage a battle against the gains in the domestic currency by initiating a number of strategies. One strategy included maintaining a 1.5% volatility ban on the currency which, if broken, results in a halt in currency trading. However, despite attempts to stall further gains, the currency reached higher levels in 1995. Analysts cited further foreign investment interest in the currency along with continued repatriation of offshore workers' remittances as the major reasons for higher levels. The currency has appreciated 13% since 1993 even though measures have been instituted to stem the rise.

Restrictions

Foreign currency for the payment of obligations related to loans and investments may be sourced from authorised agent banks only upon presentation of Central Bank approval. A documentary stamp of US$0.15 for every 300 pesos is imposed on bills of exchange or acceptance of payments that are to be paid in and out of the Philippines.

The registration of foreign investments with the Central Bank is required only if foreign exchange is to be sourced from the banking system. A documentary stamp tax of US$0.20 for every 200 pesos, or a fraction thereof, is levied on deposit substitute instruments. In addition, a 20% final withholding tax is levied on interest earned from the money markets.

THE MONEY MARKET

The interbank market is limited to government, commercial and development banks, and investment houses doing business in the Philippines. The interbank market for term deposits is not very liquid because interest earned on deposits which are booked beyond five days are subject to a 20% final withholding tax (no tax on interest earned on deposits booked within five days).

The market for interbank overnight deposits is used by banks to borrow or lend excess funds to cover prior days' reserve requirements for CMA accounting purposes. The daily turnover is between P6 billion to P18 billion. Transactions are settled through call slips submitted to the CMA between 9.00 a.m. to 12.00 noon local time.

Government Securities/Bond Market

The two types of securities offered are either peso- or dollar-denominated. For the peso-denominated securities, the main participants are authorised agent banks, insurance companies, institutional investors, offshore banks and portfolio managers. The secondary market for government treasury bills is very active. In addition to being an investment product of banks, this instrument also competes with the banks' product lines and crowds out banks sourcing for funds.

Monetary Policies

Price stability was the primary objective of monetary policies in 1994. Prudent management of monetary aggregates kept the inflation rate at single-digit levels and maintained the liquidity requirements of the country's growth objective. With accelerating inflationary conditions threatening the achievement of monetary policy goals, the BSP responded promptly and adopted tighter monetary policy measures in the second half of 1994. Measures were also adopted to lower market interest rates. Recognising the importance of market forces in increasing efficiency in the economy, the BSP continued to introduce financial sector reforms.

Open Market Operations

Open market operations continued to be the major instrument of monetary policy in 1994. These operations primarily involved borrowings under the reverse repurchase facility. These increased shortly during the third quarter of 1993 in order to absorb the increase in liquidity caused by the huge withdrawals of national government (NG) deposits from the BSP.

In December 1993, the BSP acquired a substantial stock of treasury securities which could be used for undertaking open market operations. These treasury securities were part of the P220.0 billion worth of NG issuances intended to cover BSP advances to the NG and the Central Bank Board of Liquidators (former Central Bank). The large volume of government securities in the BSP portfolio will enable the BSP to retire its own debt instruments which is not prohibited, except in cases of extraordinary movement in price levels.

Treasury Bill

Government securities consist mainly of treasury bills, Central Bank bills and reserve eligible bills. The most widely traded, and watched, is the treasury bill. The auction date for treasury bills is every Friday and its size is P8 billion. The settlement date is on the following Wednesday, and it comes with terms of 90, 180 and 360 days.

The primary market consists of a pool of accredited government securities dealers and the secondary market consists of banks, financial institutions, corporations and individuals. There is a very active secondary market.

THE DERIVATIVES MARKET

A derivative is a financial instrument which has a value that is dependent on the value of another variable. The list of instruments that qualify as derivatives differs from country to country depending on the development stage of derivative products in that country. As a financial product, derivatives have not yet gained wide acceptance in the Philippines compared to other financial centres of the world.

Demand and Growth of the Derivatives Market

The market demand for derivatives in the Philippines increased as a result of liberalisation of the financial markets in the country. Theoretically, foreign exchange rates and interest rates are free floating, except for Central Bank initiatives to calm a runaway market. For example, the Central Bank intervened noticeably in the wake of the recent Mexico debt crisis. In the period following deregulation, there has been increased volatility in equity, foreign exchange and money markets.

With political stability and reduction in the national debt, there has been a return of Philippine borrowers in the international capital markets and the emergence of local dollar funding. The deregulation of the banking industry allowed the entry of ten new foreign bank branches which will bring in a whole new spectrum of financial services and the related expertise.

Despite these deregulations, however, there has been a lack of long-term, fixed-rate local funding, which means that there is no guarantee of any cost of borrowing for huge infrastructure needs. Paradoxically, it is the lack of fixed long-term local funding that has led to the development of the derivatives market. Traditionally, there must be a certain depth to the capital markets before any development of derivatives can come into existence.

The demand for cross-border derivatives so far can be traced to interest rate hedging for dollar borrowers, currency derivatives (non-peso dollar) for borrowers with non-dollar loans, derivatives for offshore investments, and hedging for commodity producers and users. The demand for local derivatives is limited to alternatives for peso–dollar forwards, peso interest rate swaps (fixed versus floating), and derivatives for local investments (i.e., equity).

The development of cross-currency interest rate swaps is a grey area since there have been no official guidelines by the Central Bank on whether it endorses derivatives trading. It is natural, therefore, that foreign banks are more active and most transactions are booked under a branch in another country, notably in Singapore. Besides the trend towards long-dated peso dollar swaps, forwards and options, there are two future developments in derivatives trading. One is the development of local options and futures exchanges, and the other is the introduction of new financial instruments (e.g., warrants).

Central Bank Policies on Derivatives

The Central Bank realises that any move to clamp down completely on derivatives will have an adverse effect on the attraction of capital funds.

However, it is still reluctant to release its grip on the derivatives market. The Central Bank has put in place a system that combines supervision and regulations. It regularly has dialogue with bank management and representatives of the banking community. There are two organisations directly responsible for overseeing banks and the banking system. They are Bangko Sentral ng Pilipinas, which has the constitutional mandate to supervise banks, and the Philippine Deposit Insurance Corporation, which is endorsed with the authority to examine the financial statements and requirements of banks.

Authorities acknowledge that Philippine banks are already engaging in derivatives transactions. However, with the recent crisis in Barings, it is likely that steps will be taken to control and regulate derivatives trading. The challenge is to strike a balance between trading, risk and management control. If properly carried out, derivatives trading will help the Philippines to become a more sophisticated financial centre and will enhance the availability of financial instruments.

LIBERALISATION OF FOREIGN BANK ENTRY LAW

Recently, some foreign banks were given offshore banking licences to operate in the Philippines. A foreign bank must belong to the top 150 banks in the world or the top five banks in their country of origin. Also, a foreign bank must have a permanent assigned capital of no less than P210 million for the first three branches, and P35 million for an additional three branches. The foreign banks which have applied for licences under bank deregulation are listed in Appendix 6–1.

There are three modes of foreign bank entry. First, it can acquire, purchase or own up to 60% of the voting stock of an existing bank. Second, it can invest up to 60% of the voting stock of a new banking subsidiary. And, finally, it can establish branches with full banking authority. However, the law empowers the Monetary Board to ensure that 70% of the resources or assets of the entire system is held by domestic banks which are owned by a Filipino majority.

CONCLUSION

The Philippines's economic and political structure has undergone tremendous changes in the last few years. Under the leadership of Fidel Ramos and his team of ministers, the Philippines has finally been able to maintain political stability and attract much-needed foreign investments. Furthermore, with less corruption and more government supervision, public projects can be more effectively developed. Power failures that disrupted business in the past have been resolved with the construction of both public and private power plants. Missions and business trips spearheaded at ministerial levels, together with the participation of the private sector, have been very successful in attracting joint ventures and direct investments.

Looking to the future, the Asia-Pacific region will continue to be a source of economic upliftment. The Philippines will have to latch onto the emerging trends which include, among others, a stable exchange rate, controlled inflation and closer regional ties within a few economic trading blocs. The current buzz word is regionalisation. The Philippines must therefore think AFTA. While the ASEAN free-trade bloc is still in its infancy, its development will have important implications for South-east Asia and, therefore, the Philippines. The new world economy appears to be moving towards three giant trading blocs – one dominated by Europe, the other by North America and the third by Asia, consisting of China, the newly industrialised countries and the emerging countries.

ACKNOWLEDGEMENTS

We wish to thank the following for their assistance: Mr. Benjo Arcinas, FVP, Treasury Manager, Metropolitan Bank, Manila; Miss Monica Ingos, Chief Trader, Standard Chartered, Manila; Mr. Clayton Lee, AVP, Derivatives Section, Bank of America, Manila; Mr. Yong Cheng, Senior Manager, Asian Development Bank, Manila; Mr. Alexandar Escucha, Corporate Planning Manager, Chinabank, Manila; Mr. John Tsao, Chief Economist, Chemical Bank, Singapore; and Mr. Alan Siew, Asian Development Bank.

REFERENCES

"All System Go", *Far East Economic Review*, December 1994.
Central Bank Review, December 1993.

Central Bank Annual Report, 1993.
"The Barriers Come Down", *Euromoney*, May 1993.
"Night into Day", *Far East Economic Review*, October 1994.
Rana Prudumna Brickran, "Exchange Rate Risk Under Generalised Floating: Eight Asia Cities", 1989.

FOREIGN DIRECT INVESTMENT, ACCOUNTING AND TAXATION

Chapter 9

Foreign Direct Investment in the Philippines

BY
Roman LAURE
LIM Chin Chuan
Kenneth LING
ONG Chin Seng

INTRODUCTION

FOREIGN DIRECT INVESTMENT is a catalyst to ignite and fuel economic growth. This has been demonstrated in South-east Asia and is currently evident in Vietnam and China. No developing country can hope to attain advancement in a relatively short period of time without foreign investment. The government of the Philippines is no exception and, after years of political and economical mismanagement, great efforts are being made to provide a climate conducive to foreign investment.

This chapter provides an overview of the current direct investment environment in the Philippines. It covers the background of the investment environment, the various legal forms of direct investment in the Philippines, and their advantages and disadvantages. It also provides a summary of the main investment incentives available, along with examples of recent direct investments by foreign companies in different industries. Finally, an attempt is made to highlight current levels of direct investment, and to analyse future trends and issues that will affect the success or failure of the Philippines in attracting foreign investment.

BACKGROUND

The Philippines, with its resurgent economy, is now in better shape and is no longer the "sick man of Asia". Thus declared President Ramos to a meeting of diplomats and businessmen in Manila in January 1995 (*Business Times,* 1995). He added that the nation's image was now that of a "young tiger or dragon" poised to join Asia's other booming, newly industrialised economies. While these statements may be somewhat premature, the general consensus of the international business community is that the Philippines has turned around and is on the road to becoming an attractive destination for investment.

The Environment

The Philippines consists of approximately 7,100 islands with a population of around 65.8 million people. It was originally colonised by Spain for a period of over 300 years before being ceded to the United States in 1898. Japan also briefly occupied the country during World War II. The Philippines finally achieved independence in 1946.

The Philippines is strategically located between East Asia and the West. With a unique blend of eastern and western culture, values and practices, it is a hospitable place for investors from all parts of the world. It offers an alternative operating base for enterprises in developed countries, and for the newly industrialised economies (NIEs) of Asia, which are now being burdened with rising costs of labour and real estate at home. Although wages are still relatively low in the Philippines, the labour force is large, productive and relatively well educated.

The Philippines has substantial natural resources, most notably timber, copper and gold. Its economy is basically agriculture-based, although the manufacturing and industrial sectors are gaining a foothold. Consequently, the Philippines, like many developing countries, is highly susceptible to the vagaries of world commodity prices. Infrastructure is still inadequate and many projects are urgently needed for effective industrialisation of the country.

Summary of Economic Progress

Under Ferdinand Marcos, the economy never achieved its full potential due to mismanagement, widespread corruption and blatant cronyism. Marcos was ousted in a popular uprising in 1986, ending a 20-year rule.

At the time, the economy was in recession, suffered high inflation, and was experiencing an extremely wide income gap between the rich and the majority of Filipinos, who lived in abject poverty. The economy turned slowly following the establishment of Corazon Aquino as President in February 1986. The economic reforms started during Aquino's term, and were continued by President Fidel Ramos from 1992. They have now started to produce tangible results.

The most up-to-date estimates from the BOI indicates that real GDP grew by around 5.1% in 1994, more than double the 1993 growth of 2.3%. *Asian Business* estimates that GDP per capita increased from US$818.00 in 1993 to an estimated US$912.00 in 1994. Foreign reserves increased from US$5.8 billion in 1993 to an estimated US$6.6 billion while inflation was kept to single digits for the past two years. Foreign direct investment increased four times, from US$0.61 billion in 1993 to an estimated US$2.4 billion in 1994. The United States continued to be the leading foreign investor in the Philippines in 1994 with an estimated total investment of US$719 million, followed by Hong Kong with a total estimated investment of US$305 million.

The economy is expected to continue this upward trend in 1995, buoyed by government-backed structural reforms aimed at maintaining sustainable growth. Interest rates are still on a downward trend, the country's fiscal position is improving and inflation appears to be under control. Furthermore, the deregulation of previously highly protected sectors, and the privatisation of inefficient state-run businesses, are stated government priorities to attract further foreign investment.

The most significant economic problem still facing the Philippines is the large foreign debt. The debt repayment burden currently accounts for around 40% of the national budget. Therefore, increased foreign investment is critical to the continued economic development of the Philippines.

Direct Investment Reforms

The foreign investment environment was liberalised following the implementation of the FIA of 1991. The FIA is the prime regulation governing foreign investment. The governing legislation for investments with incentives is the Omnibus Investments Code of 1987 (OIC). Both the FIA and the OIC establish a foreign investment climate and incentives similar to those of other ASEAN countries.

The FIA aims to attract productive investments from foreign individuals, partnerships, corporations and governments. The new law broadened the areas of investments available to non-Filipino nationals and simplified their entry. Generally, there are no restrictions on the extent of foreign ownership of export enterprises. For domestic enterprises, foreigners can invest up to 100% equity. Exceptions are included in the foreign investments negative list (see below for more detail).

The BOI now incorporates a "one-stop action centre for investment". This department renders front-line investment services and assistance for walk-in investors, and houses different government agency representatives to accept and process investment applications. These representatives possess authority to act on all investment matters under their jurisdiction. Other reforms which are either completed, or in the pipeline, cover the following areas:

1. The lifting of all foreign exchange controls after forty years.
2. Tariff reductions under the CEPT Scheme of AFTA.
3. The granting of long-term leases (75 years) for private lands to foreign investors.
4. Accession to MIGA (Multilateral Investment Guarantee Agreement) to provide coverage to foreign investors for political and non-commercial risks.
5. The promotion of infrastructure facilities.
6. Removal of barriers to entry in key domestic industries such as banking, shipping, retail trade and telecommunications.
7. The enforcement of regulations on intellectual property rights.

FOREIGN DIRECT INVESTMENT

Definition

FDI conceptually involves whole or partial ownership of a business entity in one country (the host country) by residents of, or a firm located in, another country (the home country) with the intention of management control, or participation in the management of the foreign business entity (USITC publication, 1993). Foreign investment is generally considered beneficial and necessary by developing countries because it can very quickly bring about the following significant benefits:

(a) expand the livelihood and employment opportunities for its people;
(b) enhance the economic value of agricultural products;
(c) expand the scope, quality, and volume of exports and their access to foreign markets;
(d) impart relevant technologies in agriculture, industry and support services; and
(e) supplement inadequate domestic capital.

The government has stated that it is committed to formulating investment rules that are fair and consistent, to encourage both local and foreign investors to bring in financing, technology and expertise that will enhance local talents and resources, ultimately to help Philippine industries reach world class standards in output.

Implementing Rules for Investment

Part II of the OIC used to contain the general law concerning foreign direct investment. In October 1991, Part II was substituted when the National Economic and Development Authority (NEDA) implemented rules and regulations under the FIA, which allows for greater participation of foreign investors in the domestic market. There are four main classes of rules:

(a) Rule I: definitions;
(b) Rules IV to VI: specific procedures for registration under the FIA;
(c) Rules VIII to XIV: procedures for formulating the transitory and regular foreign investment negative lists; and
(d) Rule XVIII: administrative sanctions.

These rules are accompanied by the foreign investment negative list which prohibits or restricts the maximum equity stake of a foreign investor to 25 or 40% for certain investments.

Registration of Investments

For entities not included in the negative list, government approvals are normally not required. Such entities simply register with the SEC and submit the documents specified in Rule IV, Section 3. A sole proprietorship, however, must register with the Bureau of Trade Regulations and Consumer Protection (BTRCP). Investors wishing to repatriate capital and remit profits must also register their investments with the Central Bank.

Presently, registration with the BOI is only necessary when the entity wishes to avail itself of incentives under the OIC, or the entity wishes to fall within the export enterprise exemption. Foreign investors planning to set up business in any of the four main EPZs located in Bataan, Mactan, Cavite and Baguio City, are required to register with the Export Processing Zone Authority (EPZA) rather than with the BOI.

Investment Protection

As a member of ASEAN, the Philippines is a party to the Convention on the Settlement of Investment Disputes Between States and Nationals of Other States (Washington, DC: 18 March 1965). This provides for arbitration of disputes between contracting parties and foreign investors. Intra-ASEAN investment is protected by the Manila Agreement of 1980. This provides for any dispute between an ASEAN investor and an ASEAN government to be ultimately settled by arbitration before a regional arbitration centre in ASEAN. At present, there are two such centres, one in Singapore and the other in Kuala Lumpur. In practice, of course, arbitration judgements are difficult to enforce in developing countries. The Philippines's constitution also provides for investors' basic rights, including repatriation of investments, remittance of earnings, foreign loans and contracts, freedom from expropriation and non-requisition of investment.

FORMS OF FOREIGN DIRECT INVESTMENT

Representative Office

A representative office is not strictly a form of direct investment but, rather it is a preliminary stepping stone to penetrate a market. The activities of a representative office in the Philippines are limited to information dissemination, promotion of products and facilitating of orders of the head office's customers. It is not allowed to intervene or take part in any manner in the pricing and distribution of the products of its head office. It is also not allowed to derive income within the Philippines. Accordingly, it is not subject to any Philippine income tax. Basically, the purpose of a representative office is to facilitate the search for investment projects, and to further the interests, products, services, etc., of the main office located abroad.

The advantages of a representative office include the following: (a) no tax or corporate reporting responsibilities; (b) a simple structure with less approval time required; (c) gives a presence in the market for name recognition; and (d) no partner is required and, thus, there is no partner risk.

Disadvantages include the following: (a) it is not a legal entity; (b) there are no tax incentives; (c) it cannot trade or carry on business; and (d) the licence can be revoked or not renewed.

Joint Venture

A joint venture can be defined as an association of independent participants in a business enterprise over which they exercise a common management control. The participants are usually corporations, but they need not be, and the venture may or may not be carried out through an incorporated vehicle. The venture may be temporary, or of indefinite duration. A joint venture is by far the most frequently used foreign investment vehicle in the Philippines. Joint ventures can take one of three forms: (a) a purely contractual joint venture (business cooperation contract); (b) a partnership, or (c) a limited liability or equity joint venture (incorporated).

1. ***Contractual Joint Venture:*** In a broad sense, a wide range of cooperative arrangements, including licensing, technical assistance agreements, contract manufacturing, and even sales agency and distributionship agreements, could be categorised as contractual, or non-equity joint ventures.
2. ***Partnership:*** In general, a partnership may be defined as a relation which exists among persons carrying on a business with a view to profit. It is sometimes difficult to determine whether a particular joint venture is merely a contractual joint venture or a partnership. In such circumstances, common law courts will examine the terms of existing documentation and the surrounding circumstances to determine whether a partnership exists. This form of operation has the advantage of being able to apply losses incurred by the joint

venture against the profits of the participants from other sources, which is a significant advantage in certain circumstances. Of course, the risk of unlimited liability exists with any partnership.

3. ***Incorporated joint venture:*** This form involves the formation of a limited liability company for the purpose of undertaking a project or establishing a business, the equity of which is held by the participants in numbers corresponding to the size of each party's commitment. Most projects beyond a limited duration are operated in this manner. The obvious advantage of proceeding in this manner is the limited liability afforded to each participant. In addition to the basic shareholder's agreement and the constituting documents for such joint ventures, the arrangements are frequently supplemented by other agreements, such as supply of products and services, and agreements dealing with industrial and other intangible property rights.

The advantages of a joint venture include the following: (a) a full range of tax concessions is available; (b) domestic market penetration is better; (c) risk is shared; and (d) local partners can look after daily operations more effectively.

Disadvantages include the following: (a) capital contributions are locked into the joint venture until the venture is liquidated; (b) shared management is required and could lead to strained relations; (c) there is partner risk; and (d) transfer of ownership is more difficult.

Build-Operate-Transfer

The BOT scheme under the BOT law, RA 6957, is a contractual arrangement between the government and a private contractor, wherein the contractor undertakes the construction and financing of an infrastructure facility for the government. The contractor then operates and maintains the facility for an agreed period of time. During this period, the contractor is allowed to charge the facility users tolls, fees, rents or other charges, to achieve a reasonable rate of return. The facility is returned to the government when the agreed period ends, normally after around five years depending on the project size and type. This structure is normal for large infrastructure projects.

Aside from the BOT scheme, there are other possible arrangements, although not seen frequently, such as: BOO (build–operate–own); ROO (rehabilitate–operate–own); and ROMT (rehabilitate–operate–maintain–transfer). BOT projects include transportation (e.g., highways, expressways, roads, bridges and interchanges), energy (e.g., power generation, distribution, electrification and related facilities), communications and water resources (e.g., educational, health, environmental and solid waste management facilities). The advantages of BOT projects include the following: (a) access to high-profile, long-term projects; and (b) reasonably fair guaranteed returns through monopoly of the industry.

Disadvantages include the following: (a) projects are selected by the government; and (b) projects must usually be transferred free at the end of the contract period.

100% Foreign-Owned Enterprise

An enterprise with 100% foreign-owned capital is a separate classification of a limited liability corporation which is established and wholly owned by a foreign organisation or individual. It is fully responsible for its own management and business results. Based on regulations in the OIC, any non-Philippine national may invest up to 100% of the equity in a Filipino enterprise under the following conditions:

- (a) the entity is a domestic market enterprise engaged in activities not included on the foreign investment negative list;
- (b) the entity is an "export enterprise" and exports at least 60% of its output;
- (c) the enterprise is considered a "pioneer enterprise"; or
- (d) the enterprise is an EPZA-registered enterprise.

The advantages here include the following: (a) 100% control with no partner risk; and (b) some, but not all, tax concessions are available.

The disadvantages include the following: (a) capital contribution is locked in until liquidation; (b) transfer of ownership is restricted; and (c) the selection of industries is restricted.

Regional Headquarters

This is usually an administration branch of a multinational company (MNC) which principally acts as a supervision, communication and coordination centre for the subsidiaries, branches or affiliates of the MNC in the Asia-Pacific region. It does not earn or derive income from the host country and all expenses are financed by the head office or parent.

Branch

This is an extension of the legal personality of the foreign corporation. It engages in business and derives income in the Philippines.

DIRECT INVESTMENT INCENTIVES

The Philippines encourages foreign investment in all sectors of the economy, provided that it offers significant employment opportunities relative to the amount of investment. In addition, projects that make use of the country's natural resources (including mineral, forest, aquatic or other resources) or add value to current production, will also be looked upon favourably. The government also encourages investments that provide training or technical skills for local workers, develop rural areas, or provide long-term benefits to the economy.

The OIC integrates the basic laws on investment and harmonises provisions for the guidance of domestic and foreign investors. It offers a comprehensive set of incentives to investors who meet the guidelines. Benefits are in the form of fiscal and non-fiscal incentives.[1] Fiscal incentives include income tax holidays, tax- and duty-free importation of capital equipment and spare parts, additional deductions from taxable income for labour expenses and exemption from national or local contractor's tax. Non-fiscal incentives are simplified customs procedures, unrestricted use of consigned equipment and employment of foreign nationals.

Furthermore, additional incentives are offered to investors who invest in what the government classifies as less developed areas. They include pioneer incentives, and full deduction from taxable income of the cost of necessary infrastructures and public facilities constructed in the area. Companies locating in export processing zones (EPZs) are offered a number of incentives outside of those offered under the OIC. The privileges include a special tax on merchandise within the zone, exemption from local taxes (except real estate tax), licences, fees and others. Additional incentives are offered to MNCs that set up their regional

1 Refer to the Investment Guidebook published by the BOI for full details of incentives.

headquarters in the Philippines as well as to their expatriate staffs. These privileges are duty exemptions, importation of materials and personal effects, and visa prerogatives.

Each March, after due consultation with the relevant government agencies and the private sector, the BOI submits to the President an investment priorities plan (IPP) which lists the areas entitled to special incentives under the OIC. The criteria to guide the BOI in deciding what should be included are the economic soundness of the activity, impact on a specific development goal, comparative advantage, the market, technical aspects and so on.

Under the IPP, foreign investment may be made in almost all areas up to the extent of 100% ownership, subject to the constitutional and/or statutory limitations. Pioneer enterprises, however, are required to attain Filipino status (60% Filipino) within 30 years, or such longer period as the BOI may determine. Companies which export 100% of their production are exempted.

CURRENT AND PROSPECTIVE LEVELS OF DIRECT INVESTMENT

Statistics

Foreign investment in new projects increased from around P7 billion in 1992 to P14.4 billion in 1993. For 1994, total foreign equity investment in new projects was expected to be around P61.8 billion. Table 9–1 shows the leading international investors in the Philippines for 1994. See The breakdown of investment by leading sectors in 1994 is shown in Table 9–2.

TABLE 9–1
Leading Investors

Country	1994 (billion pesos)
United States	17.787
Hong Kong	7.607
Taiwan	7.076
Bermuda	5.324
Malaysia	4.233
Singapore	4.232

Source: Board of Investments

TABLE 9–2
Investment by Sectors

Sector	1994 Total Projects*	1994 Foreign Equity*
Energy	118.037	21.741
Public Utility	85.863	3.431
Construction	78.566	15.078
Petroleum	28.374	1.501
Electronics	25.895	11.610
Infrastructure	21.879	0.725
Synthetic Resins	19.068	0.768
Chemicals	19.031	0.387
Metals/Machinery	10.423	0.799
Textile/Wearables	8.800	0.815
Tourism	8.730	2.213
Others	30.185	2.697
TOTAL	**454.851**	**61.765**

* billion pesos
Source: Board of Investments

By comparison in 1993, total equity investment was P33.94 billion which comprised P14.41 billion of foreign equity. Clearly, in 1994, both local and foreign equity investments had increased substantially, in line with the improving business climate. A breakdown of investment by location in the Philippines is shown in Table 9–3.

Trends

Certainly the reforms which have been put in place bode well for higher levels of foreign investment in the future. Further emphasis on participation in AFTA, APEC initiatives, a shift towards technical and apprenticeship education, government decentralisation, and accelerated privatisation, will continue the momentum of the initial policies.

Furthermore, high-profile trade delegation visits (e.g., the Singapore President's visit in mid-February 1995 where he called for greater exchange between Singapore and the Philippines) will add increased impetus to invest in the Philippines. The Philippine government is well aware of the increasing competition for direct investment among the regional countries and has set a course to being as attractive as possible to a foreign investor.

TABLE 9–3
Investment by Location

Location	1994 Total Projects*	1994 Foreign Equity*
Ilocos	56.638	17.214
Cagayan Valley	1.090	0.045
Central Luzon	73.865	4.923
Southern Tagalog	71.146	11.067
Bicol	1.018	0.019
Western Visayas	0.831	0.003
Central Visayas	45.472	3.989
Eastern Visayas	14.122	2.367
Western Mindanao	10.733	1.070
Northern Mindanao	15.671	1.233
Southern Mindanao	4.478	0.057
Central Mindanao	6.371	0.057
Cordillera Autonomous	1.554	0.387
Metropolitan Manila	58.091	12.056
Others	93.771	7.278
TOTAL	**454.851**	**61.765**

* billion pesos
Source: Board of Investments

Key Issues

Key issues which will affect the level of direct foreign investment in the Philippines include several factors. These are described below.

1. ***Deficiency of the Infrastructure System:*** Brownouts in the Philippines were common in the recent past. Such disruptions affect production planning, transportation of goods and individuals' health. Several power-generating projects have been started to increase power capacity, the first of which is a coal-fired power plant being built by Hopewell Energy of Hong Kong.
2. ***Kidnappings and Disruptions to Peace and Order:*** In 1993 and 1994, there was a spate of high-profile kidnappings of Chinese businessmen, or their family members, for extortion of money. To counteract this, the government has attempted to tighten police control.
3. ***Devaluation of Peso:*** Unless investment is in a company earning

strictly foreign currency, devaluation of the peso is a problem for potential investors, particularly in the wake of the Mexican peso crisis. The Central Bank currently maintains a hands-off policy and only intervenes if the peso crosses a volatility band of 1.5% in a day, in which case trading will be suspended. With the Philippines's trade deficit widening by more than 27% to US$7.22 billion in the first 11 months of 1994, further devaluations continued in 1995. Investors can only take appropriate hedging action on major trade flows and build a depreciation factor into capital budgets.

4. ***Political Stability and Succession:*** Clearly, Ramos has done much towards creating an environment more friendly to the foreign investor. However, he can only serve one term which ends in 1998. It is believed that most current government officials are behind Ramos's reforms and, whoever succeeds him, will continue the liberalisation and deregulation policies.
5. ***Repatriation of Capital and Profit:*** The OIC guarantees investors the right to repatriate profit and capital at the exchange rate prevailing at the time of repatriation. However, it does not guarantee a right to immediate repatriation upon divestment of the original investment. Article 38 of the OIC reiterates the role of the Central Bank in determining the timing of remittances. Only investments registered with the Central Bank are entitled to full and immediate remittance of capital and profits, and they are able to source foreign exchange to accomplish this in the local market. An investor, therefore, is advised to register with the Central Bank although this is not compulsory.

EXAMPLES OF DIRECT INVESTMENT

Primofina Oleochemicals, Inc.

Primofina Oleochemicals, Inc. (Primofina) was established in 1991 as a coconut oil production mill. The original shareholders were New Lucena Oil Producers and the Chua family of Lucena City. Foreign direct investment was secured in November 1993 for a new plant under construction in Jose Panganiban, Camarines Norte. When it is completed at the end of 1996, it will be one of the world's largest oleochemical production facilities. It will convert coconut oil into basic oleochemicals for export and domestic markets. The range of products includes coconut oil, coconut cake, refined cooking oil, cocofatty alcohol, methyl ester and fatty acids.

Oleochemicals are completely biodegradable and, with growing environmental concerns around the world, the trend is for oleochemicals to gradually replace partially biodegradable petrochemicals as raw materials for the production of household cleaning and personal care products. Primofina will export 70% of its total coco chemical production to detergent and personal care manufacturers in the United States, Europe and Asia, with the remainder to be sold in the domestic market as mandated by the BOI.

The project is estimated to cost approximately US$80 million and it is expected to generate foreign exchange earnings of US$400 million from oleochemical sales during the first ten years of operations. The chairman of the company, Mr. Francisco Chua, stated in November 1993 that the investment was expected to be recouped within five years from the time commercial operations begin in 1996.

The coco chemical plant was financed through equity and loans from various sources. Of the US$80 million, approximately 60% was funded by debt and 40% by equity. These sources included the following:

(a) Asian Development Bank (ADB) – debt and equity;
(b) Asian Finance and Investment Corporation (AFIC) – debt and equity;
(c) Commonwealth Development Corporation (CDC) – debt and equity;
(d) Philippine National Bank – debt;
(e) Prudential Asset Management Asia (PAMA) – equity; and
(f) FMO Netherlands Development Corporation – debt.

The ADB, together with the CDC, provided approximately US$25 million in loan financing and US$6 million in equity. PAMA is a foreign direct investor (venture capital) and provided around US$5 million in equity.

Projects such as this, which tap into agricultural resources where the Philippines is strong, also have many other beneficial flows to the local community, both quantifiable and unquantifiable. These benefits include average annual salaries and wages for skilled and unskilled labour of

P30 million, taxes to local governments at an average of P7 million per annum, and security for coconut farmers and cooperative members because of a reliable and consistent buyer.

Having lifted off the ground through institutional support, Primofina anticipates a listing on the Manila Stock Exchange once production and earnings are established. Thereafter, the company will be able to tap the Philippine capital market for further financing from both local and foreign investors. Despite the inherent project development risks and commodity price risk, PAMA chose to invest based on the expected return to investors, the growth potential for oleochemical products in Asia, abundant local supply of raw material, professional management and consultants, participation by the ADB, and tax holidays for the project once products are generated. In summary, the benefits outweighed the project risks.

Mercedes-Benz

Despite the current euphoria of doing business in the Philippines, Mercedes-Benz is not convinced at this time that the Philippines is a ready market for their commercial vehicles. The outlook is somewhat better for their luxury vehicles. In both cases, Mercedes-Benz has decided against direct investment in assembly and manufacturing plants. Mercedes-Benz is dependent on a certain level of development in the market including an infrastructure suitable for its products.

At present in the Philippines, Mercedes-Benz is concentrating on the sale of buses for the public transport system. Mercedes-Benz sells the chassis and motor, but the superstructure is built by a local producer. The volume is small, at about 300 units per year. For other new commercial vehicles, such as heavy trucks, the demand is very small. The Philippine truck market is characterised by the import of second-hand heavy trucks from Japan, which totals approximately 6,000 per year. As in Vietnam at present, the Japanese uses the Philippines as a market "to get rid of obsolete scrap". The situation in the Philippines is made worse by the use of right-hand-steering units in a mainly left-hand-drive market.

With respect to the market for luxury cars, the situation is slightly better because of the rising desire of successful and wealthy individuals to showcase their achievements in what they drive. However, unlike the more developed and prosperous nations of Asia, the general purchasing power in the Philippines is still low and, hence, the market remains limited but is continually growing.

Accordingly, Mercedes-Benz has chosen not to invest directly in production facilities in the Philippines until such time as the market demand for trucks and luxury cars is warranted. Mercedes-Benz, instead, has chosen to maintain a presence through a cooperation with a general representative on a contractual base. This representative, Commercial Motors in Manila, exclusively sells and distributes Mercedes-Benz through their branches. Approximately 70% of total sales are made in Metropolitan Manila.

Hopewell Holdings

Hopewell Holdings (HH) entered the Philippines in the 1980s when the country had been written off by most foreign investors. It was the first to operate a BOT power project in the operation of the 210-megawatt Narotas gas turbine 1–3. HH is also involved in the rehabilitation of nine 30-megawatt power barges, which is considered to be the first successful rehabilitation sector. Currently, HH is building the 700-megawatt Pagbilao coal thermal plant in Quezon province at a cost of US$933 million and for a completion date of mid 1996.

HH also won the bidding for the 1000-megawatt coal-fired power plant project in Sual, Pangasinan. The project's estimated cost is US$2 billion. The plant is expected to begin operations in 1999. The Pangasinan project was the fifth power project by HH (now called Cepa) in the Philippines. This would make Cepa possibly the largest foreign investor in the Philippines with an investment of more than US$2.5 billion.

Besides the power projects, Cepa is also involved in other infrastructure projects in the Philippines. These include the construction of an international seaport, reclamation of 800 hectares of land for conversion into an industrial estate and the extension of the South Expressway. Cepa is the nation's leading BOT proponent and was probably able to achieve this position through its faith in the Philippines prior to the recent boom.

CONCLUSION

In summary, the Philippines can expect more in the way of BOT projects. In a speech before the "BOT Asia 1995: Focus on the Philippines" forum held in Manila in February 1995, President Ramos urged businessmen from Europe, the United States and Asia to invest via infrastructure development schemes, particularly the BOT. The BOT programme in the Philippines is recognised as one of the most successful in the world. Of course, joint ventures in appropriate markets remain an extremely viable investment option in the Philippines.

REFERENCES

General

"Conclusions Paper, 17th Annual Heads of Asia/Pacific Roundtable", *Economist*, 1994.

"Doing Business in the Philippines", Ernst & Young, December 1992.

"East Asia: Regional Economic Integration and Implications for the United States", USITC Publication 2621, May 1993.

Evans Keith R., "Joint Ventures within ASEAN".

"Foreign Investments Act of 1991", Board of Investments, RA 7042.

Irani Phiroze K., "Foreign Investment in ASEAN: Recent Developments", 1994.

Loke Alexander, "Direct Foreign Investment in the Philippines", 1994.

"Manila Central Bank Will Not Alter Hands Off Peso Policy", *The Straits Times,* 23 January 1995.

"Philippines New Young Tiger, Not Asia's Sick Man: Ramos", *Business Times*, 5 January 1995.

"Philippines – Open Arms for Foreign Resources", *Asian Business*, April 1994.

"Philippines Statistics", *Asian Business*, January 1995, p. 51.

"Primer on Investment Policies in the Philippines", Board of Investments, January 1995.

"The Licensing and Joint Venture Guide, 1983", Stitt & Baker, Ontario Ministry of Trade and Industry, p. 38.

Mercedes-Benz

Interview with Hermann Knoeckel, Deputy General Manager/Re-gional Manager of Mercedes-Benz Asia Pte. Ltd., Singapore.

Primofina Oleochemicals, Inc.

"ADB, Others to Build $80-M Oleochemical Plant in RP", *The Philippine Star,* 19 November 1993.
"Group Builds New Oleochem Plant in Bicol", *Manila Bulletin*, 29 November 1993.
Interview with Edwina Lee, Director, Prudential Asset Management Asia Hong Kong Ltd.
"PrimeChem Goes Full Blast in 1996", *Business World*, 19 November 1993.

Hopewell Holdings

"Gordon Wu Takes His Business to Southeast Asia", *Far Eastern Economic Review*, 12 May 1994.
"Hopewell Bags $2 Billion Power Plant Project in Pangasinan", *Philippine Daily Inquirer*, 2 March 1994.
"Hopewell to Build $2 Billion Coal Plant", *Manila Chronicle,* 2 March 1994.
"Hopewell Wins 3 Infrastructure Projects in the Philippines", *Business Times*, 19 September 1994.

Chapter 10

Accounting Standards in the Philippines

BY
CHAN Seet Meng
Anthony CHEW
TAN Geok Cheng

INTRODUCTION

THIS CHAPTER PROVIDES potential investors with a general overview of accounting standards in the Philippines. To facilitate understanding, we compare the Philippines's Statements of Financial Accounting Standards (SFAS) with Singapore's Statements of Accounting Standards (SAS), and International Accounting Standards (IAS).

By "potential investor", we refer to a person who is interested in general business with the exclusion of insurance companies and banks. These two business lines are deliberately left out because, in addition to being governed by accounting standards, they are also regulated by other professional bodies and, hence, would require more specialised treatment beyond our intended general perspective.

In providing an overview of accounting standards and practices in the Philippines in relation to Singapore and international standards, we first compare the regulatory framework governing accounting standards/practices in both countries. The role of the SEC in the Philippines is discussed in relation to the reporting requirements of publicly listed companies. This is followed by a comparison of Generally Accepted

Accounting Principles (GAAP) between the two countries. The focus is on accounting practices which are fundamental in nature and, hence, of general interest to the average investor. These include valuation of assets, accounting for business combinations, consolidation, provisions and reserves, footnote disclosure and recording of income. The chapter concludes with some observations on the convergence of accounting standards between the two countries.

THE REGULATORY FRAMEWORK IN SINGAPORE AND THE PHILIPPINES

Financial reporting in the Philippines is influenced primarily by American financial reporting practices in contrast to Singapore's predominantly British influence. The Company's Act in Singapore prescribes the requirements of financial reporting while the Corporation Code in the Philippines serves a similar mandate. However, unlike the former, the Corporation Code does not prescribe measurement or disclosure requirements. The regulation of financial reporting comes under the auspices of the private sector through two professional bodies.

The Philippines Institute of Certified Public Accountants (PICPA) undertakes to promote the professional interests of its members. Unlike Singapore's Institute of Certified Public Accountants (ICPAS), the PICPA is not a standard-setting body. The SFAS are issued by an independent standard-setting body, the Accounting Standards Council (ASC). With the establishment and improvement of accounting principles as its core function, the ASC comprised members from the PICPA, SEC, the Central Bank, the Financial Executives Institute of the Philippines (FINEX) and the Professional Regulation Commission (PRC).

State regulation in the Philippines is similar to that in the United States in that standard setting is vested in an governmental agencies. The government's indirect influence is exerted through the PRC, but its surveillance over business entities is handled through agencies such as the SEC and the Central Bank.

The SFAS are mandatory for any commercial, industrial or business enterprise which purports to prepare their financial statements in accordance with GAAP for issuance to other persons, such as stockholders, creditors, employees and the public at large. On the issue of authority of the SFAS, the PRC acts as a government watchdog in that all approved accounting standards must be submitted to the commission for their final approval. Hence, the PRC's stamp of approval lends formal authority to the standards.

SECURITIES EXCHANGE COMMISSION

The legislation that regulates the issue and trading of securities in the Philippines is the Revised Securities Act and the enforcement agency of the Act is the SEC. Within its general powers to regulate the securities industry, the SEC has specific powers that pertain to the area of financial reporting. Specifications concerning the form and content of financial information are not themselves written into statute, but are incorporated in directives issued by the SEC. In particular, Section 48 of the Revised Securities Act grants authority to the SEC, subject to the approval of the Minister of Finance, to do the following:

(a) make, amend, and rescind such accounting rules and regulations as may be necessary to carry out the provisions of this Act, including rules and regulations governing registration statements and prospectuses for the various classes of securities and issuers;
(b) define accounting terms used in this Act; and
(c) prescribe the form(s) in which required information shall be set forth; the items or details to be shown in the balance-sheet and earnings statement; the methods to be followed in the preparation of accounts, appraisal or valuation of assets and liabilities; determination of depreciation and depletion; differentiation of recurring and non-recurring income; differentiation of investment and operating income; and the preparation of consolidated accounts where deemed necessary.

The SEC also derives authority from the Corporation Code (Section 143) which gives the SEC power and authority to implement the provisions of the Code. The SEC issues regulations applicable to the form and content of financial statements, and other periodic information to be filed by issuers of securities traded in the exchanges or over-the-counter markets, as well as by corporations with 20 or more shareholders. The rules and regulations issued by the SEC are primarily an authoritative reinforcement of the accounting standards issued by the ASC.

In Singapore, companies that wish to list on the Stock Exchange of Singapore (SES) must obtain approval of the Securities Industry Council (SIC) and the SES for complying with the listing manual of the SES. The SIC is the regulatory agency for the securities industry which was established under the Securities Industry Act 1973. Since then, all listed companies, in addition to being governed by the Companies Act, have been subject to the rules and regulations of the SES. These listed companies are required to make prompt disclosure of all material developments which are likely to affect the market values of their securities. The corporate disclosure manual sets out the kind, and manner, of required disclosures.

As a result of its authority to specify reporting requirements considered necessary for disclosure, the SES has considerable influence over the SAS and disclosure requirements for financial statements. The ICPAS works closely with the SES in making their pronouncements on accounting principles and standards in Singapore.

GAAP IN THE PHILIPPINES AND SINGAPORE COMPARED TO IAS

Valuation of Assets

1. ***Inventories:*** Accounting for inventories in the Philippines is governed by SFAS 2. In general, the cost of inventories, which includes both direct and indirect charges, requires the use of cost-flow assumptions such as specific identification, average cost, first-in first-out (FIFO) and last-in first-out (LIFO). These are spelt out in IAS 2. While all of these assumptions are available options in Singapore under SAS 2, the LIFO method is disallowed in the Philippines because it is prohibited by the Bureau of Internal Revenue (BIR).

   Another glaring dissimilarity relates to the valuation of inventories. The rule in the Philippines under SFAS 4 is the lower of cost or market, in contrast to Singapore's lower of cost and market (SAS 2). Essentially, the "or" method allows the rule to be applied either on an item-by-item basis, in subgroups or in total. The "and" method, which is stricter, requires the rule to be applied individually.

In this respect, IAS 23 holds that it is "usual" to apply the rule on an item-by-item basis (i.e., the "and" method) although sometimes, it may be appropriate to group similar items or related items.

It should be noted that in the Philippines, any change in valuation method needs BIR approval before a new method can be used for tax purposes. Furthermore, the inventory valuation method for tax purposes must conform with that used for book purposes.

2. ***Marketable Securities:*** In the Philippines, under SFAS 10, marketable securities held for working capital purposes should be valued at the lower of aggregate cost or fair market value. But SAS 25, which is consistent with international standards (IAS 25), holds that either the lower-of-cost and fair-market-value method (i.e., value investments either in total or by category of investments), or the fair market value may be used.
3. ***Property, Plant and Equipment (PPE) and Depreciation:*** Included in this category are intangible fixed assets like land, buildings, machinery and equipment, furniture and fixtures, and leasehold improvements. Cost, less allowance for depreciation, is the generally accepted method of reporting PPE in both the Philippines and Singapore (SFAS 6 and SAS 14, respectively, and consistent with international standards IAS 16). Both standards require the depreciation of PPE (except non-exhaustible assets such as land) on a systematic basis over the life of the asset. Methods used in Singapore (straight-line, units of production, sum-of-digits and the declining balance) are equally acceptable in the Philippines. The straight-line method is widely used in the Philippines because of its simplicity. Depreciation rates are not prescribed but should be reasonable and consistently used.

   On the revaluation of PPE, SFAS 12 requires that the following must be observed:

   (a) appraisals must be made by recognised and independent specialists;
   (b) depreciation charges must be based on appraised values for financial statement presentation purposes;
   (c) revaluation increments should be shown separately under shareholders' equity; and
   (d) adequate disclosures of the revaluation basis, as well as the original cost and depreciation of assets, must be made.

These requirements are generally consistent with SAS 14, except that in point (b), it should be noted that while depreciation is based on appraised values for financial statement reporting, it should be based on cost for income tax purposes (another requirement by BIR).

4. ***Depletion:*** Accounting for depletion is more applicable in the Philippines, which is well endowed with minerals and timber land. For financial reporting, depletion is usually recorded on a percentage-of-completion basis. However, for tax purposes, only cost depletion is allowed, and the argument is similar to the preceding paragraph on depreciation. The annual allowable cost depletion should not exceed the market value of the gross output of minerals.
5. ***Accounting for Business Combinations:*** Business combinations may be classified into two categories: acquisition and merger. The two methods of accounting for business combinations are the purchase method and the pooling-of-interests method.

The Singapore and Philippines' standards under SAS 22 and SFAS 20, respectively, are similar to international standards (IAS 22). It should be noted, however, that goodwill in the Philippines is amortised over a useful life not exceeding 40 years. This is in contrast to Singapore's Provisional Accounting Standards (PAS) 26, which recommends that the amortisation period should not exceed five years, unless there are grounds to justify a longer period which must not exceed 20 years.

Consolidation

The generally accepted accounting principles on the consolidation of financial statements in the Philippines are embodied in SFAS 21. The statement adopts similar definitions of parent company, subsidiary company and control, as SAS 26 and IAS 27. Provisions on the procedures of consolidation and disclosure requirements are also similar. A noticeable difference, however, is the scope which a parent company has in presenting consolidated financial statements.

According to SFAS 21, a parent should present consolidated financial statements in the following circumstances:

1. When the total liabilities of any one entity in the group is more than P50 million, or when total liabilities of the group is more than P150 million, as shown in the balance sheets at the beginning of the most

recently completed fiscal year.

2. When it falls under one of the following categories whether or not it meets the condition set forth in (1) above:

   (a) companies whose securities are traded on securities exchanges or over-the-counter markets;
   (b) the following financial intermediaries: banks, financing companies, investment houses or investment companies; or
   (c) companies issuing commercial papers or other securities registered with the Securities and Exchange Commission.

A parent company that is a subsidiary is not required to present consolidated financial statements unless it falls under one of the categories in (2) above. However, a parent company that is a subsidiary of a foreign entity is required to present consolidated financial statements.

Provisions and Reserves

1. ***Contingency Provisions:*** The requirements on contingency provisions, as found under SFAS 7, are similar to Singapore's SAS 10 and IAS 10. Loss contingencies are accrued as a charge to income if the following conditions are met:

   (a) information available prior to the issuance of financial statements indicates that it is probable that an asset had been impaired or a liability had been incurred at the date of the financial statements;
   (b) the amount of the loss can be reasonably estimated.

   If no accrual is made, disclosure of the contingency should be made when there is at least a reasonable possibility that a loss may have been incurred. Contingencies that might result in gains are not accrued but may be disclosed if material.

2. ***Reserves:*** Reserves for general contingencies, such as strikes, business recessions and losses from catastrophes not ordinarily insured against, are not allowed. An enterprise, however, may set aside a portion of its retained earnings for future expenses, contingencies and other purposes, or as required by law.

Footnote Disclosures

1. ***Summary of Accounting Policies:*** In most financial statements of corporations in the Philippines, a typical footnote disclosure is a summary of accounting policies. This is the same as for the financial statements of companies incorporated in Singapore.
2. ***Post-Balance-Sheet Events:*** SFAS 7 of the Philippines requires disclosure of post-balance-sheet occurrences of material significance such as serious loss or damages from fire, flood or other casualties, and the sale of an important investment or capital assets, among others. This is similar to SAS 10. Both standards require disclosure of events which occur between the balance-sheet date and the date on which the financial statements are authorised for issue.

   To enable users of financial statements to make proper evaluations and decisions, IAS 10 states that when the effects of events occurring after the balance-sheet date are disclosed in the notes to the financial statements, the information given must include a description of the events and an estimation, if possible, of their financial effects. This is also required in both SAS and SFAS.
3. ***Related Party Disclosure:*** Disclosure of material-related party transactions are required in both the Singapore and the Philippines standards. This is similar to the requirement of IAS 10. SFAS 16 however, does not define the meaning of "related parties" but describes the possible entities that may be described as "related parties". In SAS 21 and IAS 24, parties are considered to be related if one party has the ability to control the other party, or exercise significant influence over the other party, in making financial and operating decisions. A related party transaction is also defined as a transfer of resources or obligations between related parties regardless of whether a price is charged or not. The disclosures required under SFAS 16 include the following:

   (a) the nature of the relationship(s);
   (b) a description of the transactions and other such information necessary for an understanding of the effects on the financial statements;
   (c) the peso amount of the transactions; and
   (d) amounts due from, or to, related parties at the balance-sheet

date and the terms of settlement.

4. ***Contingencies:*** This is the same as discussed under "Provisions and Reserves: Contingency Provisions".
5. ***Other Footnote Disclosures:*** SFAS 15, SAS 5 and IAS 5 are similar in setting forth the following disclosures:

   (a) restrictions on the title of assets;
   (b) security given in respect of liabilities;
   (c) the methods of providing for pension and retirement plans;
   (d) contingent assets and contingent liabilities, quantified if possible; and
   (e) amounts committed for future capital expenditure.

The following are some financial statement disclosure requirements that may be of particular interest to a foreign investor: name of the holding company, description, related-party transactions and sharing of expenses with affiliated companies.

Recording of income

Income is universally recognised when the earnings process is complete, or virtually complete, and an exchange has taken place. For income determination purposes, the general practice of matching income with related expenses through accrual accounting, insofar as practicable, is widely followed. A calendar year or a fiscal year may be adopted as the accounting period.

CONCLUSION

The regulation of financial reporting in the Philippines operates largely within a cooperative framework between the government and the private sector. The standard-setting body is represented by both the private sector and government agencies, and its pronouncements have mandatory status. The SEC has been vested with broad powers by the company and security laws to carry out the regulation of financial reporting.

The nature of GAAP for valuation of assets, accounting for business combinations, consolidation, provisions and reserves, footnote disclosures and recognition of income, are generally consistent with the IAS and Singapore's statements of accounting standards in broad terms, except for some slight differences in details.

REFERENCES

Companies Act, Chapter 50, Singapore.

"Doing Business in the Philippines", Price Waterhouse, 1993.

Foo S. L. and Tan P., "The Auditing Regulatory Framework In The Philippines", Research in Third World Accounting, 1995.

"International Accounting Standards", International Accounting Standards Committee, England, 1994.

Preface to Statements of Financial Accounting Standards of the Accounting Standards Council of the Philippines, Manila, 1983.

"Statements of Accounting Standards", Institute of Certified Public Accountants of Singapore, Singapore.

"Statements of Financial Accounting Standards", Accounting Standards Council of the Philippines, Manila.

Stock Exchange of Singapore Listing Manual, Singapore.

Tan P., "The Philippines", Financial Reporting in the West Pacific Rim.

Tan P. and Wong K. J., "A Comparative Study of Financial Reporting Practices in Singapore and the Philippines", 1993.

The Corporation Code of the Philippines, Manila.

Chapter 11

Taxation Aspects of Foreign Investment in the Philippines

BY
Victor LOO
SIAK Li Peng
TAN Wee Hui

INTRODUCTION

AFTER A DECADE of sluggish performance, the Philippines executed a turnabout in 1986 and 1987 when it registered respectable GNP growth. There is general consensus that such growth is not only sustainable but may very well make the Philippines the next newly industrialised country in the Asian region.

This chapter highlights the tax structure in the Philippines. In addition, it explores certain types of concessions available to companies setting up operations in the Philippines. Also, it examines the best form of profit remittance method to be used and, finally, it considers several practical problems associated with investments in the Philippines.

The chapter attempts to cover the general investment climate in the Philippines. It has intentionally left out specific industries such as banking, insurance and infrastructure projects. Discussion on regional incentives has also been omitted. Hopefully, the focus adopted here will assist investors to assess the investment climate in the Philippines based on the tax incentives and the types of concessions that are available.

FORMS OF DOING BUSINESS IN THE PHILIPPINES

To decide on a structure to conduct business, a few of the factors that investors need to consider include the liability of owners, tax considerations and capital requirements. An investor may carry out business in the Philippines using the following forms:

(a) sole proprietorship;
(b) partnership;
(c) corporation; or
(d) joint venture.

Since sole proprietorships and partnerships carry with them the risk of unlimited liability, we do not feel that these modes are advisable in a foreign country. Hence, our discussion will focus on the tax implications associated with the third form of business structure (i.e., corporation). As most joint ventures are likely to be incorporated, the discussion pertaining to corporations should subsume the issues involving joint ventures.

Under the Omnibus Investment Code (OIC), foreign ownership is generally limited to 40%. However, 100% ownership is allowed in the case of "pioneer" enterprises, enterprises exporting at least 70% of their total production, and enterprises registered with the EPZA.

GENERAL DISCUSSION ON TAXABILITY OF INCOME AND TAX DEDUCTIBILITY OF EXPENSES

Taxability of Income

Under the income tax law, taxable corporations include not only the corporate organisations or aggregation of persons contemplated under the Corporation Law but also all partnerships no matter how they are created or organised. In the Philippines, companies are taxed according to their status which involves the following:

1. ***Domestic Corporation:*** This is one which is created or organised in the Philippines or under its laws.
2. ***Foreign Corporation:*** This is one which is founded, organised or

exists under laws other than those of the Philippines. Resident foreign corporations engaged in trade or business in the Philippines are taxed on net domestic income. Non-resident foreign corporations not engaged in trade or business in the Philippines are taxed on gross domestic income. The current corporate tax rate is 35%.

Tax Deductibility of Expenses

The Philippines, like Singapore, allows all ordinary and necessary expenses actually incurred by the taxpayer in the operation of a trade, a business, or the practice of a profession, to be deductible.

The principles governing the deductibility of expenses are similar to Singapore, but it is necessary to highlight some unique features of the Philippines tax system.

1. ***Employee Remuneration:*** Excessive compensation paid to an employee–shareholder may be disallowed as a deduction and treated as an indirect dividend. Moreover, the Corporation Code limits compensation of a corporation's pre-tax income during the preceding year. Hence, this will have implications on remuneration planning for the company's personnel.
2. ***Taxes Other than Income Tax, Gift Tax, etc.:*** Unlike Singapore, which does not allow tax payable to be a tax-deductible expense for the organisation, the Philippines allows taxes paid or accrued within the taxable year to be deductible with the following exceptions: Philippine income tax, estate and gift tax, special assessment tax, taxes paid on articles imported by the tax payer that are not in connection with trade or energy, and an excess energy consumption tax. Foreign income tax, war profits tax and excess profits tax are allowable deductions only if the corporation does not make use of tax credit privileges.
3. ***Charitable Contributions:*** Contributions actually paid within the taxable year to the government, or any of its political subdivisions, and to religious, charitable, educational, scientific, athletic or cultural organisations, are deductible to the extent of 3% of net taxable income. Contributions to certain institutions are deductible in full. To make full use of this benefit, the company may have to do advance planning to determine the optimum charitable contributions to be made.

4. ***Depreciation:*** In the case of a resident foreign corporation, depreciation is allowed when the property is located within the Philippines. Depreciation rates are not prescribed but are generally based on the estimated economic or useful lives of the assets. Intangibles with limited life, such as patents, copyrights and franchises, can be amortised. Those with unlimited life, such as goodwill, trade names and formulae, are not ordinarily subject to amortisation. Gains and losses on the sale of depreciated assets are considered taxable income/deductible items, respectively.
5. ***Capital Gains:*** Capital gains arise from the sale or exchange of capital assets. Capital gains, except those arising from stock transactions, are taxed as ordinary income. Capital gains on stock transfer are taxed at preferential rates. Capital losses are deductible only to the extent of capital gains.
6. ***Losses:*** Generally, all losses actually sustained and charged off within the taxable year, and not compensated for by insurance or otherwise, are deductible. However, capital losses are deductible only to the extent of capital gains. There is no net loss carry-forward or carry-back provision.

TYPES OF INCENTIVES AVAILABLE

The Omnibus Investments Code of 1987 integrated and consolidated the investment incentive laws of the Philippines. It offers tax and non-tax incentives to registered enterprises, whether pioneer, non-pioneer or expanding, and enterprises that are located in the four EPZs. The tax incentives are available for a maximum period of ten years from the registration or startup of operations, unless another period is specified.

Eligibility

To be eligible for the main programme of incentives, firms must qualify for registration with the BOI. Preferred activities are spelt out in the annual IPP. In 1994, IPP emphasis was placed primarily on broad economic development aligned with the adoption of appropriate technology and regional development.

The BOI may classify an approved project as “pioneer”, which entitles it to enhanced incentives. Pioneer status is awarded to an enterprise that produces goods not formerly produced in the country on a commercial scale; introduces a technology, design, process or other method new to the country; is highly essential in the attainment of national economic goals; or entails substantial investment and above-normal risk. Even if the activity is not listed in the IPP, enterprises can still apply for incentives under the following conditions:

(a) at least 50% of production is for export, for Philippine-owned enterprises; or
(b) at least 70% of production is for export if the majority of equity is foreign-owned (i.e., more than 40% foreign equity).

Incentives to Registered Enterprises

1. ***Income Tax Holiday:*** New registered enterprises are fully exempt from income tax for a certain time period. For pioneer enterprises, the tax holiday is six years from the commencement of commercial operation and for non-pioneer enterprises, it is four years. The tax holiday may be extended for an extra year in each case if certain conditions (e.g., desired capital-to-workers ratio, rate of utilisation of indigenous raw materials, etc.) are satisfied. However, the maximum length of tax holiday for a pioneer enterprise is eight years.
2. ***Additional Deduction for Labour Cost:*** For the first five years of registration, a registered enterprise is allowed an additional deduction from taxable income of 50% of the wages corresponding to the increment in the number of workers, if the project meets the prescribed ratio of capital equipment to number of workers set by the BOI.
3. ***Expanding Enterprises:*** Registered expanding enterprises are entitled to an exemption from income tax, proportionate to their expansion under the terms and conditions set by BOI, for a period of three years from the commencement of commercial operation. They are not entitled, however, to an additional deduction for incremental labour expenses during the period within which the exemption is enjoyed.
4. ***Tax and Duty Exemption on Imported Capital Equipment:*** A 100% exemption from customs duties and value-added tax (VAT) on imported machinery, equipment and accompanying spare parts, is granted to new and expanding registered enterprises. One condi-

tion is that the machinery must not be manufactured domestically in sufficient quantity, or of comparable quality at reasonable prices.

5. ***Tax Credit on Domestic Capital Equipment:*** A 100% tax credit is granted in respect of machinery, equipment and spare parts purchased by a new or expanding registered enterprise from a domestic manufacturer. The amount of credit is based on how much the VAT and customs duty exemption would have been if the capital equipment had been imported.
6. ***Exemption from Contractor's Tax:*** This incentive is available to export-oriented firms both at the national and local levels.
7. ***Tax- and Duty-Free Importation of Breeding Stocks and Genetic Materials:*** This applies for the first ten years from the registration or commercial operation for agricultural producers.
8. ***Tax Credit for Taxes and Duties on Raw Materials:*** A tax credit is granted to registered enterprises equivalent to the VAT and customs duties paid on supplies, raw materials and semi-manufactured products used in the manufacture, processing or production of their export products and items forming part of those products.
9. ***Exemption from Taxes and Duties on Imported Spare Parts:*** Imported required supplies and spare parts for consigned equipment, or those imported tax and duty-free by a registered enterprise with a bonded manufacturing warehouse, are exempt from customs duties and VAT if certain conditions are satisfied. For example, at least 70% of production must be exported and spare parts and supplies must not be available locally at reasonable prices.
10. ***Exemption from Wharfage Dues and any Export Tax, Duty, Impost and Fees:*** Exports by a registered enterprise of its non-traditional export products are exempt from any wharfage dues, and any export tax, duty, impost and fees.

Incentives to Registered Enterprises in Less Developed Areas

The nationality requirement on non-pioneer activities locating in less developed areas can be waived. In other words, 100% foreign ownership is allowed. In addition, enterprises located in such areas are entitled to extra incentives:

1. ***Same Set of Incentives for Pioneer Registered Enterprises:*** Regardless of the pioneer or non-pioneer status of the enterprise, en-

terprises located in less developed areas are given the same set of incentives as the pioneer registered enterprises.

2. ***Additional Deduction for Labour Cost:*** The additional deduction for labour cost is up to 100% of the wages corresponding to the increment in the number of workers, if the project meets the prescribed ratio of capital equipment to number of workers set by the BOI.
3. ***Deduction for Infrastructure Construction:*** Deduction from taxable income of an amount equivalent to 100% of necessary and major infrastructure construction undertaken by the registered enterprise is allowed, with the prior approval of the BOI. The amount not deducted for a particular year may be carried over for deduction for not more than ten years from the commencement of commercial operations.

Incentives for Export Processing Zone (EPZ) Enterprises

Enterprises located in the EPZs are entitled to all the incentives applicable to all registered companies. In addition, they are entitled to the following:

(a) exemption from taxes and duties, which includes income tax for newly registered firms, export taxes and fees, local taxes and fees, contractors' tax, wharfage, storage and other dues under the Tariff and Customs Code, and the 15% branch profits tax for profits remitted abroad;
(b) exemption in varying rates for customs duties and VAT; and
(c) no VAT for raw materials and supplies purchased from local suppliers.

PROCEDURES INVOLVED IN REMITTING FOREIGN CURRENCIES TO HOME COUNTRY

All foreign investors in the Philippines are given rights and guarantees with respect to their investments. These rights include repatriation of investment, remittance of earnings, foreign loans and contracts, freedom from expropriation and non-requisition of investments.

Basically, these rights translate into safeguarding investments from expropriation or requisition by the Philippine government, and the ability of investors to remit capital, earnings and other cash flows related to investments. However, investors must register with certain bodies to enjoy these rights. These are shown in Table 11–1.

The investor's funds may be repatriated in several forms, the most common being dividends, royalties, interests, management fees and capital repatriation. During the incentive period, when tax is low or nil, it is to an investor's advantage to repatriate funds through dividends since dividends are not an expense item in determining taxable income. However, when the incentive period is over and the tax rate is at a higher level, funds should be remitted by way of expense-related means (e.g., royalties, management fees, etc.).

TABLE 11–1
Rights and Registration Bodies

Body	Prerequisite
Central Bank	Capital repatriation and profit remittance rights, distribution of after-tax profits and dividends to non-residents.
Technology Transfer Board	Royalty and technical service contracts.
Central Bank	Remittance of the above fees.

PRACTICAL ISSUES ENCOUNTERED BY FOREIGN INVESTORS

Three practical issues with regard to the taxation of foreign investors need to be mentioned, namely, the application for tax incentives, the tax holiday period and the annual tax audits.

1. ***Application for Tax Incentives***: Before investors can enjoy tax incentives, they first have to put up a notice in a major Philippine newspaper to inform the public of the intended application. Within seven days of the notice, any objections to the application would require a public hearing to resolve the objection. The application for tax incentives may be delayed for several months to a year, or more,

due to several consecutive objections and related public hearings. When the public hearings are satisfactorily resolved, the application can then be reviewed by the BOI. The application rejection rate by the BOI resulting from public hearings is about 30 to 40%.[1]

2. ***Tax Holidays:*** Tax holidays are given to three groups of qualifying investments as shown in Table 11–2.

TABLE 11–2
Tax Holidays

Qualifying Status	No. of Years
Pioneer	6–8
Non-pioneer	4–6
Expanding	3

Although this arrangement seems attractive at first glance, in actual fact, most foreign investors will find that they do not get the full benefit of this arrangement. Most investments are not likely to make any profits during the initial years of setting up, and due to the fact that tax losses during the tax holiday period cannot be carried forward for offsetting in future years, this tax holiday can only be enjoyed if profits are made during the years of the tax holidays.

3. ***Annual Tax Audits:*** Unlike Singapore, companies are subject to annual tax audits by the tax authorities and, although this may serve as a good method of ensuring that the annual tax returns are properly filed, it may seem a bother to investors not used to annual tax audits.

CONCLUSION

The choice of investing locally, or abroad, depends on a multitude of factors such as costs of raw materials, labour, technology, infrastructure and taxation. This chapter only focused on one aspect of investment choice, namely, taxation. We found that the Philippine government has

1 Rejection range is an unofficial estimate by a BOI spokesperson.

made many tax benefits available to foreign investors in the hope of attracting more foreign investments. However, like many countries, certain local procedures, whether social or bureaucratic, have to be followed in order to enjoy these benefits. Overall, the tax benefits appear to be very attractive to investors and they should not be a major hindrance to the decision to invest in the Philippines.

REFERENCES

AP Supplement No. 120, International Bureau of Fiscal Documentation, Philippine Government, August 1994.

"Doing Business in the Philippines", Price Waterhouse, 1993.

"Doing Business in the Philippines", Carlos J. Valdes & Co., 1993.

Singapore Income Tax Act, 1994.

"The Philippines, Your Competitive Advantage", Board of Investments, Government of the Philippines, 1993.

INDUSTRY ANALYSES

Chapter 12

The Impact of Tourism on the Philippines

BY
NG Lee Keng
Ann TAN Hon-Mui
Jeffrey ONG

INTRODUCTION

TOURISM IS THE world's largest industry, surpassing even the oil and automobile industries. It accounts for 10.2% of the world's GDP and one in ten jobs. In 1994, it was estimated that tourism contributed S$5.5 trillion to the world's economy. Worldwide, travel and tourism provide direct and indirect employment for more than 200 million people, and the income generated is expected to reach S$12.4 trillion by the year 2005. According to the World Travel and Tourism Council (WTTC), tourism growth will double in the next ten years. An estimated £460 billion (S$1,012 billion) will be invested in new travel and tourism facilities around the world, and the industry will contribute a total of £445 billion (S$979 billion) in tax revenue next year.

International tourism in the Asia-Pacific region has grown rapidly since the 1960s, primarily because of increased intra-regional travel among residents in this region. Tourism has grown fastest in Asia and the Pacific when compared to all other regions. Arrivals in Asia-Pacific destinations now account for nearly 11% of total international visitor arrivals as compared with only 1% in 1960. Caught in this regional growth is the Philippines, with its vast potential of attracting arrivals anchored in more than 7,000 islands. In 1993, visitor arrivals were 1.4 million, which contributed US$2.5 billion to the economy. By 1998, earnings are expected to reach US$6 billion, creating 1.44 million jobs in the process.

However, performance has lagged behind potential in comparison to neighbouring countries. For example, visitor arrivals were far behind Singapore (6.4 million), Malaysia (6.3 million) and Indonesia (3.5 million). Although the country has a long way to go, the challenges and payoffs are enormous. Under the present Philippine policy for the year 2000, the target is to reach newly industrialised country (NIC) status. Under this policy, 19 industries have been earmarked as catalysts to carry the country forward, and tourism is one of them.

The objectives of this chapter are two-fold. First, it examines the significance of tourism's impact on the Philippines. An understanding of impact issues can help business investors to be more aware of potential regulations and policies facing the industry. A second focus is to compare the impacts with neighbouring countries and look for solutions to minimise these impacts. Several remedial measures are suggested which serve to heighten the awareness of business investors, and the relevant authorities, in order to better manage tourism developments.

THE IMPACT OF TOURISM IN THE PHILIPPINES

Only in recent years has the negative effect of tourism on destinations been set more fully against the tangible economic gains. The rise of environmentalism, or the green movement in the mid-1980s, sets the background for a reassessment of the role and value of tourism on various destinations.

Since the Philippines is only in the developmental stage of the destination life cycle, it is important for policy makers, and the business community, to understand and judiciously apply the concepts of sustainable development and carrying capacity as guiding principles for the 1990s and beyond. The Brundtland Report (World Commission on Environment and Development, 1987) defines sustainability as meeting the needs of the present without compromising the ability of future generations to meet their own needs. The concept of sustainability demands a long-term view of tourism to ensure that the consumption of tourists does not exceed the ability of a host destination to provide for future tourists. In other words, it represents a trade-off between present and future needs. Sustainability cannot be accorded low priority as compared with the short-term drive for profitability and growth.

Going hand in hand with sustainable development is the notion of carrying capacity. As defined by Cooper *et al.* (1993), the carrying capacity of a site, resort or region refers to the ability to absorb tourism without deteriorating. This is a simple resource management principle. Carrying capacity is often a conscious management decision. The authorities and visitors often have to decide what is unacceptable, and when the quality of experience has declined.

Within the context of the Philippines, the impact of tourism can be identified by several factors:

(a) the volume of visitor arrivals;
(b) the structure of the host economy;
(c) the types of tourism activities;
(d) the difference in socio-cultural characteristics between the hosts and visitors; and
(e) the fragility of the local environment.

These factors give rise to four major impacts which are discussed sequentially: economic, environmental, social and cultural.

ECONOMIC IMPACTS

According to Dr. K. Raguraman, geography lecturer at the National University of Singapore: "A good measure of the net economic impact of tourism in the country is to look specifically at two types of multipliers – income (GDP at factor cost) and imports." Before examining these impacts, it is useful to highlight the recent performance of the tourism sector of the Philippines.

In 1994, there were 1,573,821 arrivals which set a new record in the history of tourism in the Philippines. Visitor traffic grew by 14.7% over the previous year's volume of 1,372,097 visitors. This impressive growth was achieved because of a stable political situation, hosting of the 1994 Miss Universe Beauty Pageant, and Leyte Gulf Landing's aggressive marketing campaigns such as the "bring home a friend programme" and sales missions abroad.

The major source markets are Japan, the United States, Hong Kong, Taiwan, Australia, Germany, the United Kingdom and ASEAN. With increased air transportation access, the development of new resort plans and related attractions in a natural setting can attract new market segments, especially from Japan, Hong Kong, Taiwan and other nearby ASEAN countries. In addition, the Philippines is increasingly attractive to the emerging Korean, Middle East, French, Italian and Swiss markets. As these markets become increasingly affluent during the 1990s, they offer significant opportunities for tourism growth in the Philippines.

There are a few important variables in the computation of economic impacts. They are as follows:

1. ***Tourism Receipts:*** International visitor receipts are calculated in order to determine the contribution and economic significance of the tourism industry to the national income accounts. In the estimation of travel receipts, the Department of Tourism (DOT) adopts the following formula:

   visitor receipts = number of visitors × average daily expenditures × average length of stay

   According to the statistical report presented by the DOT in 1993, the contribution of the industry to the country's economy, in terms of foreign exchange earnings in 1992, amounted to US$1.67 billion. Total visitor receipts registered a remarkable increase of 30.64% as compared to the previous year's earnings of US$1.28 billion.
2. ***Occupancy Report of Classified Hotels:*** The statistics generated are occupancy rates, average length of stay of guests (in terms of nights) and the number of rooms available. The average number of saleable rooms reported by all the classified hotel establishments in Metropolitan Manila was 8,127. This showed an addition of 404 rooms, or a 5.23% increase, over the 7,723 room capacity in 1992.

A study conducted by the Department of Tourism (DOT) in 1993 reported some of the major economic benefits from tourism which are listed in Table 12–1. As mentioned earlier, Dr. Raguraman conducted a study of the multiplier effects, and the major findings are shown in Table 12–2.

TABLE 12–1
Economic Impact of Tourism on The Economy (1993 Estimate)

Impact Element	Foreign Tourism
Gross Revenue (billion pesos)	40.95
Gross Revenue (billion US$)	1.49
GDP Contribution (billion pesos)	34.81
Percentage of GDP	3.24
Persons Employed	373,000
Employment % of Labour Force	1.46
Net Foreign Exchange Earnings	
(billion pesos)	26.21
(billion US$)	0.9538

Source: Department of Tourism (1993).

TABLE 12–2
Multiplier Effects

Impact	Multiplier	Impact On Economy (thousand US$)
Direct Visitor	1.000	15,916.5
Total Output	1.692	26,930.8
GDP at Factor Cost	1.792	12,605.9
Imports	0.146	1,027.1
Employment (Jobs)	711.183*	11,320

* Number of jobs generated per US$1 million direct expenditure.

ENVIRONMENTAL IMPACTS

The Philippines contains a diverse natural heritage that provides a sound base for the development of tourism. This includes the following:

1. A marine environment filled with coral and marine life such as that

found in northern Palawan.

2. Coastal areas containing many excellent white sandy beaches, often in dramatic settings, such as the blue limestone bluffs of Palawan and the Hundred Islands of Pangasinan.
3. Spectacular inland features such as the mountain areas of northern Luzon, with the resort city of Baguio, the active Taal Volcano and the oval sloped limestone mould of Bohol called the Chocolate Hills.

To preserve and develop some of these islands, while minimising the environmental impacts of tourism, it would be extremely useful to look briefly into the five major clusters of tourism development as stipulated in the master plan drawn up by the DOT.

Luzon Cluster

This group, which contains the pristine attractions of Palawan, the rustic charm of the Bohol area, the cool mountain climate of Baguio, and business and entertainment facilities, will be positioned as a multifaceted destination with combined attractions for all markets. Given the diversity of attractions that can be encouraged in northern Luzon, its tourism potential is high, particularly among East Asian, ASEAN and resort holiday markets.

Northern Palawan

This rates as one of the most beautiful places in the Philippines. The northern Palawan area represents one of the most environmentally and culturally sensitive areas. Its ecological wilderness and anthropological values have attracted world attention, which is why any tourism development plan must contribute to the preservation of the environment and the ethnic heritage of these islands. Northern Palawan is not earmarked for mass markets; instead, its primary goal is to develop a tourism sector that is environmentally and socially sensitive, sustainable, and internationally recognised. As a special-interest, low-volume and high-value destination, northern Palawan promises to be an adventure of a lifetime for visitors and a source of considerable profit for suitable investors.

Taal, Batangas, Tagaytay, Baguio, La Union, Ilocos Norte and Sur Cluster

The proximity of these areas to Manila, coupled with their diversity of attractions and relative ease of access to domestic and foreign markets, make them some of the major destination areas in the country.

Visayas Cluster

This cluster will be positioned for sports, cultural heritage and historic tourism activities. Cebu, Panglao Island in Bohol, Bacolod, Iloilo and Boracay are identified as priority areas.

Mindanoa Cluster

The offering here is skewed towards exotic wilderness destinations and showcases the rich Muslim culture of the seafaring Filipinos. Davao, based on Samal Island, Mt. Apo and Zamboanga City are the key destinations. Other centres include Bakak and the islands near Cagayan de Oro.

The Philippines is a vast country, with distinct differences in the stages of development of the city (Metropolitan Manila) and outlying islands. Environmental impacts are manifested in varying ways in both the undeveloped and developed regions. In the underdeveloped areas, tourism development is seen as an answer to some of the prevalent life-threatening environmental problems, such as poor water supplies, inadequate sanitation and sewage facilities, deficient nutrition, bad housing conditions, sickness and disease, and vulnerability to natural disasters.

Tourism development projects, which are to be located in declared tourist zones and in classified environmentally critical areas, require an environmental compliance certificate (ECC) from the Environmental Management Bureau (EMB) of the Department of Environment and Natural Resources (DENR). Such stringent rules will ensure that tourism development enhances, and does not destroy, the ecology of the area. This policy was clearly spelt out in President Ramos's economic policy which was announced at the 1992 Earth Summit in Rio de Janeiro.

SOCIAL IMPACTS

Positive Social Impacts

Since tourism is a people industry, it entails numerous social impacts. One macro benefit asserted by the World Tourism Organisation (WTO) is that tourism contributes to international understanding, peace, prosperity and universal respect for the observance of human rights and fundamental freedom for all, without distinction as to race, sex, language or religion. With 1.6 million tourists in 1994, and an even higher projected figure for 1995, tourism in the Philippines will be another contributing player on the global tourism platform.

Tourism also fosters a sense of national identity and pride. This, in turn, encourages the preservation of heritage in the form of encouraging artistic activities and restoration of historical landmarks. The Filipino *Barong Tagalog* is an internationally recognisable piece of attire that graces occasions of all sorts and stimulates local pride.

In a country of 60 million, in which both unemployment and underemployment are serious problems, the employment-generating capability of the tourism industry is of particular significance. With more than 350,000 university graduates each year, the tourism industry certainly serves as a formidable employer. Employment in the tourism industry represents between 2 and 3% of the workforce and it is expected that the industry will generate 1.44 million jobs by 1998. Alongside the availability of more job opportunities is the opportunity to learn new skills. Currently, human resource development in the tourism sector is carried out on three levels: the baccalaureate degree (4-year course), the associate degree (2-year course) and vocational training. These tourism training programmes will certainly help to produce a more efficient, effective and competitive manpower supply.

Tourism may also trigger the desire of local people in less developed areas to aspire to a higher standard of living. Coming into contact with visitors who are obviously on a higher income level (able to travel, dress and dine well), may motivate them to strive harder to afford the same luxuries.

Upgrading of the infrastructure for visitors invariably results in spill-over advantages for the local population. There are about 26 infrastructure projects outlined in the Tourism Master Plan which include the upgrading of airports (Manila's Ninoy Aquino International airport, Davao Airport and Cebu's Mactan airport), roads (Subic expressway) and ancillary services (sewage and utilities). These improvements will provide an increased standard of living for the local people.

The development of tourist spots also serves to discourage the depopulation of remote areas. Take, for example, the Boracay Islands project by Ayala Land Inc. Apart from the development work, the company has also provided the local inhabitants with skills training and helped them to set up shops in the resorts. The provision of training and a livelihood will certainly help to curb the migration of individuals to the already congested urban cities.

Negative Social Impacts

Benefits aside, tourism does contribute to negative social impacts. At a conference on The Social and Economic Impact of Tourism on Pacific Communities held in the 1970s, an unanimous conclusion was that tourism promises dreams but produces nightmares. Two decades since then, the social ills of tourism are still as prevalent.

One disadvantage that tourism brings is overcrowding. After only a few years, Cebu is already reported to be overheated by Japanese tourists. Overcrowding puts a strain on the visitors as well as the visited. Resources are overtaxed, privacy in rural communities is lost, and claustrophobic feelings can lead to the erosion of goodwill.

Through contact with visitors who have higher spending power, local people can subsequently acquire new greed and desires. According to a 1993 visitor survey, the average daily expenditure for all visitors to the Philippines was US$131 as compared to the daily income of about US$5 for the Filipino blue-collar worker (in Cavite, for instance). This disparity can develop envy, jealousy and, most importantly, new wants and expectations, all of which can culminate in increased crime and misdemeanours. It was reported in *PATA Travel News* (January 1994) that there were near-daily complaints by tour operators of Japanese tourists being harassed. The DOT even has a tourism police force operating in the capital to fight urban crime.

In addition, moral behaviour may be less restrained where anonymity prevails, and prostitution is a common by-product of mass tourism. The powerful tourist dollar enhances further the Filipino image of Manila being a City of the Males. In 1988, the Police Chief of Manila, Alfred Lim, attempted to shut down the Ermita girlie bar strip with the aim of making Manila the first city in the country without prostitution. But seven years later, evidence shows that his attempts did not end the country's reputation for sex tours. The strong tourist dollar simply shifted the base to neighbouring cities such as Pasay, Makati and Angeles.

Although the tourism industry is often hailed as a big source of employment, many tourism jobs are unskilled, lowly paid and part-time. Much tourism employment is also highly seasonal and this can present social problems not detected at the surface. Last, but not least, all too frequently, traditional employment in the agriculture and fishing industries can be forsaken for the perceived glamour of a tourist job.

There are opportunity costs involved in the development of tourist attractions. First, the provision of infrastructure to support tourism may be carried out at the expense of other worthy projects such as health facilities. Second, tourist attractions that reap high profits, such as casinos, may have an impact on the social habits of the local people. Already there are casino branches which have sprouted in several areas including Manila Bay, Tagaytay, Laoag, Baguio, Angeles, Cebu, Olongapo and Davao. Third, land development necessitates the displacement of farmers' land. In Panglao, Bohol, for instance, the development work did not proceed beyond the planning stage because of resistance from the local community. These examples are just a few of the potential social costs attributable to expanded tourism.

CULTURAL IMPACTS

Positive Cultural Impacts

The tourism market has been viewed as a saviour of indigenous art and craft traditions. Most tourists have a desire to acquire some tangible momentos of their visit. The advent of video cameras still cannot beat the satisfaction of purchasing art work. Native Filipino dances, with their strong influence from the Spanish era, are also popular with tourists. Here, too, tourism is partially responsible for their continued development. Besides art and crafts, interest in the local cuisine is also being revived and sustained. The Filipino *kare-kare* and crispy pata dishes, for example, have become mandatory food items.

Other obvious benefits are the conservation and restoration of historic sites and buildings. Not only does tourism give a reason for preservation, but it generates income that can also provide the means to achieve these objectives.

Negative Cultural Impacts

As mentioned in the previous sections, the clamour for the tourist dollar is most understandable and, in many situations, it makes common sense. However, there are valid causes for concern. One of the most visible areas of tourism's downside involves the commercialisation and trivialisation of dance, music, art and crafts. Ritual dances performed on the hour to suit tour-bus operators lose much of their true significance. What used to be festivals of historical and religious significance, like the Mardi-Gras style Ati-Atihan festival in Aklan, have degenerated into a mere show for tourists. Similarly, there is pressure to make souvenir objects suitcase-sized and cheap. A higher importance inevitably is placed on saleability rather than on authenticity.

REMEDIAL ACTIONS FOR SOCIAL AND CULTURAL NEGATIVE IMPACTS

There is no simple panacea for the problems of tourism. It takes conscientious, long-term planning and management to keep the disadvantages in perspective. Tourism planning is not just opening hotels, promoting airlines, mounting promotional campaigns and, then, counting the revenue.

A standard set of actions is necessary to remedy the disadvantages of tourism. Laws need to be passed to protect the environment, funds need to be set up to preserve historic buildings, and educational programmes need to be established to foster pride in the local people and to encourage respect from tourists. But the underlying premise is that tourism can benefit a country or community more economically, and at less cost, if individual participation and local involvement are broadly based.

Integrated Planning and Development

Tourism planning requires careful cooperation and coordination from both the private and public sectors across three different layers: international, national and regional/local. It is advocated that the development plan team be comprised of market analysts, physical planners, economists, infrastructure engineers, transport specialists and legal experts to collectively identify, inventorise, make forecasts, plan and implement decisions.

Many countries have plunged into tourism following the jump-on-the-bandwagon syndrome. The realisation that conditions and programmes are not uniform knowledge disappears. The words of the former Minister, Jose D. Aspiras, in his speech during the PATA Seminar on Tourism Investment and Finance in the early 1980s, are telling: "The tourism industry in this region (Asia and the Pacific) managed to survive and grew quite spontaneously with very little coordination and planning, by merely playing the rules of supply and demand by ear. But finally the age of innocence and abundance of tourism is over, and we must now begin to contend with the realities of our trade...." Indeed, there must be efforts guided by clear tourism policies and systematic plans, which can then result in viable developments that are in close harmony with the local culture. This is true, not only in the Philippines, but in any destination.

Involvement of the local community

The involvement of the local people cannot be overemphasised. Mr. Renton de Alwis, PATA vice-president (Asia), said at the Second Pan-Asia Hotel and Tourism Technology Conference: "...as more and more land areas open up for tourism and related activities, the impact these activities have on the local community and their lifestyles may create negative feelings. We need to take these sensitivities into account and develop models of tourism that have total participation of the community as much as possible." And it is very encouraging to note that the Under-secretary, Ramona Lopez-Ty, when interviewed by *Asia Money* in 1993, mentioned: "We are integrating the resident community. We are not going to freeze them out. They will be part and parcel of the development."

Towards this end, the Philippines's 20-year Tourism Master Plan has two key people-related objectives. One is to provide livelihood opportunities to the community while the other is to train the community in native craft-making and developing skills.

CONCLUSION

Tourism is necessary and inevitable. And in the case of the Philippines, as for many other countries, there is no turning back as far as tourism development is concerned. However, there is no denying that tourism brings more non-pecuniary benefits and costs than any other export industry. Thus, governments should not be dazzled by the benefits, but should be proactive in coping with the changes and stresses, and institute policies and programmes to ensure long-term viability from their tourism investments.

The catalogue of impacts mentioned in this paper is by no means exhaustive. It merely serves to highlight some of the industry's attendant problems. It is unfortunate that these issues are little understood, downplayed or ignored. But the good news is that there are solutions to the problems. It is merely a question of whether to act or not to act.

REFERENCES

ASEAN Tourism Training Directory 1992/3, pp. 61–5.

Cooper C., J. Fletcher, D. Gilbert and S. Wanhill, Tourism Principles & Practice, Pitman Publishing, London, 1993.

Edgell D. L. and J. Smith, "Tourism Milestones for the Millennium: Projections and Implications of International Tourism for the United States Through the Year 2000", *Journal of Travel Research,* 1993, pp. 42–7.

EIU International Tourism Reports No. 3, The Economist Intelligence Unit Limited, 1994, pp. 47–70.

Gee C. Y., J. C. Makens and D. J. L Choy, The Travel Industry, Van Nostrand Reinhold, New York, 2nd edition, 1989.

Gimenez Teresa E., "A Feasibility Study on the Sustainable Tourism Development of Barangay Laiya–Aplaya, San Juan, Batangas", Dissertation, San Juan, Batangas, 1993/1994, pp. 1–26, 54–5.

Investment Opportunities In Tourism Industry, Board of Tourists, 1994.

Ludszuweit Daniel, "Night Life, Philippine Guides", Cockatoo Press Inc., Manila, 1988, pp. 119–20.

Mak James and Kenneth White, "Comparative Tourism Development in Asia and the Pacific", *Journal of Travel Research,* 1992, pp. 14–22.

"Philippines, Poor Image Still Nags", *PATA Travel News,* January 1994, pp. 15–16.

Press Release, 1992/1993 Tourism Year End Report, Department of Tourism.

Press Release, 17 March 1995, Life Section p. 7.

"Prospects and Challenges for Tourism to the Millennium", *Tourism Management*, October 1993, pp. 392–5.

"Social and Economic Impacts of Tourism on Asia–Pacific", A publication sponsored by Asia Productivity Organisation, 1982, pp. 215–27.

"World Tourism Expected to Double in Ten Years", *Business Times*, 18 November, 1994.

Chapter 13

Towards Sustained Competitive Advantage in the Philippine Hotel Industry

BY
CHAN Mei Wah
Gerard Dionicio GONZALES
EOON Hoon Eng

INTRODUCTION

THIS CHAPTER REVIEWS the competitive strengths and weaknesses in the Philippine hotel industry. The review sets the stage for a discussion of key issues that need to be tackled by the industry in order to compete successfully in the region. It concludes with practical strategies that the hotel industry can implement to enhance its competitive advantage. The objectives addressed in the paper are: (a) factors that determine the competitiveness of the hotel industry; (b) key issues influencing the long-term growth of the industry; and (c) practical recommendations to achieve competitive advantage in the region. The data come from a review of current literature, interviews with persons familiar with and involved in the hospitality industry, and real-estate developers in the Philippines. Michael Porter's diamond framework, relating to the competitiveness of nations, is extended to determine the competitive strengths and weaknesses of the Philippines as a tourist destination.

The Philippines's master plan for tourism,

developed in conjunction with the United Nations Development Programme and the World Tourist Organisation, projects that the country will receive 5.4 million visitor arrivals by 2010, an average annual increase of 15% from the 1.6 million visitor arrivals in 1994. As arrivals continue to climb, industry members see a definite trend in favour of the Philippines. Key markets are responding well to political reforms that started two years ago, and the stable political situation in the Philippines today has helped in easing concerns about generating markets. To achieve the 2010 visitor target, the government plans to undertake massive redevelopment of the country's infrastructure and provide incentives to attract local and foreign participation in developing attractions, hotels, resorts and other supporting tourism amenities. The master plan projects that a total of 17,950 rooms for hotels, resorts and budget accommodations will be needed in the form of private-sector investment.

Future growth of the tourism and hotel industry in the Philippines is undoubtedly bright. However, the threat of competition from other ASEAN countries, as well as Vietnam and Myanmar, is growing as these countries are planning to attract the same base of visitors and investors. Consequently, visitors and investors (developers, owners or managers of hotels) have a wide choice of regional destinations in which to enhance their psychic and economic wealth. How to achieve competitive advantage in a region undergoing unprecedented economic and tourism growth, is the primary challenge facing the Philippine hotel industry.

COMPETITIVE STRENGTHS AND WEAKNESSES

Porter's "diamond" consists of four broad attributes that influence an industry's ability to innovate and upgrade its competitive advantages over time:

1. ***Factor Conditions:*** These involve the contributions to production, such as skilled labour or infrastructure, necessary to compete in a given industry.
2. ***Demand Conditions:*** These concern the nature of demand for the industry's product.
3. ***Related and Supporting Industries:*** These relate to the presence or

absence of supplier and related industries that are internationally competitive.

4. ***Context for Competition:*** This concerns conditions in the industry governing the nature of competition, and the ways in which companies are created, organised and managed.

Factor Conditions

1. ***Skilled Labour:*** Although the Philippines has an abundance of relatively inexpensive labour, skilled labour is in short supply. Since the hotel industry is a labour-intensive one, the lack of well-trained staff is a serious threat to the industry's competitiveness. The industry has been losing trained employees to other burgeoning industries in the country, and to countries such as Malaysia and Hong Kong. To counter these effects, the Hotel and Restaurant Association of the Philippines has planned a joint public/private venture to tackle the problem. In 1994, a small 25-room hotel and an associated hotel school, the Hotel and Tourism Institute of the Philippines, were opened to train 720 students within three years.
2. ***Infrastructure:*** Ninoy Aquino International Airport, the country's main ingress and egress point, has reached full capacity, and its facilities are a pale comparison to the airports of competing countries. Some minor improvements have taken place recently, and a major upgrading programme has been delayed due to political infighting. The massive upgrading was to have included a new terminal building and additional facilities to enable a passenger throughput increase from the current five million to 12 million by the year 2010 at an expected cost of US$535 million. This decision, however, has been put on hold because the government is considering the conversion of Clark Air Base into a major international airport. Across the country, the airport infrastructure remains inadequate, which is a serious cause of concern to both government and industry. Of the approximately 100 airports in the country, only 70 are operational. Four domestic airports were reported to have been shut down by the Air Transportation Office due to poor safety standards.

   Around 34 foreign airlines now fly to the Philippines and new domestic carriers have begun operations. All these have contributed to increased flight frequencies and air capacity, both domestically and internationally. The open-skies policy appears to be paying off judging by the double-digit growth in international visitor arrivals since 1992, and the sprouting of hotels and resorts in remote locations that were once inaccessible.

3. ***Attractions:*** The country's primary attraction lies in its tropical island setting, mountains, culture, festivals, shopping, music, night life, sea sports and warm Filipino hospitality. Spanish, American, Malay and Chinese influences all combine to make the country's culture an intriguing one for tourists. A diverse natural and cultural heritage provides a sound base for tourism.

Demand Conditions

1. ***Visitor Arrivals:*** In terms of visitor arrivals to ASEAN countries, the Philippines's mark of 1.4 million in 1993 lagged far behind Singapore's 6.4 million, Malaysia's 6.3 million, Thailand's 5.5 million and Indonesia's 3.5 million. The Philippines managed to beat only Brunei, which reported 900,000 visitor arrivals for 1993.

   Still, 1993's performance increased 19% over 1992's 1.15 million. Just over one-half of all arrivals (52.7%) were from the Asia-Pacific region with a significant proportion (40.7%) from East Asia (Japan, Hong Kong, South Korea and Taiwan), which is growing in market share. North America's share was an above-average 22.4% of all arrivals, followed by Europe (13.1%) and ASEAN (5%). A fairly large percentage of arrivals were "balikbayans" (former Filipino nationals with foreign citizenship and their families), a market that resiliently weathered the poor publicity and safety concerns that plagued the country.

   According to one report, the industry is on target to reach 2.0 million visitors in 1995 and is expected to break the three million mark in 1998. The DOT said that the growth rate of arrivals would continue, with 1995 set to register the biggest increase (up 25%) and 1997 the lowest (13%). Actual visitor arrivals from 1989 to 1993, and DOT's visitor arrival projections for the period 1994 to 1998, are shown in Table 13–1. If the projections are on target, then the impact on the Philippine hotel industry will be substantial.

2. ***Purpose of Visit:*** The highest proportion of arrivals (31.4%) to the Philippines in 1993 were of the VFR (visit friends and relatives) variety as compared to 24.6% in 1992, and 28.9% in 1991. This

reflects an industry in a stage of infancy as well as the high "balikbayan" content. Visiting for business and leisure purposes has an almost equal share, but vary among the different geographical markets. About 62% of arrivals in 1993 were repeat visitors, most of whom were from the United States, Hong Kong and Singapore. This reflects the strong VFR and business component, but the fairly weak leisure travel share.

TABLE 13–1
Actual and Projected Arrivals: 1989 to 1998

Year	Volume	Growth Rate
Actual		
1989	1,187,719	
1990	1,024,520	–14%
1991	951,365	–7%
1992	1,152,952	21%
1993	1,372,097	19%
1994	1,608,058	17%
Projected		
1995	2,000,000	24%
1996	2,300,000	15%
1997	2,600,000	13%
1998	3,100,000	19%

Source: Philippines Department of Tourism.

3. ***Visitor Expenditure:*** The average daily expenditure for all visitors in 1993 was US$131, an increase of 2.9% over 1992. Singapore, Germany and Hong Kong reported the highest growth. As expected, travellers on package tours spent less than independent travellers, or US$116 per person as compared to US$132 per person, respectively. Most of the package travellers' spendings were on shopping, entertainment and recreation, while accommodation and shopping were the main expenditures of business travellers.
4. ***Hotel Occupancy:*** No data is available for the occupancy levels of hotels in the various cities and regions, except for Metropolitan Manila. Table 13–2 shows that the average hotel occupancy levels in Metropolitan Manila have been declining since 1989, a result of increased hotel supply over the last five years and an increasing VFR component. Only the deluxe hotels increased their average occupancy level in 1993 because no new buildings of this class

entered the market except for an additional 179 rooms. Based on a sample survey, approximately 56% of foreign visitors stayed in hotels in 1993, with large differences in the geographic origins of these visitors (refer to Table 13–3). Resorts account for only a small proportion of hotel room nights as this sector is relatively small, though growing fast.

TABLE 13–2
Average Hotel Occupancy Rates in Metropolitan Manila: 1989 to 1993 (Percentages)

Classification	1989	1990	1991	1992	1993
Deluxe	81.0	68.4	66.7	70.2	62.9
First Class	77.7	67.7	59.3	60.6	62.4
Standard	70.2	70.1	65.8	58.9	53.2
Economy	60.8	57.4	65.3	53.1	46.0
Overall Average	**76.4**	**67.6**	**64.8**	**64.9**	**59.9**

Source: Philippines Department of Tourism.

TABLE 13–3
Accommodation Choice in the Philippines by Selected Markets: 1992 to 1993 (Percentages)

	Hotels		Resorts		Homes of Relatives/Friends	
	1992	1993	1992	1993	1992	1993
United States	51.8	39.6	2.4	1.8	35.0	49.4
Japan	61.4	64.2	5.0	3.3	21.6	21.8
Hong Kong	73.3	73.0	12.1	6.1	9.9	10.9
Taiwan	81.8	72.9	2.2	5.0	12.1	16.0
Australia	52.2	51.1	7.6	6.2	23.2	23.7
South Korea	62.9	64.4	4.5	2.5	18.3	17.3
United Kingdom	48.5	47.6	11.2	4.7	20.6	34.7
Germany	32.6	42.1	22.4	16.7	26.8	22.0
Canada	51.7	32.8	9.2	4.2	21.8	49.6
Singapore	81.8	86.1	1.1	1.2	11.4	7.3
Overseas Filipinos	4.2	5.3	1.2	0.0	90.4	91.2
All Markets	**55.5**	**51.4**	**7.7**	**4.4**	**23.3**	**32.4**

Source: Annual visits sample survey, The Asia-Pacific Centre for Research.

Supporting Industries

The burgeoning economy has given rise to increased local and foreign investments in nearly all industry sectors. The growth of these industries will continue to stimulate business travel to the country's hotels.

Context for Competition

According to a recent report by the Economist Intelligence Unit (EIU) International Tourism, there is no accurate record of the total accommodation stock in the Philippines and detailed statistics are available for Metropolitan Manila only. The number of rooms in the country at the end of 1993 was reported to be 33,250. This includes both existing stock and committed projects, with 24,100 in the Luzon region, 6,300 in the Visayas and 2,900 in Mindanao.

The last hotel-building boom was in the mid-1970s in Manila when developers rushed to accommodate delegates of the 1976 annual IMF conference held in the Philippines. It was an ambitious plan for 14 hotels to provide 11,000 rooms. Although not all were completed for financial reasons, it was sufficient to cause a dramatic drop in occupancy rates as well as room rates after the event. The situation did not improve until the early 1990s because of the unsettled political situation which depressed the tourism industry at large.

However, there has been a recent surge in new capacity, particularly of deluxe hotels, with three completed in 1993 alone. This has added an additional 1,430 rooms to the available capacity. The newly opened upmarket Shangri-La hotels, the EDSA Plaza Hotel and the Shangri-La Manila in the Makati business district, and one other luxury 468-room Manila Diamond Hotel (which was funded by the Japanese) have further boosted confidence in the country's stability and prospects for tourism growth. The new investment has also led to the refurbishment of a number of the city's older hotels. The Manila Hotel, the city's best-known historical hotel, has undergone extensive renovation to compete with the new market entrants.

One industry observer believes that the hotel industry will become more concentrated and dominated by a number of international chain hotels. The intense rivalry among the bigger chains, especially in the Metropolitan Manila area, has already led to down-market segmentation (i.e., competition in the two- and three-star hotel segments) by some of the international chains as well as local chains. This is currently the trend in countries such as Singapore, Malaysia and Indonesia.

CURRENT ISSUES UNDERLYING THE HOTEL INDUSTRY

The Philippines is currently undergoing major economic reform and policy changes under the Ramos administration, and the way in which these factors are affecting the hotel industry needs to be addressed. Some of the key issues involved are dealt with below.

Major Players and Ownership

It is interesting to note that the major players and owners in the hotel industry are predominantly wealthy Filipinos. This is probably because of the conservative land laws in the past which prohibited foreign ownership of land. Therefore, the development of hotels was confined to the Filipino land owners.

According to one of the senior executives from a major real-estate developer, most of the standard and economy class hotels are owned by single proprietors. The first-class and deluxe hotels are mainly owned by big corporations because of the need for large capital investment and management skills. The majority of the deluxe hotels are located in Manila. They were built in the mid-1970s to accommodate delegates attending the annual IMF conference as mentioned earlier. A world recession, and the unsettled political situation in the country, curtailed capacity development until the early 1990s.

At this point, new economic reforms and policies have been successful in attracting new investment into the country. Experienced hoteliers and investors, like the Shangri-La group and some Japanese groups, were quick in responding to the liberalisation of business laws, and in 1993 alone, three new deluxe hotels were added to the existing capacity in Manila. The new investment has also led to refurbishment and upgrading of existing hotels to compete with the newcomers.

It is now believed that these investors are enjoying the benefits of the economic reforms and government policy changes. The hotels in the deluxe class are now experiencing above-average occupancy rates (70% as compared to about 63% in 1993). This is even higher for premium business hotels because of the substantial increase in the number of business travellers and the frequency of travelling. Food and beverage revenues have also increased substantially, with more companies hosting business functions in hotels. Apart from the substantial increases in operating profits, these hoteliers are also enjoying high capital gains in their hotel properties. This can be translated into higher net worth which is useful for financing business expansion.

However, it should be recognised that continuing reforms can have a negative impact as well. More hotel development can be expected in the near future. However, it takes several years to construct and complete a new development. Therefore, existing owners should be searching for geographical diversification and, perhaps, upgrading their existing capacity.

Market Potential

The surge in foreign investment in all sectors, from high-technology agricultural products to telecommunications, is creating excellent market potential for hoteliers. This has been confirmed by statistics on visitor arrivals to the Philippines from the DOT which shows consistent increases since 1991. The statistics also indicate that business travelling is on the rise, especially from countries such as Taiwan, Hong Kong, South Korea, Australia and the United Kingdom. Business travellers from these countries account for 30 to 47% of total travel. The number of leisure travellers is also expected to increase with government efforts to promote tourism.

The recent multibillion-peso Fort Bonifacio redevelopment project is another vote of confidence by prominent business groups in the Pacific Rim, which includes the Salim group of Indonesia, Malaysia's Robert Kuok and the Chinese-Filipino tycoons, Lucio Tan and Andrew Gotianum. Apart from these, the World Bank is setting up some special private-sector, long-term funding arrangements to help finance major infrastructure projects in transportation, communications, sanitation and water supply. Investment is now being gradually translated into firm commitments, and the government is also responding by continuing to take steps to improve the investment environment.

It should be noted that there is also a multiplier effect on inward travelling from place to place which may not have been accounted for in the DOT's statistics. In addition to business travel, it is expected that tourism and leisure travel will flourish next, with the current influx of investment and government effort in promoting tourism. In other words, demand for hotel accommodation will continue to rise in the future. This creates an excellent market opportunity for investors.

Human Resources

Having a large workforce which is educated, and highly competent in English, has been the marketing tool and competitive advantage of the Philippines. An annual supply of 350,000 graduates to various industries is another plus factor.

However, human resource requirements in the hotel industry differ from other industries. Most hotels prefer to start the staff afresh and go through their own in-house training programmes. Staffing is a key issue in the hotel industry because it is service-oriented. Hotels earn their reputation from the service level that is accorded to guests.

Although the hotel industry has been losing trained staff to other countries, the overall situation in the hotel industry is not overly pessimistic. From feedback received, hoteliers appear prepared to reward staff with higher wages and extra bonuses for profitable operations. Currently, the situation is under control. Looking ahead a few years, however, the situation may be different. If the Philippines is successful in economic reforms, there will be an acute shortage of manpower resources in the domestic market, with strong demand for skilled labour for various industries. It will replicate the labour problems of other newly industrialised countries. With more hotels opening, existing staff will be pirated, and there will be pressure on staffing costs. These are realities which the industry has to go through in a normal business cycle. Thus, hoteliers need to be proactive in resolving the labour problem to remain profitable.

Investment Incentives

The new liberal foreign investment policies are creating a more hospitable climate. New laws make it possible for foreign investors to own 100% equity in many domestic ventures, except those expressly reserved by the Philippines's constitution. The new laws also simplify the procedure for doing business in the Philippines by requiring new investors to register solely with the SEC. They are not required to register with the BOI unless they are seeking incentives.

The investment incentives given to foreigners for new hotel

development and investment are also very attractive. Apart from 100% equity ownership, the government is setting aside land in special processing zones and specific free port areas like Subic Bay. And, potential developers can approach the government agencies directly for site acquisition and development. The government is also throwing in other incentives such as income tax holidays, equipment incentives, and tax credits on capital equipment.

Generally speaking, the investment incentives are very attractive and have been very successful in attracting many investors. Consequently, it is a win–win situation for everybody, and it is generating a large volume of business transactions. The hotel industry is experiencing high occupancy rates and record high operating profits.

When asked about the continuity of these trends, hoteliers were optimistic. They contend that location is important, and it is difficult for new investors to secure good sites in cities like Manila and Cebu. New developments in the special zones are not a threat to existing hotels. In fact, developers with large land banks are quite comfortable about new investments in hotels. The returns from leasing land sites to potential hotel investors exist. It appears that the return from leasing land is better than operating a hotel which is cyclical and capital intensive.

Cost of Financing

Financing cost is a major issue for investment in hotel development projects. In the first place, the capital outlay is very high. Potential investors must first acquire the land, following it with design, construction and commission, which will take a few years to complete. Costly pre-opening commitments are necessary to train staff and to test-run operations before opening. The usual time frame for pre-opening is three months but in some cases where staffing is a problem, it may take a much longer time.

Investors also must ensure that the right leverage is used as high gearing will ultimately affect profits. In general, it takes about eight to ten years for a hotel to break even, given an optimistic scenario of over 70% average occupancy rate with matching food, beverage and other departmental income. Unfortunately, these conditions are not always manifested. The hotel business is cyclical and subject to many uncontrollable external factors. It is generally ideal for big corporations to include hotels as part of an investment portfolio for diversification purposes. This is exactly the reason why most deluxe hotels in the Philippines are owned by large corporations and not wealthy individuals.

On this issue of financing, the Filipinos are in a better position because they are able to obtain loans from the local banks. However, the financing cost is relatively high. The feedback we have from local developers indicates that financing costs are as high as 12 to 14% per annum. This may explain why most local developers prefer to lease their land rather than to develop it. Foreign investors must acquire financing through offshore banks, and use foreign currency. Interest rates may be lower in some cases but investors are exposed to exchange risks for their repayments.

Returns

Hoteliers report a fairly high gross operating profit (GOP) as compared to Singapore. The GOP average appears to be around 40% for the deluxe hotels in Manila. In Singapore, the corresponding GOP is approximately 30%.

SUSTAINING A COMPETITIVE ADVANTAGE

The competitive advantage of the hotel industry stems from many discrete activities. Each activity can contribute to the industry's relative cost position and create a basis for differentiation. The value chain therefore provides a systematic way to examine all the activities that the industry performs, and how they interact with each other, in order to analyse the sources of competitive advantage. For the hotel industry, operations, marketing and sales are examples of vital categories.

Human Resources

As a service industry, human resource activities support the entire value chain. A highly motivated and competent workforce can lead to high differentiation, or cost reduction, in operations and marketing activities. The impact is on every interaction with a customer. Proper recruitment and training can help hotels in achieving and sustaining differentiation. The retention of marketing and sales staff is also essential because of the need for maximising strong client relations which are developed as a result of dominant personal selling. The Philippines's workforce, most of whom are English-speaking and educated, will serve this strategy best in sustaining the competitive edge.

Marketing

Market segmentation is also an important factor in determining the competitiveness of the Philippine hotel industry. The hotels will need to aim for high occupancy and offer low room rates to tourists, especially corporate clients and business travellers. Considering the prime location and accessibility of major international hotels, the industry can focus on corporate clients. Major players, like the Mandarin Oriental and Manila Peninsula, have about 65 to 80% roomnights from corporate clients. These hotels focus on strategies such as superior personalised service, superior facilities, image and so forth and, yet, their pricing is competitive among similar hotels in the region.

The industry must also be competitive in the tourist segment, particularly those markets which are price sensitive like the United States and Europe. These groups continue to be a major source of business for tour operators.

The major strength of a hotel lies in the group that it belongs to and the respective image. Hotels in the Philippines need to position themselves in the region from a cost-competitive angle and get a niche, particularly in the business segment. This is crucial with the economy in the recovery stage and given the expected increase in economic activity.

Infrastructure

Infrastructure can affect the hotel industry. At present, there is some concern about the inadequacy of infrastructural standards in the Philippines, such as road congestion. This deters investors which, in turn, has a dampening effect on the hotel industry.

Technology

Another major area where the industry can sustain its competitiveness in the region is through technological improvements. There is a range of activities that can be broadly grouped into efforts to improve the hotels' products and processes. These include product design, service procedures and media research. In relation to these, the hotel industry will need to invest sufficiently in areas such as advertising and creative marketing.

Better products and services will be the new battleground among hotels in the Philippines and the region, with the target being business travellers. Service differentiation will be instrumental for the hotel industry in its efforts to sustain any competitive advantage, particularly with new emerging destinations such as Vietnam, Myanmar and Cambodia. In the process, there is a need to keep prices on par with other cities in the region.

EXPANSION STRATEGIES

There has been considerable growth in the tourism industry in the Philippines which has fuelled the growth in the hotel industry. The government has begun laying the groundwork for implementing an ambitious 20-year master plan for the development of the industry. No doubt, this has attracted investors who see opportunities in the tourism industry.

Tourist arrivals for 1994 were 1.6 million, and projected arrivals for 1996 and 1998 are 2 million and 3 million arrivals, respectively. Tourism receipts for 1994 were P2 billion, and the projected receipts for 1996 and 1998 are P3.03 billion and P4.6 billion, respectively. Currently, there are more than 93,000 deluxe, first-class, standard and economy rooms in Metropolitan Manila. At the end of 1994, it was estimated that there would be an additional 1,200 to 1,300 rooms. The new rooms in the New World Hotel, which opened in June 1994, cater to business travellers, and two more new hotels, the Bay View Park and Manila Clarion, are also expected to cater to this category.

The increase in opportunities in the tourism and hotel industry stems in a large part from government efforts. The unique opportunities include low-entry cost for tourism projects. The government offers tax exemptions on imported capital equipment, tax credits on domestic capital equipment, and income tax holidays for projects in less developed areas. Incentives cover hotel projects that cost US$100,000 per room for projects in Manila and US$50,000 per room for projects outside Manila, provided that a project's total cost is at least US$5 million. For resorts, the requirement is US$10 million per project for those in Manila and US$5 million for those outside Manila. Added to these incentives, foreigners are now allowed 100% equity in tourism projects.

In line with boosting the tourism and hotel industry, the government is also making a concerted effort to develop infrastructure, particularly airline-carrying capacity. New gateways have reduced the heavy dependence on Manila's international airport, and they provide some immunity from adverse developments in the capital. For example, Cebu is being served by direct flights from Singapore, and in Davao there are weekly flights, with prospects of connections to cities such as Singapore, Kota Kinabalu and Kuching. The DOT plans to develop a hub in each of the country's geographical regions. These hubs are expected to provide the type of service which is presently offered by Metropolitan Manila, including scheduled domestic and international flights.

These infrastructure plans need to be in place in the next three to five years for the Philippines to be competitive with ASEAN neighbours. A vital part of the whole development plan is the creation of resort areas in Bohol and Samal Island, for example.

On the hotel front, there has been a building boom in Metropolitan Manila. Since 1993, three deluxe hotels have opened – the 440-room Shangri-La EDSA Plaza, the 703-room Shangri-La Hotel Manila, and the 500-room Manila Diamond. These hotels represent an investment of about US$230 million by the Kuok Group. Other major international groups have also joined in the opportunities offered in the Philippines tourism and hotel industry. The ITT Sheraton is attempting to become the leading international chain in the Philippines. It is bidding for the Manila Hotel, with plans to convert it into a flagship Philippine property. Mimosa Resorts plans to develop a 125-hectare property at Clark Air Base, Pampanga, into a tourism complex managed by the Holiday Inn. The complex is scheduled for completion in 1996 and will include a 324-room hotel. Hilton Hotel is looking for sites in Manila, Cebu and the Hundred Islands cluster of islets in northern Luzon.

There is great potential for the long-term expansion of the hotel industry and the travel industry in the Philippines. The success of expansion lies in developing the infrastructure and access. Over the next five years, the DOT has estimated that an investment of about US$1.8 billion will be required to develop the tourism industry.

CONCLUSION

In the long term, infrastructure bottlenecks from inadequate planning and rapid growth will ease. A major focus is to spread tourism and hotel development across many regions and, thus, reduce the congestive pressures on Manila.

With relatively inexpensive accommodation and ancillary facilities, first-class hospitality, an increase in international flights (both within and outside of airports in Manila), a growing economy and infrastructure improvements, the prospects for the hotel industry are sound.

Crucial to the hotel industry are human resources, or the hospitality workforce, of the Philippines. This sector of the workforce is in short supply and needs to be addressed. Successful hotel operations require managers who are well-acquainted with local and non-local culture. Thus, there is a need for concerted government-sponsored programmes in the hospitality area as well as effective in-house training by the hotels.

With incentives offered by the government, continuing stability in the political climate, and support of the private sector, the future bodes well for the hotel, and the related tourism, industry in the Philippines.

REFERENCES

Bing Man, "The President's Jaleco", *Asia Travel Trade*, January 1993.

Brennan Eamonn, "Trends and Markets for the Philippines Hotel Industry", *Hotelier*, March 1995.

Cruz Patricia Alaina, "Doing Business in the Philippines", *Directions*, November/December 1994.

Focus of The Philippines, *Travel News Asia*, 3–16 October 1994.

Hong Kong: "Sustaining Competitive Advantage in Asia's Hotel Industry", *The Cornell H.R.A. Quarterly*, October 1994.

"Hotel Opportunities In Thailand", *The Cornell H.R.A. Quarterly*, June 1993

"Hotel Operators and Investors Recognise the Great Opportunity Presented in Southeast Asia – But Do They Recognise the Specific Challenges of Each Destination, As in the Case of Thailand", *The Cornell H.R.A. Quarterly*, June 1993.

"Industry Follows in Ramos' Footsteps", *Travel News Asia*, 7–20 November 1994.

Jaleco Bing, "Philippines – Strategy for Success", *PATA Travel News*, October 1994.

"Korea's Hotel and Tourism Industry", *The Cornell H.R.A. Quarterly*, May 1990.

Kye-Sung Chon, Amrik Singh and James R Mikula, "Thailand's Tourism and Hotel Industry", *The Cornell H.R.A. Quarterly*, June 1993.

"Philippines – Get Infrastructure Plan Moving", *PATA Travel News*, March 1994.

"Philippines Plans Asia's Biggest Casino", *Travel News Asia*, 5–11 December 1994.

"Philippines Rides Crest of a Wave", *Travel News Asia*, 7–20 November 1994.

"Philippines Wants More Capacity", *Travel News Asia,* 5–11 December 1994.

Philippines, EIU International Tourism Reports, The Economist Intelligence Unit Limited, No. 3, 1994.

"Poor Image Still Nags", *PATA Travel News*, January 1994.

Santos Carlos B., "Philippines: Tourism – Ushering in the Good Times", *Asia Travel Trade*, August 1994.

Santos Carlos B., "Manila: Dressing Up for Miss Universe", *Asia Travel Trade*, April 1994.

Santos Carlos B., "Philippines: Aviation – On a Wing and a Prayer", *Asia Travel Trade*, August 1994.

Santos Carlos B., "Philippines: Hotel – The Right Formula", *Asia Travel Trade*, August 1994.

"South Korea's Emerging Tourism Industry", *The Cornell H.R.A. Quarterly*, April 1994.

"Vietnam's Tourism Industry: Can It be Kept Afloat?", *The Cornell H.R.A. Quarterly*, October 1994.

Villegas Bernardo M., "Turning Bullish on the Philippine Economy", *Directions,* November/December 1994.

Chapter 14

Human Resource Quality in the Philippines

BY
GAN Chin Yean
LIM Kok Khen
TAN Ming Chian

INTRODUCTION

AN APPRECIATION OF Filipino workers appears to be growing throughout Asia. Apart from political and socio-economic factors, the human resource dimension is one of the essential underpinnings for the growth process and, therefore, should be assessed and understood in conjunction with starting new business ventures in the Philippines. The increasing mobility of capital and technology globally can also affect labour to a considerable extent. The literature on human capital concludes that investment in human resources raises labour productivity and entrepreneurial skills. As general levels of education increase, there is more rapid advancement in production and consumption activities because scientific and technological innovations are more readily understood and accepted. Given these premises, management and labour in the Philippines have a significant role to play in stimulating and sustaining the growth of the economy.

Philippine labour consists of English-speaking, dependable, well-trained and highly qualified professional, technical and managerial talent, as well as skilled and semi-skilled manpower (Hubbard, 1994). According to one survey of company managers in Asia, the Philippine workforce is the best in the region in terms of quality, availability and cost. When an earthquake struck the Philippine island of Luzon four years ago, Texas Instrument Inc.'s experience with the Filipino workers in the semiconductor-packaging industry illustrated the sentiment of "dedication and teaming" of the people. Instead of the headquarters' estimate that the Philippine subsidiary would require six months to commence operations after the shutdown due to the earthquake, Texas Instrument Philippine took only 23 days to get the plant fully operational. Although many Filipinos have sought employment overseas, the country still has a surplus of manpower.

In view of the mobility of labour in the Philippines, this chapter discusses information on human resources needed by business executives and prospective investors. It also gives a macro understanding of the Filipino workforce so that an objective assessment of its quality can be made. Overall, the chapter addresses some of the important issues that may augment growth and drive the development programme.

The chapter relies upon secondary data collected through a literature search pertaining to issues on human resources and includes published statistics, indices and research reports. Three visits were scheduled during the BSM to Manila. These included the University of Philippines School of Labor and Industrial Relations, Asian Institute of Management, and SGV & Co. Through structured interviews and dialogue with the hosts, primary data on labour relations, human resource management and practices were obtained. This information is used throughout the chapter.

QUALITY OF THE LABOUR FORCE

General

The Philippines's population was estimated to be 66.2 million in 1994 with an annual growth rate averaging 2.3%. The Philippines's labour force expanded at a higher rate in the 1980s and early 1990s (4.4%) as a result of the cumulative effect of high population growth rates during the 1960s (3.0%) and the 1970s (3.0%). The working-age population aged over 14 years was 39.831 million in 1992, and 26.290 million constituted the Philippines's labour force.

In 1992, the prime working group of 25 to 54 years of age was the largest (60%), followed by the 15 to 24 age group (25.9%), and the older age group of 55 years and over (13.5%). The Philippines's labour force is dominated by males (62.9%), with females accounting for 37.1%. While participation rates of males and females both grew over the period from 1980 to 1992, the increase was higher for females than males (48.5% versus 41.6%).

Employment is the outcome of demand and supply. However, for the Philippines, demand basically determines the level of employment because of the large labour supply.

Employment increased from 1980 to 1992. The level rose from 15.900 million in 1980 to 23.696 million in 1992 and grew at an annual rate of 4.1% (i.e., 650,000) each year. However, employment has failed to keep up with the annual 4.4% growth of the labour force, resulting in higher unemployment. A more serious problem confronting the labour force is underemployment. By definition, underemployment relates to the proportion of the labour force which is underutilised, meaning they work less than the normal 40 hours per week (Serrano, 1994).

Labour costs in the Philippines remain competitive relative to many South-east Asian countries but lag behind Indonesia and Vietnam. In the Cavite EPZ, the minimum wage for a production operator is P138 per day (S$8.62) for eight hours of work. The monthly wage for an engineer and a production supervisor ranges from P6,000 (S$375) to P12,000 (S$750) and P4,500 (S$280) to P8,000 (S$500), respectively.

Sources of Employment

Because the Philippines's economy is primarily rural-based, the agriculture, fishery and forestry sectors accounted for nearly one-half (48.5%) of total employment for the period from 1980 to 1992. The service sector accounted for over one-third (36.6%) and the industrial sector only 14.9%.

Throughout the 1980s, there was a declining trend in the proportion of total employment for the agricultural sector. It decreased from 53.7% in 1980 to 45.3% in 1992. But the rate of decline has been marginal, averaging about 0.7% per year. This reflects the labour market consequences of a slow-developing economy. However, the proportion of the labour force shifting out of agriculture has become more pronounced since 1987.

Employment growth in the industrial sector lags behind neighbouring South-east Asian countries. The industrial sector has failed to provide employment opportunities to absorb those moving out of the agricultural sector plus new entrants to the labour market. The ratio of industrial sector employment to total employment has remained consistently low, averaging 14.9% for the period 1980 to 1992. The ratio declined in 1986 but in 1989 it improved to 16%.

The performance of the manufacturing sector is the main focus of the government's industrialisation policies. From 10.2% of total employment in 1980, the ratio moved to a low of 8.7% in 1986. This discouraging performance can be attributed to previous industrial policies which were biased toward capital-intensive, large-scale, urban-based enterprises. Furthermore, the adverse economic recessions of the 1980s seriously affected industrial output and employment.

The net transfer of employment has been from agriculture to the service sector. The service-sector employment ratio increased from 31.5% in 1980 to 38.6% in 1992. This expansion has been more pronounced in the subsectors of wholesale and retail trade (9.8%); transportation, storage and communication (6.1%); and community, social and personal services (5.7%). The service subsectors of financial services, real estate and business services, grew at a slower rate of 3.8%.

Another source of employment is the informal sector, known as the underground economy. It includes the self-employed and unpaid family workers in the non-agricultural sector. In 1992, the informal sector was 4.222 million and accounted for 17.8% of total employment. The majority of workers in this sector engage in trading and they account for 58.7% of the total informal sector workforce.

Unemployment and Underemployment

Unemployment and underemployment are dominant issues facing the Filipino workforce. The unemployment rate was 10% at the beginning of 1995. The unemployed labour force comprises predominantly male workers. However, their share relative to total unemployment has decreased from 58.4% in 1980 to 56.6% in 1992. The share of unemployed females has increased from 41.6 to 43.4%, respectively.

The distribution of unemployed over the past 12 years has shifted to urban areas. Specifically, the proportion of urban unemployment increased from 43.1 to 63.4% relative to the share of rural unemployed which declined from 56.9 to 36.6%. Moreover, the urban unemployment rate (12.9%) in 1992 was nearly twice the rural area (7.0%) and the discrepancy is worse now.

The unemployed are concentrated in the younger age group (15 to 24 years of age) and are mostly school drop-outs. This group accounts for about 55% of unemployment. The majority of unemployed are relatively well educated while those with lower education tend to have jobs.

In 1992, more than two-fifths (42.1%) of the unemployed earned at least a high school education, and about one-third (32.5%) were college educated. During the same year, those with elementary education accounted for only 22.9% of the unemployed while those with no formal education accounted for 2.1%. This phenomenon arose because of the easy absorption of less educated individuals into the informal and service sectors.

While unemployment is more of an urban phenomenon, underemployment is more prevalent in the rural areas and it affects all ages. The underemployment rate was 20.6% in 1992. The relationship between underemployment and education is the opposite of that between unemployment and education. From elementary to college education levels, the ratio of underemployed to total employed in each education group declined: 23.8% with elementary education, 20.3% with high school education, and 13.8% with college education. Only a relatively small group without any formal education deviated from this trend.

Given the unemployment problem, Filipino workers are realistic. Many college graduates are employed in jobs that clearly underutilise their training and abilities. For instance, a front-desk cashier at a hotel in Makati has a college degree in management. The human resource director of SGV & Co., a management consulting firm in Metropolitan Manila, said: “If they feel that they are overqualified for the jobs, there are many more people of similar background vying for the same jobs.” Her colleague, a manager with the same consulting firm, added: “If they don’t work, they don’t eat.” Hence, Filipinos tend to treasure their jobs because they are difficult to find. Dr. Gloria De Guzman of the Asian Institute of Management pointed out that a proverbial saying among the Filipinos is: “If one does not have a large enough blanket, one has to squeeze oneself under the blanket.” This simply means that one has to make do with the available resources. The lack of up-to-date equipment does not seem to deter Filipino workers from performing well under adverse circumstances.

The Education Profile

The Philippines's education system is, in many ways, patterned after the American system. Primary education involves elementary school for six years. Secondary education requires another four years in high school. Except for a few government-funded universities, many of the colleges are private institutions. There are about six colleges offering MBA courses and the Asian Institute of Management attracts students from the richest families in ASEAN countries.

To ensure quality graduates, the government regulates admission to colleges and universities by requiring high school graduates to pass the national entrance examination. Those who do well in these examinations gain admission to the university of their choice. Those who fail to gain admission to the university have the option of applying to private colleges or technical schools.

The quality of the Philippines's education policy is evidenced by a literacy rate of 93.5% as well as a large supply of workers who have received tertiary and secondary education. In 1992, 21.3% of the total workforce had a college education.

Filipinos value education a great deal. There are numerous accounts of sacrifices made for children to obtain an education up to the tertiary level. It is no surprise, therefore, that the Philippines has the highest percentage of enrolment for tertiary education (28% in 1989) among all ASEAN countries. Each year there are approximately 300,000 graduates produced by the Philippines's universities and colleges. The Philippines also has the highest percentage of enrolment for secondary education (73% in 1989) from among South-east Asian countries. Furthermore, the use of English as a medium of instruction in the educational system makes the Filipino workforce internationally mobile since English is the *lingua franca* of the world.

On a negative note, expenditures on education by the government in 1991 amounted to only US$21 per capita. By comparison, expenditures on education by the Singaporean government in the same year was US$322 per capita, more than 15-fold greater. The education system in the Philippines is largely decentralised and is not controlled by the central government. As a result, the education system is unable to meet the demands of the labour market efficiently (The World Competitiveness Report, 1994).

Training

Training practices in the Philippines are associated with the culture and education system. Filipino workers value training and consider it a vehicle for career advancement and improved social status.

Among the proposals for a long-term national manpower plan are the establishment of manpower committees and training centres at the regional and congressional district levels. Also proposed is a special training fund to assist training institutions, industries, and local government units, in upgrading their capabilities to develop and implement training activities. The Philippines ranks fourth in the region behind Singapore, Malaysia and Thailand, for corporate investment in employee training.

Foreign employers, especially those in manufacturing and the service industries, are encouraged to provide employee training programmes to train local staff for administration, supervisory and technical positions. Incentives are granted for government-approved employee training programmes. An incentive equivalent to 50% of labour training expenses incurred for approved development programmes is allowed as an additional deduction from taxable income subject to certain limitations.

Training programmes are generally categorised into three levels: initial entry-level training (recruitment training); retraining to improve job performance or to enable workers to move between jobs of a similar grade and status (retraining I); and retraining to upgrade for purposes of promotion, higher status, and so on (retraining II). An ideal human resource-oriented enterprise should possess the following complementary characteristics (Standing, 1992):

(a) adequate initial training for all new recruits;
(b) opportunity for, and encouragement of, retraining for improved work performance and task enhancement;
(c) retraining for promotion and career mobility;
(d) a deliberate and collectively negotiated policy to upgrade the skill composition of tasks and of the workforce;

(e) a policy of job rotation, if feasible and negotiated;
(f) an orientation towards work reorganisation so as to ensure that jobs are adapted to workers' needs and aspirations; and
(g) established procedures for collective negotiation over important aspects of the work process.

Surveys show that large-scale firms with more than 1000 employees, foreign-owned firms, and firms with industrial unions, are far more likely to possess these characteristics. In addition, these firms are more likely to have higher sales growth, carry out work reorganisations, and introduce technological changes, all signs of dynamic enterprises. In short, firms that possess the complementary characteristics are economically dynamic and efficient.

In view of their educational background and proficiency in English, Filipino workers are easily trainable. Thomson Audio established an assembly plant in mid-1994 in Subic Bay Freeport to produce telephones. According to the manager of Thomson Audio: "The learning curve of the Filipino production operators is two weeks while their counterparts in Malaysia might take up to four weeks."

Labour/Management Relations

Filipino workers tend to question authority more than workers from other South-east Asian countries. An autocratic style of management creates an adversarial impression, especially for foreign bosses. A more successful approach is the participative style of management. The receptiveness of the labour force to total quality management (TQM) practices and principles is particularly interesting.

There are numerous accounts of successful implementations of quality control in the manufacturing sector. One noteworthy example involves a group of janitors at Motorola Philippines that gained recognition for winning the worldwide quality control circle competition among all the Motorola plants. A new corporation, Gateway Electronics Corporation, plans to start a new semiconductor manufacturing facility with TQM principles from the commencement of operations.

Filipino workers display high loyalty to their employers in return for good welfare and proper motivation. They expect a paternalistic employer who understands their problems. As the human resource director of SGV & Co. consulting firm pointed out, when an employer decides to take in a new employee, the relationship often includes a network of relationships with the employee's family. If a family member is ill and the family lacks financial resources, then the employee approaches the employer for assistance. The employer usually honours the request. Benefits for employees tend to be family-oriented in nature. There are "rice subsidies" and family allowances given to employees on a monthly basis, in addition to the usual wages.

Unions

Another indication of the quality of the Filipino workforce is the trend of trade unionism in the Philippines. Colonised by the Spanish and the Americans, the Philippines has inherited ideals like freedom of speech and the right of the individual. The protection of the worker is provided in the Labour Code and it covers policies on pre-employment, wages, labour standards, health and safety, post-employment benefits, conciliation, and arbitration procedures for the solution of labour–management disputes. The Labour Code also grants workers and employees the right to form or join a union of their own choice for the purpose of collective bargaining. Except for the period when the Philippines was under martial law during the Marcos rule, workers' rights are deeply imbued in Filipino society.

Trade unions in the Philippines are classified as labour federations, trade union centres and local unions organised at the plant or enterprise level. The percentage of unionised workers declined from 1990 to 1992. There were 152 labour federations with 2.257 million workers, or 72.1% of the total workforce in 1992. Local unions numbered 4,965 and had a membership of 766,000, mostly organised at the plant or firm level.

Trade unionism is at a crossroads. In the past, trade unions were highly politicised, borrowing heavily from the ideals of communism and, as a result, tended to be more adversarial in their relationships with management. There was also an expectation, being a litigious society, of relying on lawyers from both unions and employers to resolve disputes. While unions in the Philippines tended to be militant in the past, there is momentum now towards a conciliatory approach to problems on the part of unions and employers.

There are several reasons for this shift. First, with the collapse of communism in Eastern Europe and the breakup of the Soviet Union, coupled with the opening up of China, the role models for left-wing trade unions have disappeared. The fall of the Western trade unions, particularly in Europe and the United States, is another factor. Third, the booming Asia-Pacific region provides opportunities for new NIEs to challenge Hong Kong, Singapore, Taiwan and South Korea, where costs are higher. To attract foreign investors, the government and trade union leaders are acutely aware of the need for harmonious industrial relations. The government also has been instrumental in influencing trade unions to shift towards a conciliatory approach. This has been done through the legislature to protect the rights of workers (an example is the minimum wage requirement), and through the establishment of the National Labor Relations Commission which has jurisdiction over cases involving employee/employer relations.

These factors have affected trade unionism in several ways. First, membership in unions in recent years has not equalled the growth of the labour force and, as a percentage, fell from 12.6% in 1990 to 11.9% in 1992. There is also a trend for trade unions to decentralise. More local unions are forming rather than being controlled by large national unions. Second, the percentage of actual strikes to notices filed dropped during the period 1985 to 1992 (see Figure 14–1). Third is the decline in actual strikes occurring without notice and the decreasing trend of the number of workers involved in strikes (see Figures 14–2 and 14–3). These trends signal a move by trade unions away from adversarial relations with employers and towards a conciliatory relationship.

The Philippine government's approach to industrial relations is to provide adequate protection under the legislature to ensure that the basic rights of workers are not violated. The employers and unions must take responsibility in resolving labour disputes, with recourse to the legal system or the arbitration system provided by the Department of Labour and Employment. This approach was used to settle the issue of contract workers versus permanent workers in a recent case.

There is a need for a more proactive approach in industrial relations with the Ramos administration actively promoting the Philippines as an emerging NIE. The emphasis is to ensure at the outset that the expectations of both workers and investors are fully communicated and communication channels are kept open to identify potential conflict areas before a crisis develops. This approach is utilised in the Cavite EPZ. Management is actively involved in matching investors with Filipino workers, and it is surprising to learn that there are no unions operating in the zone. Companies locating in the zone are encouraged to establish labour management councils within their factories. Active support is provided by zone authorities through a field assistance office located next to the main administration office.

Presently, trade unionism in the Philippines has shifted towards a collaborative approach. In industrial relations, the 1994 World Competitiveness Report ranked the Philippines 26th out of 43 countries, ahead of India, China, and even Korea. On industrial disputes in 1992, as measured by the working days lost per 1,000 inhabitants, the Philippines ranked 18th, ahead of Singapore and Korea.

The following recommendations are important to potential investors. First, investors cannot exploit Filipino workers by paying the minimum legal wage, and expecting high productivity. Second, investors should make use of the services provided by the export zones or the BOI in the area of industrial relations. These services include familiarisation of employer/employee expectations, styles of management, attitudes of Filipino workers, collective bargaining, conflict management and resolution. Third, open and continuous communication is an important element in industrial relations. It is possible for investors to bypass unions but it is necessary to form a labour management council with representatives from both workers and management.

Lastly, investors need to understand the attitudes of Filipino workers with regard to work rules, training, productivity and long-term employment. Due process must be adhered to in dealing with violations of work rules, with sufficient time given for counselling. Training is viewed as an incentive and, if packaged properly, then it is a great motivator. Filipinos generally are receptive to efforts for improving productivity; again, the key is to communicate adequately. Most workers view their employment as long term thereby creating some inflexibility on the part of employers in responding to changing external conditions. A worker cannot be fired for reasons of redundancy. This will change rapidly if the economy continues to grow and unemployment and underemployment decreases.

QUALITY OF MANAGEMENT

The quality of management in the Philippines can be analysed in several contexts. First, there are sources of managerial expertise from the education system, external sources and changing socio-economic conditions. Second, organisations with good management practices can be considered. Third, an analysis of how management practices in the Philippines are ranked in comparison to other countries can be presented. Fourth, the transfer of corporate technology from MNCs operating in the Philippines since World War II can be discussed. For example, approximately two-thirds of the chief executive officers at commercial banks started their banking careers with Citibank Philippines.

There are other factors responsible for the continued development of managerial talent. Perhaps the most important one is a younger generation imbued with professionalism in business. The economic crisis since 1981 has jeopardised family-run corporations and many elite families are handing over control to executive teams from outside. This is evident in 25 domestic commercial banks managed by professionals who are not major shareholders. Another related factor is the expansion of corporations either through listing on the stock exchange or through alliances with other conglomerates. This expansion provides more opportunities for Filipino managerial ranks to develop, grow and serve as managerial talent for foreign investors.

Examples from MNCs

At Intel Philippines, the twin emphasis of empowerment and training is part of the organisation's strategy to remain competitive. Employment seeks to achieve two objectives: to encourage innovation and to tap leadership potentials as responsibilities increase. Teams in Intel are called "bayanihan/balikatan" (BBs) and quality improvement process (QIP) teams. BBs consist of production operators who are trained to participate, to be assertive, and to become decision makers in their own right through the use of problem-solving tools. QIP teams comprise multifunctional employees who form groups to solve problems or make improvements. It is a reflection of the quality of management that the employee suggestion programme attracts an average of 250 entries per quarter, with a 90% implementation rate.

Intel management recognises the importance of continuous training and development, and several company programmes are designed to help employees achieve personal and professional goals. The MOVE-ON programme is an in-house training programme for operators to gain technician skills. The New College Graduate Programme trains new employees in a variety of jobs over a six-month period before placement in the organisation.

The Management and Supervisory Development Core Programmes are Intel-designed programmes for three levels of management training: senior managers, middle managers and first-line managers. These are one-week residential programmes required for all managers and supervisors. All senior Intel Philippines employees in the programme are sent for training overseas in the United States, Macau or Singapore. Overall, an average of 200 employees per year are sent for training. In 1994, Intel Philippines won the coveted Intel Quality Award bestowed by Intel Corporation.

Motorola Philippines is an excellent illustration of how MNCs should conduct themselves in the Philippines. An example of a particular team empowered to start up a PLCC (plastic leadless chip carrier) line, and have it qualified on the first attempt, tells a story of the transformation of a group of production operators into a self-directed, high-performance team. The team went through the processes of forming, "storming", "norming" and, ultimately, performing. The target set at the beginning of 1991 was for the line to be qualified by October 1991, with a ramp-up in production by November 1991 and a three-shift operation by December of the same year. Each member of the team was trained in the total quality management (TQM) courses offered by Motorola.

The team proceeded to benchmark all existing lines and incorporated the best practices in documentation and process controls. A performance-tracking system was also set up by the team and technical know-how, such as failure mode and effects analysis (FMEA) and *poka yoke*, was learned. Motorola management provided the basic training and guidance and, most importantly, the trust that the team would be able to meet the challenge.

Beginning in early 1991, the team members gradually assumed most of the roles usually assigned to supervisors, including scheduling vacations, making work assignments, recognising achievers, training operators and conducting performance appraisals. The PLCC operation was qualified in June 1991 on the first pass, with the three-shift operation running by December 1991. This feat would not have been possible without the enlightened management of Motorola Philippines, and it clearly demonstrates the capabilities of the Filipino workforce.

Examples from Indigenous Corporations

At San Miguel Corporation, there is a similar emphasis on training although the focus on employee involvement is much less than at Intel. Training at San Miguel is focused on managerial staff, with the San Miguel Corporation Management Training Center serving two objectives. First, it imparts concepts, skills and practices needed by management to perform effectively in current and potential jobs. Second, it communicates a code of behaviour that encourages all employees to operate by the same core values and standards of excellence.

The San Miguel Corporation Management System II borrowed the "seven basic habits" from Dr. Stephen Covey to help supervisors develop a managerial mind-set, managerial skills, self-management and interpersonal effectiveness. While the effectiveness of such a programme is difficult to assess, a survey conducted in July 1994 by middle managers and officers of the San Miguel Group cited the training centre's programme as the most-favoured means of developing managerial capabilities, ahead of education courses, task forces, special projects, coaching and job rotation. An important development is the planned programme for managers assigned to San Miguel China. This programme will combine classroom instruction in language, literature, history, business practices and commercial law, with observation tours, visits and meetings with potential partners, business-venture managers and government officials.

Stanfilco, a division of Dole Philippines, approaches empowerment in a different way. It proceeded with the assistance of a regional office of the Department of Labor and Employment (DOLE). This is one of the few examples in which the government assisted indirectly in a productivity movement of an organisation. The programme initiated by the DOLE in 1987 was called the Kaibigan Programme. It was adopted by Stanfilco to allow each employee to study the company indepth, particularly its goals, problems and future direction. Management recognised the usefulness of the programme and established a new division called "Dole Number One Division". It has the responsibility of coordinating all departments into a unified effort centred on quality, productivity, cost and efficiency. Top management support is demonstrated by the division manager reporting directly to the general manager.

With the strong foundation necessary for openness and communication provided by the Kaibigan Programme, the next stage established the Stanfilco Quality Circle Programme as a preliminary step towards empowerment. Since 1989, a total of 192 quality circle projects have been presented to management and projects from Stanfilco and Growers (another Dole division) won the National Quality Circle Competition in 1992 and 1993.

In 1993, the company formally launched its empowerment programme by treating the packing plants as "empowered packing plants". By August 1994, about 80% of Stanfilco workers, including packing plant crews, harvesting crews, banana gardeners and office workers, were empowered. Supervisors play the role of a coach, no longer dictating to workers. The empowered workers elected from among themselves a set of officers consisting of a chairman, vice-chairman, secretary, treasurer and auditor. The elected chairman assumed 70% of the former supervisor's job.

With success in the field, the company institutionalised the programmes by establishing a Stanfilco Management Quality Council. Twenty-five high-ranking staff comprise the council and the general manager acts as chairman. The active participation of workers in the quality circle is credited for the company becoming the leader in the Philippine banana industry.

At the Victorias Milling Company, emphasis is on communication channels between management and labour. Although workers in the company have been unionised since 1976, the Labor Management Council (LMC) was formally established on 27 June 1987. The LMC is composed of 12 permanent members divided equally between union and management that meets once every quarter or as, and when, the need arises. The LMC also serves as the vehicle for collective bargaining agreements. At Victorias, management conveys its expectations through the employee's handbook on matters of personnel, employment policies, rules and regulations, guidelines and procedures.

The company has improved relations with the unionised workforce and this is reflected in the goals set for the Productivity Improvement Incentive Programme launched in 1986–1987. This programme provides procedures whereby employees submit constructive ideas designed to increase productivity and operating efficiency, yield earnings for the company, or improve employee/management relations. There is a strong paternalistic element in the company, instilling in the minds of employees that the "father" (the employer) is responsible and caring for his "children" (the employees), and that this approach is best for both corporate and employee growth.

Evaluating the Two Types of Corporations

The above cases reveal differences in management approaches by multinational and indigenous Filipino companies. Intel's comprehensive, multiprong approach ensures that all levels of employees are involved in value-added training, development and overall organisational effectiveness. As one of the top semiconductor companies in the world, substantial resources and a reputation for excellence are obvious strengths for Intel Philippines and these are reflected by the quality of the training and management programmes.

At Motorola, the objective was to transfer a product line successfully to the Philippines. Instead of a conventional straightforward transfer, they chose to mobilise the Filipino workforce through teams and empowerment. The fact that the product transfer and the formation and functioning of empowered work teams were a success is a reflection of quality management at Motorola.

There are three reasons for these two successful experiences. First, large and successful MNCs have readily available resources. Second, because of their reputation, they are able to attract the best available talent. Third, the Filipino workers are more than willing to be trained, knowing that it enhances future job opportunities. In fact, corporate site visits revealed that workers from better-known MNCs receive comprehensive training and are more mobile than other workers.

On the other hand, there is a different focus in the three Filipino companies. At San Miguel, emphasis is on managerial training and development, with no indication of training for lower-level staff. San Miguel still adheres to a hierarchical style of management with a top-down approach.

Stanfilco is an interesting example of empowerment in the Filipino way. Empowerment started from the field and took almost seven years from inception to implementation. The establishment of a steering council was formed after the operations had been successfully empowered. This is unlike in the West, or in Japan, where team-building and empowerment is generally driven by top management. This approach may be appropriate for the agricultural industry where competition is not as intense as in the manufacturing sector.

At Victorias, a tense labour/management relationship is apparent. There is a strong focus on open communications since improving employee/management relations is one of the goals of a productivity improvement programme. The management style is one of paternalism, with the employer treating employees as "children" and workers relying on employers to look after their economic and social needs.

Clearly, management styles vary from modern techniques such as "management by objectives" (MBO) and TQM adopted in MNCs to paternalistic and hierarchical styles practised by Filipino companies. The latter approach is experiencing pressure to change because more foreign investors are entering the Philippines and bringing the latest management techniques. More Filipinos, who will eventually form the managerial backbone of indigenous and foreign firms, are being trained with these new techniques.

CONCLUSION

Filipino workers have a competitive advantage relative to some countries in the ASEAN region which are experiencing labour shortages. The abundant labour supply is conducive to labour-intensive operations. Manufacturing companies can readily acquire a blue-collar workforce. However, labour outflow from the Philippines must be closely monitored. In the long run, overseas employment should be used only to absorb excess labour. There is an increasing number of Filipinos sending their children overseas for education which has resulted in a brain drain. In light of the rapidly changing economic and political scene in the Philippines, there should be plans to draw this talent back home.

The characteristics of Filipino workers make them an attractive workforce. Many possess highly developed managerial skills. They are typically pragmatic and perform the jobs assigned to them to the best of their abilities. Many executives in the Philippines claim that Filipino workers are quite creative. Of course, opportunities follow product development and the potential here is just beginning to unfold.

Labour unions in the Philippines resolve disputes through communication and negotiation. A combination of internal and external factors have changed militant unions into more conciliatory, decentralised local unions. With continued economic growth, the role of trade unions will continue to change. While unemployment and underemployment are the dominant problems plaguing the Philippines's labour force, they also present enormous opportunities for foreign investors.

On the other hand, human resource management requires an understanding of Filipino culture, character and history. Virtually all of the companies interviewed stressed the importance of human resources. Employers must be culturally sensitive and empathetic. Salaries and bonuses should be truly performance-driven to motivate the workforce and to develop empowerment. Overall, the quality of management in the Philippines has improved significantly and this feature is an asset for potential investors.

FIGURE 14–1
Percentage of Actual Strikes to Notices Filed

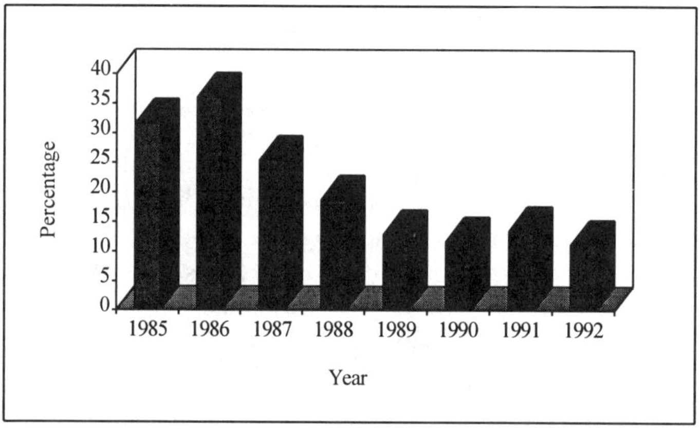

FIGURE 14–2
Strikes Occurring Without Notice

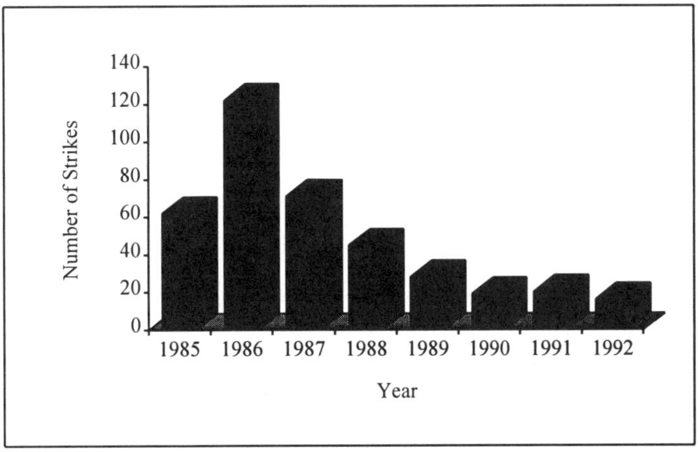

FIGURE 14–3
Number of Workers Involved in Strikes

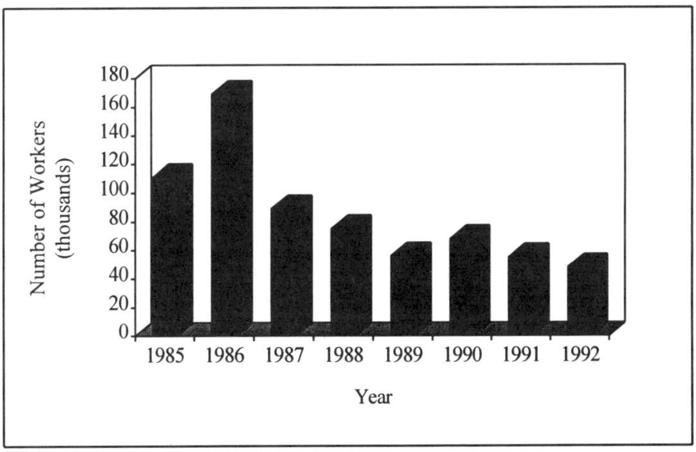

REFERENCES

"A PMAP Heritage", Personnel Management Association of the

Philippines, Eastgate Publishing Corporation, Philippines, 1994.

Business Environment Risk Indicator Report, *Quality of Workforce Index*, 1994.

"Doing Business in the Philippines", Joaquin Cunanan & Co./Price Waterhouse – Philippines Information Guide, 1994.

"Focus Philippines: New Upwardly Mobile Tycoons", *Far East Economic Review*, September 1992.

Hubbard Clarry, "An Abundance of Working Capital", *Electronic Business Asia*, June 1994.

Serrano M. R., "The Implications of Labor Flexibility to Unions in Selected Establishments in Metropolitan Manila", University of the Philippines, School of Labor and Industrial Relations, 1994.

Standing Guy, "Identifying the 'Human Resource Enterprise': A South-east Asian Example", *International Labor Review*, Vol. 131, No. 3, 1992.

The World Competitiveness Report, 1994.

Chapter 15

Telecommunications in the Philippines

BY
TOO Shiun Jye
LOW Kim Lian
LOW Wah Chai

INTRODUCTION

THE STATE OF the telecommunications industry is changing fast worldwide. With the advent of new digital technologies for switching and transmission, the development of telecommunications is now more in tune with the fast-changing world of computing rather than the long investment cycle of an utility industry.

The impact brought about by technological change spreads far beyond the purely technical and engineering arena. The opportunities created by the availability of new telecommunication services range from new data and electronic mail services to highly sophisticated managed network services which can be packaged for major corporate customers to meet their individual needs. Even for traditional telephone services, the basic economics have changed radically. It is now possible for new telecommunication infrastructures to be implemented at a fraction of the capital cost required a decade or two ago.

Long-held ideas of telecommunications as a natural monopoly have been questioned and abandoned, or modified, not only in developed countries like the United States, United Kingdom and Japan, but also in many developing countries. All of these countries now allow competition in telecommunication services in one form or another. The Philippines is no exception.

This chapter examines various issues surrounding business and investment opportunities for the telecommunications market in the Philippines. Specifically, the following issues are addressed. First, the government's framework for deregulation of the telecommunications industry is examined. A comparison is made between the pre-deregulated era and the present. Second, the current and future telecommunications needs of the country and how the government plans to achieve these goals are discussed. Third, the actual management of Globe Telecom in providing telecommunication services is examined. This company is a joint venture between the Ayala Group and Singapore Telecom International (STI).

BACKGROUND AND METHOD

Between 1975 and 1984, the combined deficits of public enterprises in the Philippines reached a staggering US$5 billion (Del Rosario, 1994). Since the presidency of Aquino, the Philippines has adopted privatisation as a strategy to reorient the economy towards market-led growth and greater efficiency in resource management. The Aquino and Ramos governments have set up a business environment conducive to foreign investment.

The Ramos administration has liberalised the country's telecommunications industry by allowing competition in a variety of services. The Philippines is expected to be among the top spending telecommunications countries in the Asia-Pacific until the end of this century. The growth forecast in the telecommunications market is an increase from US$98 million in 1986 to US$204 million in the year 2000 (Research Logistics, 1994).

Data was collected mainly from secondary sources. The other source of data was from a presentation and discussion with staff from Globe Telecom and Andersen Consulting in the Philippines. The visit provided a clearer understanding of a joint venture telecommunications company in the Philippines. The interview with the president of Globe Telecom, who is STI's resident director, revealed indepth knowledge about a joint venture between a local Philippine company and a foreign organisation.

THE TELECOMMUNICATIONS INDUSTRY

Overview

The Philippines has one of the lowest telephone density rates in the region with 1.8 telephones per 100 people. This is only higher than Indonesia (0.60) and China (0.86), and it compares quite poorly with other peers in the ASEAN region, not to mention more developed countries such as Japan, Hong Kong, South Korea and Taiwan (*Asia Week*, 1992).

Table 15–1 shows a breakdown of the telephone density in the Philippines by region as of the first quarter of 1990. The national capital region (NCR), as expected, has the highest telephone density with 8.3 telephone per 100 population. This translates into about 650,000 telephones serving 7.9 million people. The region with the next highest index is region VII (central Visayas) with a lower index of only 0.93. All other regions have even lower indices.

TABLE 15–1
Telephone Density By Region (As of 1st Quarter 1990)

Region	Total Connections	Population (thousands)	Telephone Density per 100 Persons
NCR	658,570	7,929	8.306
CAR	7,191	1,146	0.628
I	15,518	3,551	0.437
II	6,033	2,341	0.258
III	31,746	6,199	0.512
IV	45,815	8,266	0.554
V	6,963	3,910	0.178
VI	33,452	5,393	0.620
VII	42,634	4,593	0.928
VIII	2,386	3,055	0.078
IX	8,088	3,159	0.256
X	7,182	3,150	0.205
XI	19,442	4,457	0.436
XII	3,944	3,171	0.124
Total	888,964	60,320	1.472

Note: NCR - National capital region
CAR - Cordillera autonomous region.

The Pre-deregulated Environment

Basic telephone services are provided by the Philippines Long Distance Telecommunications (PLDT), 63 smaller telephone operators and, in areas where there is no private operator present, the government through the Telecommunications Office of the Department of Transportation and Communications. PLDT (including Piltel) dominates the market for telephone service with a 94% market share.

The low level of investment in the basic public switched telephone network telecommunications infrastructure (*vis-à-vis* the total requirements for an acceptable nationwide service) is due to a host of factors including the archipelagic and volcanic nature of the topography, predominantly agricultural nature of the economy, and low income levels. These factors make land-line service in many rural areas non-viable.

Thus, the pre-deregulated environment of the Philippine telecommunications industry was heavily dominated by PLDT. There was inadequate infrastructure and facilities, and the grade of service was generally poor. Major development was concentrated in the NCR. Little was done to improve the long-established indifference to customer needs and satisfaction. All these problems were manifested in the huge subscriber backlog and long waiting list for telephone service, crossed lines and interference in telephone conversations, network inaccessibility and congestion, inaccurate billing statements, and slow customer service response time.

GOVERNMENT FRAMEWORK FOR DEREGULATION OF THE TELECOMMUNICATIONS INDUSTRY

General

The government, in its effort towards improving and enhancing basic infrastructure such as power, roads and education, recognised that telecommunications is a vital sector for economic development. It realised that the Philippines, as with any developing economy, could not rise from such a poor economic status, much less aspire to be one of the region's new economic tigers, without dramatically improving the availability and quality of telecommunication services.

Executive Orders

Under the charge of two successive executive orders, the government defined a framework for the deregulation of telecommunications in the Philippines. EO 109 compels existing operators of International Gateway Facilities (IGF) to install 300,000 local exchange lines within three years of receiving the grant of the Provisional Authority. It also requires the existing operators of Cellular Mobile Telephone Service (CMTS) to install 400,000 local exchange lines within five years from receiving the grant of the Provisional Authority. This order was established to increase the telephone density of the Philippines.

EO 59 mandates interconnection among all of the authorised telecommunications carriers. It compels bilateral and multilateral negotiations between interconnecting parties by stipulating a 90-day agreement period upon mutual exchange of all required interconnection documents.

Service Areas

Further to the executive orders, the government carved the country into 14 (including NCR and CAR) service areas. The NCR was divided into four areas and each area was paired with a less developed region. Operators of IGF and CMTS were entitled to two service areas each. The division of service areas was the result of a series of workshops held between the National Telecommunications Commission (NTC) and the private sector. Thus, the aim of these moves by the government is to create a strong environment to stimulate competition in telecommunications products and services.

If the government is successful, then it will bring about new telecommunications and information technology applications to business and residential telephone subscribers. This will create competition among operators to innovate and differentiate intercarrier services, leading to more customer and market focus by operators and, finally, to intense time-based competition, namely, reduced cycle time for application processing and improved response time for customer service.

RISKS AND OPPORTUNITIES FOR NEW TELEPHONE OPERATORS

General

As of the first quarter of 1990, the Philippines had an estimated 900,000 telephones in service all over the country. Naturally, there is a great clamour for service which the existing operators have not been able to fulfil. In Metropolitan Manila alone, with the highest telephone density in the country, the backlog is estimated at 600,000. Many residences and new commercial developments wait for months, even years, for an application to be serviced. This situation is expected to improve only with the infusion of massive amounts of investment spending by existing telecommunications operators. If the present operators of basic telephone service are unable or unwilling to make the necessary investments, then there will be strong pressure on the government to explore other ways of channelling funds into this essential industry.

Estimated Size of the Telephone Market

There are varying estimates of telephone demand in the Philippines. In the National Telephone Development Plan for the period from 1991 to 2010, the telephone demand in 1995 was 1,346,000 according to the forecast of PLDT; 1,181,000 according to the study made by Sycip, Gorres, Velayo and Co. and Teleconsult Inc., and 1,300,000 according to the projections made by NEDA. Globe Telecom's projection is 1,079,052. Furthermore, these studies show that demand will increase over the years due to population growth, the availability of basic service in previously unserved areas (which will give more people an appreciation of the benefits of having a telephone), and the development and availability of new improved services (which will increase usage levels of current subscribers).

Current Operators

Basic telephone service is divided into two major offerings: local exchange service and long-distance service. Local exchange service operators include the PLDT, which has the biggest market share at 94%. Small private carriers and the Telecommunications Office (TELOF) divide what remains of the market. On the long-distance side of the service, again it is PLDT that has the largest market share. At present, the PLDT owns and operates all the national backbone transmission networks. PLDT and TELOF operate public long-distance calling booths in various parts of the country and compete with some franchised local operators.

Government Solutions

Recognising that telecommunications is a vital ingredient in the country's drive for modernisation, the government put forward several measures aimed at improving the state of the communications industry in the Philippines. The government is encouraging the entry of more operators to the telephone industry. However, new operators cannot provide only the more lucrative international gateway and cellular mobile telephone services which are the acknowledged money-earning sectors of the industry. They are also required to operate local telephone services, not only to the urban areas, but to the previously unserved areas as well.

Risks

It is highly unlikely that all of the operators of the 14 service areas will survive. Two crucial factors will determine the survival of the new operators. First, there is the potential share of the international telephone traffic and revenue. Second, they need to consider the capability of introducing and marketing new value-added services to their users promptly. Ironically, the most important prerequisite in achieving these success factors is to generate the largest possible subscriber base for local telephone service, which is the most capital-intensive portion of the investment in the telecommunications business.

A successful new venture in this industry, therefore, calls for a carefully considered and well-developed long-term plan, incorporating large initial investment and capital commitments. This may not bring about positive earnings in the short run. Considering the uncertainty surrounding the political and economic climate, the risk of such a venture is high.

GLOBE TELECOM: A NEW JOINT VENTURE

Globe Telecom (GT) resulted from the merger of Globe Mackay Cable and Radio Corporation (an international record carrier) and Clavecilla Radio Systems. The merger was approved by both Houses of Congress and was signed into law in March 1992. This merger, together with the entry of STI as the company's foreign stockholder and technology partner, makes GT one of the most capable and credible applicants for a nationwide integrated telephone network. Among the distinctive advantages that GT can cite are the following factors.

Franchise

GT has an all-encompassing franchise to offer all types of telecommunication services. It can thus offer voice and data services domestically and internationally. This franchise is valid until the year 2030.

Track Record

GT began operations in the Philippines in 1928 (the same time that PLDT began) and has operated continuously since then. The company has a long history of innovation and of introducing the latest services allowed by its franchise. The introduction of computerised telex services in 1975, Intelsat Business Service in 1990, and very small aperture terminals in 1991, are some of the innovations.

Solid Stockholder Base

Telecommunications is a capital-intensive business which requires a massive amount of capital. To initiate any new project and maintain viability over the long run, any telecommunications company must rely on solid domestic and foreign shareholders. Having a solid stockholder base is one of Globe Telecom's major advantages over the other applicants.

The 1994 entry of STI into GT, via the acquisition of the holdings of ITT Communications and Information Services, completes the impressive line-up of GT's stockholder base. The combined resources of these stockholders (domestic and foreign) enables the funding of any type of capital-intensive telecommunications venture. GT's shares have been listed on the Makati and Manila Stock Exchanges since 1974.

Large Financial Resources

As at 31 December 1992, GT had a total asset base of P1.15 billion and stockholders' equity of P418 million. These figures were significantly increased by the first half of 1993 with an equity infusion totalling P690 million. As at 31 March 1993, more than P500 million of this equity has already been paid. As at 31 December 1994, total assets were close to P6.0 billion and stockholders' equity was P4.5 billion.

Strong Technology Partner

The equity infusion of STI into GT provides access to the vast pool of telecommunications expertise and experience of the Singapore Telecom group which operates one of the most sophisticated telecommunications networks in the world. Singapore Telecom has established the world's first fully push-button domestic telephone network, and has the highest density of public telephones and optical fibres networking in the world.

STI is the overseas investment arm of Singapore Telecom which has equity investments in overseas telecommunication companies. Four are in the United States and one is in Thailand. STI also has joint ventures with telecommunications companies in Thailand, Indonesia, Hong Kong, Vietnam, Sri Lanka, the United Kingdom, Mauritius, Australia, Malaysia and Norway.

More important to GT than the vast operating experience of the Singapore Telecom group in many countries, is the Singapore Telecom Academy (STA). The STA is a telecommunications university (bigger than the Asian Institute of Management (AIM) campus) with a full-time faculty and complete facilities which offer a wide selection of telecommunications courses ranging from basic maintenance to executive development. The proximity of the Philippines to Singapore means easy access to the facilities of this unique institution for the training of hundreds of new technical staff that GT will be hiring for new projects.

With these distinct advantages, GT is in a unique position of strength to implement a nationwide, integrated local telephone network. However, it needs the assistance of the government and this aspect is addressed in the following section.

DISCUSSION

Investment and Business Environment

Committed to the concept of free enterprise, the Philippine government is determined to reduce its presence in business and to transfer more government entities through the privatisation programme. Telecommunications is one industry undergoing rapid privatisation.

The government is also formulating investment rules that are fair and consistent in order to attract both local and foreign investors. Towards this end, the government has produced a package of incentives to foster business growth in the country from both local and foreign investors. These moves encourage foreign investors to bring in the financing, technology and expertise that will enhance local talents and resources. They also help more Philippine industries reach world class standards in output.

The Philippines offers investors a favourable business atmosphere in the country. Located between the East and the West, it also offers a strategic location in Asia with the potential of an important telecommunications hub/gateway for Asia. With an interesting blend of Eastern and Western culture, values and practices, it is a hospitable place for investors from all parts of the world. The NTC regulates the rates for broadcasting and telecommunications as part of the government encouragement towards privatisation of the telecommunications industry.

The Omnibus Investment Code

EO 226, otherwise known as the OIC of 1987, integrates the country's basic laws on investments and clarifies their provisions for guiding domestic and foreign investors. It contains incentives available to business organisations engaged in preferred areas of investment.

Telecommunications Business

The telecommunications industry is currently saturated with new operators competing side-by-side with the incumbent PLDT. Business opportunities focus on value-added services such as high-speed, leased-circuit network, supplementary telephone services and intelligent networks.

PLDT's Position

Similar to other countries, PLDT, as the established provider of telecommunication services in the Philippines, now faces a completely new operating environment. There are new threats to established positions in home markets because of the deregulation of the telecommunications industry. Previously, it operated within closely defined boundaries, both geographically and in product terms. The job was largely an engineering one of providing a network and equipment that could service the area. Now two important additional functions are needed for survival. First, strategic planning is necessary to specify the markets in which to operate and how to approach them. Second, marketing is needed to ensure that the company's products are well matched to the demands of customers. With the removal of a monopoly environment, business will be lost if the product mix is wrong.

Under a deregulated environment, mounting pressure on improving and changing to match new competitors gives PLDT an impetus to leapfrog in all aspects pertaining to the management of the telecommunications business. Thus, deregulation could well be a blessing in disguise for PLDT since it forces the organisation to venture into the global telecommunications market.

The New Operators

With deregulation, companies originally outside the telecommunications industry now have new opportunities to enter and they can offer voice, data or value-added services. These companies are used to operating within competitive environments, such as the computer industry, and may be better equipped with marketing skills than existing carriers. However, they need to build market share rapidly if they are to achieve a competitive level of operating costs. For existing world class players, such as AT&T, strong global coverage and linkages may provide an advantage to them as new operators.

The Regulator

Perhaps the most difficult job is regulating activity in these new markets. Each issue seems more complex than the last one, as technology opens up new avenues of development. Moreover, the time available to consider decisions becomes shorter and shorter. If the pace of regulatory change is too far out of step with technological change, then the development of real benefits is delayed and the whole regulated market structure experiences chaos.

CONCLUSION

More and more developing countries are following developed countries by introducing competition into telecommunication services. The Philippines is no exception. However, the regulatory provisions for competition in individual countries reflects technical and economic realities which are common to all countries. It is expected that the provision of local access will remain closely regulated for the foreseeable future while long-distance service will become a market divided among a few large competing players.

Furthermore, the definition of value-added services is becoming increasingly liberal and providing them will be almost totally deregulated. It is expected that the market for value-added services will polarise into two distinct segments: lower-level services offering transport and protocol conversion only, and application-level services. Large voice-based carriers will play an increasing role in value-added markets. Lower-level services will become increasingly standardised, making it difficult for vendors to differentiate their products. Price is becoming the most important competitive factor and it will concentrate business in the hands of a few large players.

Application-level service will be provided by a large number of suppliers, with many of them specialising in a particular industry sector. For applications which are not confined to specialist areas, such as electronic mail or Electronic Data Information (EDI), there will be considerable pressure from users for the interconnection of independent systems so that a public any-to-any service becomes available. Since telecommunication traffic across the Atlantic Ocean and Pacific Ocean is growing at 15 to 20% per annum, new operators will have to compete with PLDT in this, the most lucrative, part of the telecommunication business.

In raising the relatively low telephone penetration, the Philippine government has drawn up 14 regions across the country, each of which was tendered separately for new operators. This was, indeed, a wise strategic move. However, given the rather limited present market potential and the nature of telecommunications service revenue which hinges significantly on international telephone traffic, most of the present nine new operators will not survive the longer term. In perhaps five to ten years, mergers and acquisitions among these organisations will be the order of the day. Finally, only two or three major stable players in the Philippine telecommunications industry can be expected to survive over the long run.

The major issues facing the new operators in the 14 regions are the economic viability of the investment and the competitive scenario *vis-à-vis* the incumbent, PLDT. These operators must achieve good market share in the relatively low-revenue local telephone services quickly in order to realise reasonable returns and satisfy the contractual obligation of providing the required local telecommunication network infrastructure. At the same time, each operator has to secure as much of the lucrative international telephone revenue as possible by providing international direct connections wherever feasible.

REFERENCES

"Asia Pacific Telecommunications Markets", Study Code AP1, Research Logistics, 1994, p. 225.

Asia Week, February 1992.

Bender Warren G., "The Outlook for the World Telecommunications Industry", 1991.

"Competition and Choice: Telecommunications Policy for the 1990's", London, HMSO, 1991.

Del Rosario Ramon R., "Time to Bet Again on the Philippines", *Asian Business*, February 1994, pp. 36–8.

"Entrepreneurial Opportunities in Telecommunications: Shifting Technology, Regulation and User Requirement Drive Opportunities", Market Intelligence Research Corporation, 1992.

Globe Telecom Annual Report, 1994.

Kitchen Malcom, David Lewin and Hans Schoof, "Telecommunications: The Opportunities of Competition", Ovum London, 1987.

"Telecommunications in the Asia Pacific: A Detailed Analysis and Assessment of 15 Telecom Markets", Research Logistic, Barnhan, West Sussex, 1989.

The Philippines' National Information Technology Plan (NITP 2000), 19 July 1994.

Chapter 16

The Philippine Electronics Industry

BY
Lionel GOUW
Kian Hui
Lawrence HON
SHEN Shu Qiao

INTRODUCTION

THE ELECTRONICS INDUSTRY in the Philippines plays a pivotal role in the development of the economy. It is one of the country's main sources of export revenues and domestic employment. A gradual 15% growth in employment from this sector alone has occurred since 1985. This is attributed to the strategic proximity of the Philippines to neighbouring industrialised economies such as Hong Kong, Korea and Taiwan. Over the past 15 years, the industry has built up an impressive export performance record and is the top revenue producer. Moreover, it offers lucrative trade and investment opportunities.

The conditions that encouraged foreign electronics companies to enter the Philippines in the mid-1970s are still intact and have been enhanced by the political democracy introduced in 1986. Strong international support for the government has raised expectations of marked improvements in the country's balance of trade and debt situation.

The Philippines is upgrading its telecommunications infrastructure at an estimated cost of US$2.0 billion per year until the year

2000. During this period, about 500,000 to 700,000 telephone lines are to be installed each year. The manufacture of personal computers and consumer electronics which are costly in developed markets, such as in Japan and Western countries, are solid investment possibilities. Also, domestic demand is growing which provides additional opportunities for domestic production. The Philippine government is aggressively promoting joint ventures with foreign electronics companies. The aim is to make the Philippines a viable and competitive manufacturer of electronics products and, ultimately, to develop the country into a leader in the design, manufacture and export of these products.

SUPPORTING INDUSTRY

The Philippine electronics industry has four subsectors, namely, consumer electronics, telecommunications and industrial electronics, computer products and peripherals, and semiconductor and components manufacturing. The industry also offers services. Local companies engaged in electronics assembly manufacturing provide facilities, manpower, utilities and administrative services while customers supply materials, equipment on consignment and process technology. Moreover, there is a growing number of local companies that provide turnkey services including component sourcing from overseas suppliers.

The Philippines imported an estimated US$2.62 billion worth of electronics components and parts such as printed circuit boards (PCBs), resistors, capacitors, motors, transformers, copper wires, gold wires, lead frames, precision metal parts and precision plastic parts, which can all be manufactured locally. There is underdevelopment in the component and supporting industries.

Electronics Components

The Philippines has the capability to manufacture transistors, diodes, light-emitting diodes (LEDs), transformers, rectifiers, PCB fabrication, wire and cable harness assembly, optic devices, opto-couplers, magnetic heads and semiconductors. Since most firms in the industry have their average voltage load (AVL) requirement, many Philippine companies usually import electronics components from overseas sources. Most semiconductor companies receive the wafers on a consignment basis. These remain the property of the customers, who have contracted

Philippine companies to assemble or encapsulate the wafers into individual chips according to specifications. The Philippine companies do not manufacture for inventory because all production outputs are presold or, more accurately, they are "job order" products.

PCB Assembly Industry

Subsidiary manufacturing transfer (SMT) contract manufacturing involves mainly third-party subcontractors, Filipino-owned companies, and multinational plants which cater to their parent companies. The bulk of the PCB assembly activities in the Philippines are primarily of high labour intensity and low value-added activity. Now, many PCB assembly houses prefer turnkey services ranging from design, development and component sourcing, to final product testing and engineering support.

Plastic and Precision Engineering Industry

Precision parts, such as tools, dies, fixtures, jigs and plastic cavity moulds to make electronics or computer parts, are usually consigned by customers. There are promising opportunities for both local and foreign investments in this area. Ocean Precision Corporation and Micro Minitech are two new entrants into the Philippine moulding industry in 1994.[1]

Because of the underdeveloped component sector in the Philippines, most companies resort to consignment kiting and have their stock of electronics components imported from overseas sources. Hence, ample lead time must be factored into the material requisition for parts to be delivered at a specified date to meet production needs. Similarly, shipment deliveries according to committed schedules of export products made in the Philippines need to be monitored due to logistic issues.

---

1 Source: BOI and EPZA.

EXPORT STRUCTURE

General Information

The Philippine electronics industry entered the export market in the early 1970s. Ten years later (1984/85), it achieved an export sales level of more than US$1.3 billion. By 1993, export sales reached a level of US$3.7 billion (nearly 30% of the total Philippine exports) with an average growth rate of 20% over the past five years.

With reference to Table 16–1, semiconductor devices (with a share of 70%) led with export sales of US$2.6 billion in 1993 followed by the telecommunications and sound recording equipment sector at 13%, with total export sales of US$506.31 million. The highest growth rate of 77% was the electrical machinery, apparatus and appliances sector. Table 16–2 shows that the United States accounted for about 45% of the overall electronics products exported from the Philippines. Japan ranks second at 11.7%, and Germany is third at 6.6%.

TABLE 16–1
Philippine Exports of Electronics Components: 1989 to 1993
(US$ millions)

Product	1989	1990	1991	1992	1993	Percentage Share 1993	Growth Rate
Electronics	1,815.54	2,044.37	2,419.55	2,970.93	3,785.66	100.00	20.14
Semi-conductor Devices	1,401.49	1,536.15	1,360.68	2,013.04	2,641.02	69.75	25.04
Electrical Machinery Apparatus/ Appliance	151.68	212.53	645.10	354.84	423.30	11.18	77.15
Telecom-munication Sound Recording Equipment	207.40	225.95	306.15	408.51	506.31	13.37	25.43
Electronics Office/ Automatic Data Processing	55.09	66.74	106.94	193.02	215.02	5.08	43.15

Source: Department of Trade and Industry.

Electronics Industry Participants

There are over 300 electronics firms, including some of the leading global companies, in the Philippines. Over 200 electronics firms are registered with the Philippines BOI and EPZA. The majority of these firms are located in the Metropolitan Manila area, as well as in the designated industrial and export zones around the country.

TABLE 16–2
Major Markets for Philippine Electronics for 1992 and 1993 (US$ millions)

Countries of Destination	1993		1992	
	Value	Percentage	Value	Percentage
Total World	3.79	100.00	2.79	100.00
United States	1.17	45.12	1.27	42.78
Japan	0.44	11.61	0.47	15.82
Germany	0.25	6.60	0.21	7.07
Hong Kong	0.24	6.33	0.18	6.06
Singapore	0.22	5.80	0.14	4.71
Taiwan	0.18	4.76	0.13	4.38
United Kingdom	0.16	4.22	0.12	4.04
Netherlands	0.11	2.90	0.12	4.04
Malaysia	0.10	2.64	0.08	2.69
France	0.09	2.37	0.06	2.02
Others	0.28	7.39	0.19	8.40

Companies in the finished electronics product sector are either subsidiaries of transnationals or joint ventures with small or medium Filipino-owned firms. This sector has insignificant exports since most of the products which are manufactured or assembled are absorbed almost entirely by the domestic market. In the electronics component sector, companies are usually third-party subcontractors, which are mainly Filipino-owned, or multinational plants which cater to the requirements of their parent companies.

PHILIPPINES FREE PORT AND EXPORT PROCESSING ZONES

The government of the Philippines is committed to developing several special economic and free port zones to serve as industrial, commercial, investment, and regional growth centres. The most famous special economic and free port zone is Subic Bay, located south-west of Luzon Island. This was a United States navel base from 1945 to 1992. It has a well-developed seaport and the second largest airport in the Philippines, capable of handling jumbo jets.

The infrastructure and facilities for industry development, worth US$8 billion, are there and available for use. They include transportation facilities such as an airport, berths and road network, fuel storage, power plants, electricity and water system, public communications system and a labour force of over 42,000 highly skilled workers formerly employed by the United States Navy. In addition, Subic Bay is mentioned by the Metropolitan Authority as one of the most orderly, peaceful and safe places in the Philippines for business operations.

One of the electronics ventures there is Thomson Consumer Electronics which is controlled by Singaporeans. It operates a new plant worth S$10.22 million and produces audio and communication products such as telephones and compact-disc players for export to the United States and Asia. The operation is using the labour force to advantage for shipping in components, assembling them in the plant, and then directly shipping to the United States and other destinations.

One of the EPZs is Cavite. Some of the ventures in this zone started operations in early 1986. It is now booming in the 1990s with investments mainly by the Japanese, Korean, Taiwanese and Americans. There are 31 electronics and electronics supporting industry companies in operation dealing with PCBs, CD-ROMs, electronics and computer components, car stereos and radios, plastic injection moulding and so forth. These companies account for 25% of the 124 companies operating in the zone.

There are other export processing zones (EPZs) and free port zones, like Baguio in the Ilocos region located in the northern part of the country. It is a 45-minute flight from Manila and is the educational centre of the north for technical and management personnel. Infrastructure facilities such as standard factory buildings, power and water supply, communication and transportation are available. Of the eight preferred industries listed by the zone authorities, electronics ranks first.

Mactan EPZ in Cebu, an island province in central Philippines, focuses on manufacturing, services and tourism. With sufficient infrastructure in place, development of the electronics engineering industry, such as silicon wafer fabrication, audio-visual equipment, quartz watch assembly and optical instruments, are the main considerations of the local government. There are many other regional growth centres, such as the Clark Special Economic Zone located in the provinces of Pampanga and Tarlac. Others, such as St. Ana Regional Industrial Centre and Port Irene EPZ in northern Luzon, Pavia Regional Agro-industrial Centre in western Visayas and Zamboanga City Regional Industrial Centre in western Mindanao, are all booming under the effective support of the state and local governments.

The major preferential policies for the free port zones and special economic zones involve taxation and trade. There is no foreign exchange control in the zones. Foreign exchange transactions relating to profit remittance and capital repatriation are free of any restrictions. There are exemptions of local and national taxes, such as customs and import duties, national internal tax (e.g., VAT) and income tax on income from business operations within the zones and foreign countries. When foreign articles are removed from the zones to a customs territory, they are subject to the payment of duties and internal revenue taxes as ordinary imports.

TWO FIRMS IN THE INDUSTRY

Integrated Microelectronics, Inc. (IMI)

IMI was incorporated in 1980 and started operations in 1981, with 78% of its share capital controlled by Ayala Corporation which is mainly in the real-estate business. In 1994, IMI's total assets were P9833.5 million (roughly S$58.3 million) and sales were P629.5 million (S$39.3 million). The main business line of IMI is the assembly of electronics products. Its subsidiary, Electronic Assemblies Inc. (EAI) does merchant PCB assembly. IMI is actually an electronics contracting firm consisting of six special business divisions dealing exclusively with the contracts of NEC/Toshiba, Matsushita, Solid State Optronics, Yamaha, Hewlett-Packard and Sunward. IMI merely assembles the products. Logistics and marketing are not relevant operations in the firm because customers ship in their own components and ship out the assembled products, for further processing, or to the target market. In this sense, the firm is like a local processing division of the offshore customers. The assembled products include paddle board, thin film head and gimbals, headstacks, flexible printed circuits, floppy disk heads, pulse transformers, hard disk drives, connector wire harnesses, LED displays and AC–DC converters.

Electronics Assembly, Inc.

This company was established in 1988 by IMI (94.4%) and Sakata (5.6%). There are five modules in EAI for different assembly functions defined by customers from Japan, such as Toshiba, Minolta and Casio, and Philips Jarafalla in Europe. EAI is an electronics assembly company like IMI, but different. It is more like an independent assembly company, which is divisionalised by functions of assembly, as compared to IMI which is divisionalised by different customers. The product lines of EAI include consumer flexible circuit assembly of hard disk drives, cameras, fax machines, pagers and battery chargers.

The most important competitive advantage of the Philippines is identical for IMI and EAI, that is, the large pool of skilled labour. The profile of operators in IMI and EAI is shown in Table 16–3. Graduates from high school are overwhelmingly female (about 90%) and they characterise the electronics industry labour force.

TABLE 16–3
Profile of Operators in IMI and EAI

Education	IMI	EAI
High School Graduate	61%	61%
College Level	24%	22%
College Graduate	15%	17%

Well-trained workers are doing extensive assembly work in place of automated machines, lowering the cost of investment and, ultimately, production. This explains why a significant percentage of worldwide merchant integrated circuit (IC) assembly is done in the Philippines. As early as 1983, the percentage was around 20%. The competitive advantages of the Philippines for the electronics industry are political stability, stable currency, logistics, previous track record, cost control, creditability of assemblers and government regulations.

Analysis

From interviews with the managements of both IMI and EAI, the benefits of their operations are two-fold. First, the foreign parent firms help to overcome marketing deficiencies. The outlet for products is guaranteed while designs and specifications are supplied by the parent firms. Information about the targeted markets and changing tastes are most important to the exporters and, yet, these are also the most difficult for the exporters from developing countries. Second, local firms supply advantages, such as land and cheap labour, while parent firms supply equipment and transfer technology through personnel training, expert supervision, technical design and specification, together with techniques such as quality control. For example, EAI was awarded the outstanding quality control company in 1991 and the ISO9000 certificate was issued to EAI by the Bureau of Product Standards of the Department of Trade and Industry.

For the export processing electronics industry, and the special cases of IMI and EAI, the advantages are a combination of the following:

(a) export-oriented industry and trade policies of the governments;
(b) abundant supply of highly disciplined and efficient labour;
(c) advantageous location of the country; and
(d) preferential economic and tax policies for the industry and free port zones, such as tax holidays, tariff-free capital goods import and priority of custom clearance for the import of raw materials and components for export processing.

The concentration of the export-oriented labour-intensive industries is encouraged by the government through schemes such as the EPZs and liberal trade policies. These are the most important factors in the Philippines electronics subcontracting industry. One of the comparative advantages of the Philippines in undertaking the export processing or subcontracting business is avoiding many of the import quotas of the European and United States export markets. Another influencing factor is that the general scheme of trade preference in the United States makes exports from the Philippines more profitable.

CONCLUSION

The electronics subcontracting work in the Philippines is highly labour intensive and is a low value-added activity. The underdeveloped component sector in the Philippines has prompted many electronics companies to adopt the consignment basis for part kiting. This involves shipping parts by customers who have contracted Philippine companies to assemble them. Such consignment arrangements are only sustainable if duties are not imposed on the import of components. The supporting industries can grow correspondingly so long as the MNCs make a commitment to stay in the Philippines.

Although there are signs that some companies are expanding their current facilities, most prospective electronics investors would rather adopt a "wait and see" attitude. Because of the strategic location of the Philippines, and the government's move to privatise and liberalise the economy, the electronics industry will grow. The entry strategies normally adopted for prospective investors are through subcontracting arrangements, so as to minimise risk, or joint ventures if there is domestic market potential. Although the electronics industry is in the initial development stage, the time is right for prospective investors to enter this segment of the economy.

REFERENCES

Board of Investments, Department of Trade and Industry of the Philippines, *Investment News*, Vol. 4, No. 1, January 1995.

Nell Guides, "Philippines", First Edition, 1994.

"International Sub-contracting: A Tool of Technology Transfer", Asian Productivity Organisation, 1978.

"Philippines Business Environment", *SEAM*, February 1995.

"Ramos Continues Marketing of 'Philippines Inc.'", *The Philippines Star*, 5 March 1995.

Subbramanian N. P., "A Strategic Plan for Sustenance of the Growth of the Semiconductor Industry in the Philippines", Asian Institute of Management, 1985.

"Subic Bay Freeport, Philippines – A Guide for the Foreign and Local Investors", Philippine Government, 1994.

Wong Poh Kam, "Technological Development Through Subcontracting Linkages", Asian Productivity Organisation, 1991.

REGIONAL GROWTH CENTRES

Chapter 17

Investment Incentives and Opportunities in Cebu

BY
ONG Tjhang Kang
CHONG Weng Yong

INTRODUCTION

WITH MANY REGIONAL growth centres, special economic zones and EPZs, the task of selecting an appropriate investment location in the Philippines is not an easy one. Many factors need to be considered. Each location has its merits and drawbacks. One location, however, is increasingly popular and rapidly becoming a centre of economic prosperity. This is the province of Cebu.

This chapter examines several factors giving Cebu a competitive advantage and making it a favourite investment site. Next, Cebu's dominant industries are analysed. Finally, some of the more important investment opportunities are evaluated.

COMPETITIVE FACTORS

Strategic Location

Cebu is located at the centre of the Philippines. The island is sheltered from seasonal storms which batter the Philippines's eastern and northern provinces. This protected, central location makes Cebu an ideal base for the distribution of goods by air or by sea.

Cebu offers easy access to foreign markets via its international airport and seaport. The Mactan International Airport in Cebu is the second international gateway to the Philippines after the Ninoy Aquino International Airport in Manila. The former handles flights to and from Japan, Hong Kong, Malaysia, Australia, Singapore and the west coast of the United States. It is also linked to 14 major cities around the world through the Philippine Airline's Cebu Express Service.

The Cebu International Port is the only seaport with international standards in the Visayas and Mindanao regions. It accommodates 85% of the country's inter-island shipping activities and it is the gateway for over US$2 billion of exports and imports annually. It has a 3,831-metre marginal wharf and three finger piers with a berthing length of four kilometres. Also, it has a 10,000-twenty-foot equivalent units (TEU) container capacity which can handle an estimated three million tonnes of cargo annually.

Large Domestic Market

Because of its strategic location, Cebu has virtually the whole southern Philippines as a domestic market. Cebu has a population of 2.5 million people, while the latter contains an estimated 22.5 million people. Having a big market brings several benefits which include the following:

1. A better capacity utilisation of capital assets and, as a consequence, economies of scale.
2. The opportunity to specialise in some products. This leads to greater productivity and lower unit costs.
3. The ability to get bulk discounts on items purchased for resale.
4. The advantage of lower transportation costs due to break-bulk and ship-load factors. It is more economical to send goods in bulk to Cebu for eventual transhipment to smaller markets.

Cebu's market is not only large but it is also diversified. In this regard, Cebu can be compared to a bank with a good loan portfolio. Diminishing purchasing power in one market segment (say, the coconut-growing region) may be offset by increases in demand from another segment (say, the gold rush areas of Davao). This market diversity, as well as integration, enables Cebu to receive income spillovers from the other regions.

Competitive Wages and Personnel

Cebu, like other regions of the Philippines, has a large pool of educated, skilled and easily trainable manpower. The labour force is abundant, with almost 20,000 graduates every year. Foreign firms can readily obtain the services of competent, mature and responsible English-speaking managerial and technical personnel at relatively low cost. In absolute figures, the differences in wage rates for similar or equivalent positions in the Philippines and more developed Asian countries are substantial. For example, a foreman in Taiwan gets as much as three to four times the annual pay of his counterpart in the Philippines (see Table 17–1).

TABLE 17–1
Annual Pay of a Foreman as of July 1988 (in US$)

Country	Salary
Hong Kong	17,000
Taiwan	12,000
Singapore	11,700–11,900
South Korea	8,500–8,700
Thailand	7,500–7,800
Philippines	3,800–4,000
Indonesia	3,200–3,500

Source: *The Economist*, 5 November 1988.

Despite the concentration of industrial workers in Cebu, the strike incidence in Cebu is comparatively low (0.29 per 100,000 workers as compared to the national average of 1.11 per 100,000 workers for the period January to September 1988).

To give a perspective on costs across the Philippines, one can compare regional family incomes. Table 17–2 shows that family income in Cebu is much lower than that in Manila.

Financial Institutions

The financial institutions in Cebu are well developed. Apart from Manila, Cebu has the largest concentration of banking institutions, making it the centre of financial transactions in the southern Philippines. There are 105 major commercial banks and money shops in Cebu. At present, two offshore banking units are operating in Cebu City, namely, Citibank NA and Standard Chartered Bank.

TABLE 17–2
Threshold Family Income as of June 1988
(pesos per month)

Source	Low	High
Metropolitan Manila	6,530.95	9,511.24
Metropolitan Cebu	5,097.89	6,304.75
Rural Cebu	1,762.37	1,965.04
Davao City	4,876.03	5,823.06

Source: CRC Corporate Planning Services Division, Manila.

Communications

Cebu has one of the most modern communication facilities in the country for both national and international connections. Services such as international direct dialling, facsimile, telex, databank access, voice data channel facilities, cable, worldwide express delivery service, postal service and telegram systems are available.

Power Supply

Cebu's electric power requirement is provided by the state-run National Power Corporation (NPC). Total capacity is well in excess of demand. Power barges, two thermal power plants, two diesel power plants and two land-based gas turbines, have a dependable generating capability of 512.7 megawatts daily. For the next 10 years, Cebu is projecting an average annual growth rate of 15% in capacity as a result of NPC's expansion programme.

BOTTLENECKS

Not everything in Cebu, however, is perfect. For example, the Metropolitan Cebu water supply is from groundwater sources which are constantly decreasing as more areas are cemented and developed, and as the demand for water increases. The Metropolitan Cebu Water District currently produces an average of 107,337 cubic metres daily. Many companies, however, must provide their own water supply. To augment production, several projects are being implemented over a six-year period which will add over 343,700 cubic metres of water daily.

Another problem is the lack of an efficient public transport system. Good roads are necessary for sustainable future developments. The island offers only thin strips of usable land on the coast which is divided by a spine of mountains. Road links and land reclamation are vital to overcome these limitations. The government is aware of this problem and is looking into major infrastructural improvements such as the Cebu circumferential road project.

INDUSTRIAL ESTABLISHMENTS

Cebu is the only non-agricultural-based economy in the Philippines. Cebu's economy has been tooled up from the beginning for developments in manufacturing, services and tourism. Cebu's industries are predominantly export-oriented. It is the only province in the Philippines which consistently exports more than it imports, thus registering the highest positive balance of trade. It has the highest growth rate in exports (29% in 1993), which is double that of the Philippines (13%). Cebu is the number one manufacturer and exporter of furniture and fashion accessories in the Philippines. It is also the number one processor and exporter of dried fruits and seaweed in the Philippines. It is well known in Europe, the United States and Japan for furniture, garments, handicrafts and fashion accessories.

Mactan Export Processing Zone (MEPZ)

Powering Cebu's growth over the years is the MEPZ. Established in 1979, the MEPZ is an ideally located industrial estate operated as a self-contained enclave for export-oriented industries. It offers 250 hectares of prime facilities on Mactan Island, 14 kilometres from Cebu City. The area is also ideal for light and medium manufacturing industries. Some of the facilities offered include standard factory buildings for lease, power supply, well-paved internal roads with drainage and modern lights, and port and wharfage facilities.

One attraction of the MEPZ includes investment incentives such as tax-free imports of equipment, raw materials and supplies needed for production, tax holidays, no limitation on foreign ownership or equity, and the employment of non-Filipinos. Other advantages include operating and capital costs. The minimum wage for a non-agricultural worker is US$5.50. Rental rates for industrial land range from US$0.35 to US$0.40 per square metre per month. Rental rates for standard factory buildings are US$1.91 per square metre per month. Construction cost for a self-designed factory building is about US$200 per square metre.

At present, more than 61 companies produce a variety of products. They range from bags, garments, and cardigan (extract of seaweed), to computer software. The majority of firms are Japanese but there are also Filipino, American, British, Swiss and Bermudan companies. Among the companies in the MEPZ are Timex, Isumi Corporation, National Semiconductor, NEC Technologies, Asahi-Pentax and Daewoo. The only Singapore investment in MEPZ is the Singapore Telecom–Ayala Group joint venture, Globe Telecom. It has recently set up a general system modulation (GSM) mobile phone cell there as part of a countrywide expansion plan.

INVESTMENT INCENTIVES

Enterprises can register with the BOI or the MEPZ Authority. Depending on the form, investment incentives can vary and some of the more important items are discussed below.

BOI Incentives

1. In terms of tax holidays, newly registered firms in commercial operations are fully exempt from income tax for six years if they qualify as pioneer firms, and four years if they are non-pioneer

firms. A pioneer firm is one that is engaged in one of the following activities:

(a) manufacturing, processing or production (not merely assembly or packaging) of goods or raw materials not produced in the Philippines on a commercial scale;
(b) transformation or production of any element, substance, or material into another raw material or finished good using a design or process that is new and untested in the Philippines;
(c) pursuit of agricultural, forestry and mining activities and/or services, including the industrial aspects of food processing as approved by BOI; or
(d) production of non-conventional fuels or equipment that either utilises non-conventional sources of energy, or converts coal, as a source of energy in production.

2. Tax-and-duty free importation of equipment.
3. Tax credits on domestic capital equipment and raw materials, and additional deductions for labour expenses.
4. Access to bonded manufacturing/trading warehouse systems.
5. Exemption from wharfage duties, and any export tax, duty or import fees.
6. Exemption from contractor's tax.
7. Tax-free exemption of imported spare parts.

MEPZ Incentives

Firms registered with the MEPZ Authority are entitled to all of the incentives available to firms registered with the BOI. In addition, they are entitled to the following:

1. Special tax treatment of merchandise within the zone.
2. Exemption from local taxes (except real estate tax) and fees.
3. Exemption of real-estate tax on production equipment and machinery not attached to real estate.
4. Profits remitted abroad by a branch office to the head office are exempt from the 15% branch office remittance tax.

Other special privileges and priorities including the following:

1. No limitation on the ownership or equity of non-Filipinos in zone enterprises.
2. Non-Filipinos may be employed in supervisory, technical or advisory positions in zone enterprises within five years from registration.
3. Zone enterprises have priority in the allocation of foreign exchange.
4. Simplified import and export procedures.
5. Imports are exempt from inspection by the Societe Generale De Surveillance (SGS).

PHILIPPINES'S EXPORT WINNERS

The Department of Trade and Industry has identified export winners for potential investments based on the criteria of high worldwide potential, less sensitivity to protectionist measures of importing countries, and minimum requirements for efficient infrastructure, production capability and highly skilled labour. The export winners include the following:

1. Agriculture-based and resource-based products, such as cardigan and seaweed, marble (tiles and slabs; novelty items), processed tropical fruits, shrimps and prawns.
2. Consumer products, such as garments and textiles, ceramics (dinnerware, bathroom accessories, etc.), furniture, gifts and houseware (basket wares, christmas decor), and jewellery (gem-set and plain gold jewellery).
3. Industrial products, such as electronic components/products; packaging of ICs and special plastics, transistors, photo-diodes/phototransistors, etc.; metal components and parts such as casted parts for various machines; and other forged components for automotive, shipping, mining, electrical utilities, agriculture, aero-space and other allied industries.

PRIORITY AREAS OF INVESTMENT

The government encourages investments in projects which will generate jobs, add value to local resources, introduce technology and skills, open new markets and develop outlying areas. In this respect, the government has set out in the 1994 IPP the preferred areas of investment it wishes to promote in the economy. The preferred investments are in the following areas:

1. ***Export Activities:*** These are the export winners mentioned above.
2. ***Agricultural and Marine Products, Inputs and Services:*** These include agricultural products, such as the production of agricultural crops; livestock, poultry, dairy, fishery and aquaculture; and agricultural/marine infrastructures for public use.
3. ***Basic Industries:*** These include primary and secondary processing of ferrous metals (specifically, iron making integrated with slab making and steel plate rolling); cement; chemical products; and refined petroleum products.
4. ***Electronics and Telecommunications Products:*** These include semiconductor devices and allied electronic products, and components and raw materials needed for their manufacture; and telecommunications, information handling equipment, and their parts and components.
5. ***Textile and Textile Products:*** These include chemical fibres and filament yarns; silk (spinning from cocoons); and textile dyeing and finishing.
6. ***Support Facilities:*** These include power-generating plants; testing and quality services; public utilities; and infrastructure projects for public use.
7. ***Environmental Conservation and Protection:*** These include forest plantation/farms, and environmental support facilities.
8. ***Projects Supporting Priority Programmes of Other Government Agencies:*** These include mining, health and tourism.

INVESTMENT POTENTIAL IN CEBU

The Cebu government welcomes any of the above preferred investments by foreign investors, corporations or governments. Investors may locate within or outside the MEPZ. However, with its competitive advantage, Cebu's main potential appears to be in light engineering, including manufacturing and precision assembly, manufacturing of spare parts and components, and subassemblies. Potential investors may wish to consider products such as silicon wafer fabrication, audio-visual equipment, quartz watch assembly and optical instruments. Other areas with potential are the following:

1. ***Plastics and Packaging:*** Over 90% of the packing needs of MEPZ firms are imported at very high cost from outside Cebu. There is a sufficient number of these firms to encourage investors to put up plants to service their needs. Potential products include precision moulded components, cartons, bags, foam and plastics.
2. ***Aircraft Maintenance and Related Activities:*** The government is actively embarking on a programme to establish Cebu as a regional aviation centre and airport maintenance centre. There is potential for services such as aircraft refurbishing, maintenance, flight training centres and so forth.
3. ***Construction:*** With increased construction activities in Cebu, there is a large need for additional cement-manufacturing companies and construction-related services.
4. ***Ship Breaking, Ship Building, Ship Repair and Maintenance:*** These areas are investment opportunities given that Cebu is the centre of inter-island shipping in the Philippines. The Keppel Group of Singapore has a ship maintenance and repair facility in Mactan with a 20,000 dead-weight tonne dry dock, six slipways and ample berthing space. The Tsuneishi group of Japan is in Balamban organising ship building and ship module manufacturing for export.
5. ***Computer Software:*** With the growing number of computer training schools, and the number of computer-literate graduates in Cebu, it is viable for investors to establish computer software and related services in Cebu. Potential products include data entry, engineering/drafting services, financial services and software development.

6. ***Electronics:*** This industry is essentially engaged in assembly, manufacturing and labour-intensive activities. The component sector, however, is underdeveloped. The plan for the year 2000 is to adopt a more focused investment programme and target leading computer, electronics and electrical equipment manufacturers. There are also intentions to increase component suppliers and upgrade support industries to add value. Key opportunities, therefore, exist in areas such as telecommunications, semiconductors, consumer electronics, hard disk drives, PCB assembly, and component manufacturing, design and logistics.
7. ***Tourism:*** Tourism will continue to boost Cebu's economy. The proximity of resorts and cultural sites, plus the amenities of modern urban life, are the key elements in Cebu's success in tourism. Local hotels and resorts are enjoying very satisfactory occupancy rates. There is great opportunity to establish Cebu as an upmarket destination in the international tourism industry. Cebu needs investments in retirement villages, eco-tourism and high-end beach resorts.

CONCLUSION

Cebu has the trappings of a newly industrialising country on a regional scale. It has been quick to capitalise on a strategic location, and many other features, to take advantage of the domestic and foreign markets. Its industrial and service sectors have sanguine market prospects and it is actively encouraging investors to match these bright prospects. Potential investors looking for a place in the Philippines need go no further. Cebu is the answer.

REFERENCES

"Doing Investment in the Philippines", Price Waterhouse, 1994.

"Make it Cebu", Notes from the Philippine Embassy, Singapore.

Manzano George N., "NIC Fever on Fiesta Island in the Making of a Vibrant Economy", CRC publication, 1988.

"The Philippine Electronics Industry", Integrated Microelectronics Inc., The Philippines, 1994.

Tiglao Rigoberto, "The Other Philippines", *Far Eastern Economic Review,* 28 November 1991.

Chapter 18

Conversion of Subic Bay

BY
CHUA Hock Lye
ER Jui Pin
TAN Teng Chong

INTRODUCTION

ON 24 NOVEMBER 1992, the United States Navy bid farewell to Subic Bay Naval Base in the Philippines. The Philippine government inherited the well-developed area but had to face the challenge of converting this once-thriving military asset into commercial use. The government has made this a high priority and allowed Subic Bay to be the country's first special economic zone. A corporation-cum-government body, Subic Bay Metropolitan Authority (SBMA) was set up to run the entire area.

For nearly a century, the economies of Subic Bay and adjoining Olongapo City depended heavily on the United States Navy which was home to the largest American military base in Asia. Some 42,000 Filipinos had jobs on the base. Another 80,000 were involved in stores, restaurants and bars that the Americans patronised. Now, they have lost their jobs overnight and their future depends on the successful conversion of Subic Bay.

Subic Bay is located 80 kilometres northwest of Manila, in the province of Zambales, and a short distance north of the entrance to Manila Bay. It is strategically located near major international shipping lanes in the South China

Sea. It offers a natural harbour which is protected on three sides by mountains, and is only a three-hour drive from Manila. The site has a land area of 16,200 hectares (40,000 acres) and an estimated English-speaking workforce of 66,000 with a wage rate of US$5 per day. It is a freeport and a special economic zone. There is a search on for investors to revive the base.

BACKGROUND OF UNITED STATES NAVY'S WITHDRAWAL

Nationalisation Movement

The United States Government was a strong supporter of the Marcos regime. When the latter fell from power, the United States was not held in high esteem by the general population. In 1986, with a new Constitution under the Aquino Government, a small group who strongly opposed the American military presence succeeded in inserting a condition in the constitution which stated that foreign military forces can be present in the country only if a two-thirds positive vote is ratified by the Senate. This set the stage in 1991 for the Senate to decide whether to renew the United States military treaty. Under the fragmented political conditions at the time, the two-thirds positive vote was not successful. This outcome culminated in the government giving formal termination notice of the Military Base Agreement of 1947 (amended in 1966).

End of Cold War Era

In 1990, the Berlin Wall came down and the reunification of Germany signified the end of the cold war between the West and the East. The communist regimes were in disarray and were no longer a potent threat to the West. Russia's economic difficulty greatly weakened her military power and presence. The United States saw that there was no need for a continual build-up of their military presence in the world. The 1980s in South-east Asia were quite peaceful with no major conflicts, especially after the Sino-Vietnam War. With a big military presence in Japan and Korea, Subic Bay was expendable.

United States Budget Deficit

The United States has been suffering budget deficits since the Carter administration and it became worse with the Reagan administration which supported a military build-up. As a result, the United States government cut back on military spending especially with the end of the Cold War. This was a disincentive for an American presence in the Philippines.

Incorrect Judgement

The United States negotiator for the renewal of the treaty assumed wrongly that the Philippine government would be forced to renew the naval base treaty on terms favourable to the United States. The Americans probably underestimated the Filipinos' sentiment in removing their presence. The United States assumed that their presence was economically very important to the government. As a result, it was not prepared to yield to the Filipinos' terms and conditions. This led to failure in the renegotiation of a new treaty.

Mount Pinatubo Eruption

In June 1991, Mt. Pinatubo erupted, covering Subic Bay with ashes and damaging several buildings. This would have required the United States to spend millions of dollars to clean up the ashes. This further prompted the United States to leave the naval base.

SUBIC BAY'S ASSETS

Port Facilities

Subic Bay has over 10,000 feet of berthing space. The depot covers 41 hectares and has a movable pier, a fixed pier and two berths, a cold storage facility, 22 warehouses, two open storage areas and a container stacking yard. Although Subic Bay was built for naval use, it is also suitable for commercial operations.

Air Facilities

The naval air field was built in the 1950s. The single runway is 9,000 feet long and is capable of handling Boeing 747s, except when they are fully loaded. The small apron and buildings limit its potential as a major commercial airport or hubbing operation, but the facilities can handle international charter flights and can support an aircraft maintenance or specialised air cargo facility.

Utilities and Services

1. ***Power:*** There are six diesel generators which produce 26 megawatts of power, assuring new locators of continuous power. As such, Subic Bay has no brownouts which is a common problem throughout the Philippines. In addition, a United States company, Enron Corporation, is constructing a 108 megawatts capacity power installation.
2. ***Water and Sewerage:*** A tropical forest provides the base with a watershed. Thus, the water supply is ample to serve the needs of a large investment community. It should remain adequate so long as the watershed remains intact and there are no heavy industrial users. There are six treatment plants to handle sewage.
3. ***Telecommunications:*** The existing telephone network capacity exceeds 15,000 lines. A new switch is to be installed to replace the one removed by the United States Navy.
4. ***Roads:*** Subic Bay has an extensive well-maintained network of approximately 100 miles of roads.
5. ***Petroleum, Oil and Lubricants (POL) Facilities:*** Subic Bay has a POL tank farm with a 2.4 million gallon capacity in 68 tanks, an unloading pier and a pumping station. The POL supply capacity is equivalent to a 14-day supply for the whole country.
6. ***Ship Repair Facilities:*** The ship repair facilities, consisting of several dozen workshops with specialised equipment and nearby piers, have extensive capabilities to repair military ships. A total of 12 ships can berth at one time, with 27 berths possessing a draft of 40 feet and a berthing of 7,065 feet. The area has facilities to accommodate three floating dry-docks, four portal cranes, five floating cranes, and 36 service crafts. There is capacity to service 20 different types of ships in over 40 permanent structures, including welding, mechanical and electrical shops, a foundry and over 2,000 pieces of plant equipment. The long-term use of these facilities is under review in consonance with the master plan of the area.

Industrial and Commercial Estates

There are approximately 100 buildings, including warehouses and workshops, which are suitable for industrial and commercial uses. There are also office buildings, barracks and hotels that can be used for administrative and housing purposes.

Residential Areas

Subic Bay has approximately 2,000 single-family housing units in two main residential areas, plus schools, swimming pools, stables, an 18-hole golf course, gasoline stations, shopping areas, parks, gymnasiums and a hospital.

Grande Island and Forest

This is a 39-hectare island near the entrance to Subic Bay which has a small hotel, yacht basin, beaches and reefs. Within the Subic Bay baselands are 3,500 hectares of virgin tropical forest. This forest offers the potential for supervised recreational and tourism development.

STRENGTHS AND ATTRACTIONS

Strategically located in South-east Asia, with impressive natural beauty and a well-developed and immaculately maintained infrastructure inherited from the United States Navy, Subic Bay has the potential to become a new centre of major economic activity during the 1990s. Some of the strengths of Subic Bay are discussed below.

Physical Assets and Facilities

One major strength of Subic Bay is the facilities left behind by the Americans. These facilities have been valued at US$8 billion. Wayne Conway, President of Subic Bay Clothing Corporation, a subsidiary of Dasuna of Tasmania, expressed the desirability of the infrastructure: "Subic has exactly what we need – a ready-made factory with air-conditioning."

High-quality Workforce

There were 42,000 English-speaking workers unemployed after the transition. Foreign firms have cited the Filipino's widespread use of English as a crucial factor in their investment decisions. Furthermore, worker productivity and quality is considered highly favourable.

Location

Subic Bay is strategically located in the centre of East Asia. It is only one hour and 50 minutes by plane from Hong Kong or Taipei. With the return of Hong Kong to China in 1997, and the unstable relationship between China and Taiwan, Taiwanese investors are looking for a nearby economic zone. Subic Bay Free Economic Zone is the nearest economic zone to Taiwan. Subic Bay is also near major international shipping lines within the Asia-Pacific region.

Leadership

The man behind Subic Bay's transformation is the charismatic, urbane 49-year-old Richard Gordon. Analysts think that Mr. Gordon's leadership will be a key factor for success. A master of public relations and hard-sell techniques, Mr. Gordon has made it work so far. Under a tight budget, he recruited 8,000 unpaid volunteers to maintain and run the base. Washington Sycip, Chairman of the auditing and consulting SGV Group, says Gordon is the right salesman for Subic Bay: "You need a person with his enthusiasm. A technocrat wouldn't have got all the volunteers." Through his efforts, Subic Bay obtained special economic zone status in 1992 under RA 7227.

Special Economic Zone Status

Subic Bay is a Special Economic Zone (SEZ) under the Base Conversion and Development Act of 1992. It became the country's first SEZ on 5 February 1992. There are many privileges and benefits associated with the SEZ status. The incentives include:

1. Duty-free import/export of goods and materials.
2. Unrestricted foreign ownership of business.
3. No foreign exchange control.
4. No taxes except for a 5% tax on gross income.

5. Tax holidays.
6. Permanent resident visas may be issued to investors bringing in US$250,000.
7. Free market for gold, futures and securities.

Government Support

The Philippine government is focusing on economic development and the conversion of Subic Bay is a high priority. In the words of President Ramos on 30 September 1992, Subic Bay is to serve as the "springboard of our economic take-off."

To support the economic reform and attract foreign investors, the government liberalised many policies. *Asia Business Week* (January 1995) commented: "Policies liberalising investments have largely benefited foreign investors, and more are expected in the future. Almost all restrictions on foreign exchange have been lifted. Most manufacturing sectors are now open to foreign investors. Banking is open to foreigners on a selective basis. There is a motion to allow foreigners into retailing. BOT schemes allow private investors in infrastructure."

CONVERSION PROBLEMS

Although Subic Bay has an excellent infrastructure, a natural deep-water port, and a big pool of skilled labour, converting a military base into a prosperous economic zone based on international private-sector activity presents a considerable challenge. SBMA has to overcome many problems, and some of the more important ones are described below.

Lack of Transport Connections and Supporting Facilities

Although Subic Bay has an airport and a deep-water port, one of the key drawbacks is the lack of other supporting activities and facilities such as shipping. The problem is that business activity has not reached the critical volume that lures shipping lines. Similarly, the air field has great potential but it will not be commercially viable until there is sufficient traffic. In the meantime, investors and goods still have to go through Manila. Taiwan Reebok Shoemaker, Subic Star, is 100 metres from a deep-water port but it must still get raw materials and send finished products via Manila. On the other hand, American President Lines can have ships calling at Subic Bay only twice a month although it had planned for once a week.

Relatively High Operating Costs

The Philippines has operating costs that are double those in China and Vietnam (Figure 18–1). This clearly reduces the attractiveness of Subic Bay.

FIGURE 18–1
Comparative Weekly Wage Rates

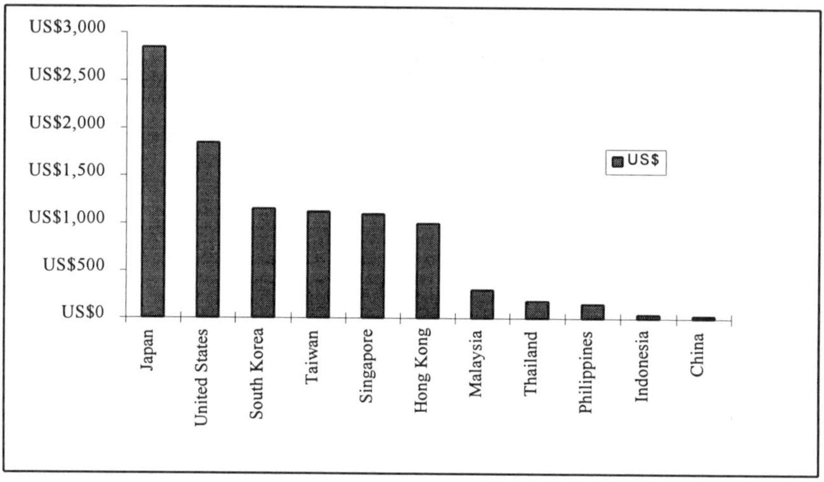

Difficulties in Converting Military Facilities to Civilian Use

SBMA is trying to convert all the military facilities to civilian use. Many difficulties have been encountered. For example, SBMA is trying to figure out how to use scores of ammunition bunkers which are underground.

It is not easy creating a business centre out of a military base, and it is a costly exercise. A 1990 government study estimated a cost of P33 billion (US$1.4 billion) to convert the base to private use. SBMA is faced with the task of raising funds for conversion.

Fund Requirement

A 1992 law requires the conversion to be financed from the sale of land which is mostly occupied by the Philippine military. But try telling that to the military, which opposes the law on the grounds that its 32.5% share of the proceeds is insufficient.

Mt. Pinatubo – A Live Volcano

Mt. Pinatubo is 32 kilometres away from Subic Bay. It erupted in June 1991, 18 months before the turnover of Subic Bay by the United States Navy, covering all of the area with ashes and damaging several buildings. Fortunately, a mountain range protected the complex from the mud flows that ravaged most of central Luzon. Scientists have not ruled out another major eruption.

Negative Image of the Philippines

Although the base is an easy sell with an excellent infrastructure, natural deep-water harbour, and skilled labour, SBMA has to overcome the problem of a negative image of the Philippines to attract investors. Political instability, inefficient government, lack of infrastructure, and power supply problems in other parts of the Philippines, do not help in this matter.

Competition from the Region

At the macro level, the Philippines needs to compete with other emerging countries in the region, such as China, Vietnam and India, as well as developing countries, such as Malaysia, Indonesia and Singapore, for investment from the same pool of investors including the United States, Japan and Taiwan. Moreover, at the micro level, Subic Bay needs to compete with other economic zones in the Philippines. Altogether, there are four regular economic zones and ten SEZs.

INVESTMENT POTENTIALS AND OPPORTUNITIES

The master plan for Subic Bay identifies light to medium industries as preferred investments. So-called "environmentally unfriendly" industries are banned. Other commercial possibilities are tourism, telecommunications and ship repair. These prospects are discussed below.

Light to Medium Manufacturing Industries

Mr. Gordon's preferences for non-polluting industries include electronics, microchips, machinery and parts, textiles and garments, light engineering, steel fabrication, software development, as well as airplane, car and yacht assembly. Subic Bay offers a complex of buildings and warehouses for light manufacturing. However, development has been so rapid that investors have reserved all of the buildings and warehouses available for lease. Prospective investors will now have to build their own structures or lease those built by other individuals.

Tourism Industry

Tourism potential is based on a natural setting. The location offers tropical weather, water sports, a virgin forest and duty-free shopping. Olongapo City has many restaurants, night clubs and one beach resort hotel. Within the former United States base are 1,876 executive homes and three-storey, 80 to 100-room international hotels. It also has sports and recreational facilities, such as an 18-hole golf course, 37 tennis courts, six swimming pools, theatre buildings, a gymnasium, a horse-riding stable, bowling alleys, football fields and parks. At the mouth of Subic Bay is Grande island which is a beach resort. Good medical and educational facilities are also available.

International Telecommunications Industry

The SBMA has the authority to offer franchises to investors interested in developing and operating the existing telecommunications system within the free port zone. A relatively low level of investment is necessary for starting up a telecommunications franchise due to the existence of some 7,000 access lines within the former United States base.

Subic Bay has many administrative buildings that can be used by firms specialising in data processing, computer software, telemarketing, customer support services, and similar export-oriented information enterprises that can employ the inexpensive, literate and English-speaking Philippine workforce. The government would have to allow the establishment of a teleport or gateway at Subic Bay, with the lowest possible international rates, to make these feasible alternatives.

Ship Repair Industry

For ship repairs, Subic Bay offers the shops, equipment and piers at the former United States Navy's ship repair facilities. The long-term use of these facilities is under review in consonance with the master plan of the area. At the north end of Subic Bay is the Philseco yard designed to repair very large and ultra large carriers. Keppel Corporation of Singapore is one of three Asian ship repair companies that has shown a strong interest in both the ship repair facilities and Philseco.

PROGRESS: THE SECOND ANNIVERSARY

On 24 November 1994, Subic Bay marked the second anniversary of the withdrawal of United States troops with the signing of another 18 new business contracts. This raised the total investment in the sprawling free port to US$657.3 million. It had already generated employment for about 11,600 workers (13,000 by March 1995), far exceeding the World Bank target of 10,000 jobs in five years. The World Bank's consultants predicted that Subic Bay could only operate the sea port after four years and the airport after six years. But the SBMA has shown the world how capable it is under the leadership of Mr. Gordon. The sea port was operating within two years, and Federal Express cargo planes were landing in 1995. Mr. Gordon expected that another 20,000 jobs would be generated by the end of 1995.

The 18,000-hectare property had lured 107 companies, with United States firms making up about 60% of the total investment, by the second anniversary date. The bulk of the investment contracts with the SBMA were signed during the first year of operation. Those deals included US$100 million worth of contracts with the United States firms of Enron Corporation, Coastal Petroleum and Federal Express.

Enron took over a 31-megawatt power station, once run by the United States military. In addition, it built a 108-megawatt power plant for US$128 million. After the existing station, which is under a 15-year BOT arrangement, this is the largest single investment in the zone so far.

Coastal Petroleum was one of the first foreign investors to move into the bay, signing a US$93 million, 25-year lease for its 2.4 million barrel oil depot. By bringing in diesel, aviation fuel and other refined products, the company is in a position to take advantage of regional marketing opportunities, particularly in southern China and Vietnam.

Federal Express is investing US$100 million to have the busiest Asian small-package transfer hub. Conditions are ideal because of the proximity to most of Asia's major trading centres, excellent infrastructure and the local government's enthusiasm. The Federal Express centre is handling a variety of trans-Pacific flights since operations began in early 1995. Flights come directly from the United States, or the Anchorage facility, which is the transshipment point for air freight moving to Asia from the United States and Europe.

Taiwanese billionaire Jeffrey Koo, chairman of Taipei's China Trust Commercial Bank, feels strongly that Subic Bay is poised to become Asia's next economic miracle city. A joint venture among the Taiwanese government, the SBMA and a private Taiwanese company has started to develop a 660-acre parcel of land at Subic Bay into an industrial park. The commercial space will then be marketed principally to Taiwanese companies. The industrial park is expected to open in December 1995.

Malaysian billionaire, Lim Goh Tong, also likes the future of Subic Bay. A group that includes Lim's Kuala Lumpur-based resort operator, Resorts World Berhad, has invested US$100 million to build a 5-star hotel, with 400 rooms, a casino and golf course. A partial list of investors in Subic Bay Freeport Zone, by project and nationality, as at 11 March 1994, is shown in Appendix 18–1.

DISCUSSION

The United States Navy's withdrawal from Subic Bay created a big challenge to the SBMA as well as to the Philippine government, but it also offered an unique opportunity. The SBMA has shown that it is able to manage the "crisis" and turn disadvantages into opportunities.

Under the leadership of Mr. Gordon, and with excellent facilities left behind by the Americans, the SBMA generally has had an easy job in attracting investors. With the government's support, and the likely further opening up of the economy, it is expected that Subic Bay will continue to expand and draw more investors. However, there are additional challenges ahead for the SBMA.

Challenges for SBMA

While the SBMA has been successful in maintaining facilities and attracting 110 companies so far, it is now facing another set of challenges. The heavy construction work and transportation will increase the need for road and environmental maintenance. The coastal highway construction, started in March 1995, will be completed only in 1997. Thus, traffic in Olongapo City is expected to increase while the inconvenience of transporting employees and supplies in and out of the city will continue for a few more years. The nature of volunteer work will also shift, from maintaining facilities and promoting investment, to working for investing companies in factory construction work and administrative tasks. Also, the number of volunteers is dwindling and SBMA needs to attract new assistance.

Moreover, SBMA is facing competition from other emerging countries, such as China and Vietnam, and other economic zones internally. SBMA has to intensify the promotion of supporting facilities and activities, such as shipping and logistics, to attract more foreign investment. To counter the relatively high operating costs, SBMA has to aggressively promote the concept of good local productivity. It may have to ask the government to provide special incentives to lure investments from Japan, Taiwan, Hong Kong, Korea and the United States. One consideration is to relax the 5% tax on gross income and adopt the same income tax holiday (four years for new non-pioneer firms and six years for new pioneer firms) provided by the BOI.

One unique strength of Subic Bay is the large technically trained workforce. SBMA hopes to use this advantage to attract electronics manufacturers and research and development investments. However, many pioneer companies still set up labour-intensive and low value-added factories, and manage their production lines to take advantage of the cheaper labour rather than higher technical skills. SBMA can develop and publish a more detailed master plan to guide and shape the appropriate types of industries for future growth.

Opportunities for Investors

We are confident that Subic Bay is going to take off successfully. However, it may take another two years or so for the critical supporting facilities to be ready, including the coastal highway, housing along the highway, shipping and logistic activities, and so forth. The issue for potential investors is one of timing. Earlier investors will have better location and workers, “free publicity” by SBMA, and possibly preferential treatment and cooperation from local networking that may extend into the future.

For investors who have decided on the Philippines, Subic Bay is a good choice. Once the coastal highway is completed, it is only an hour’s drive to Manila, free from traffic congestion. We agree with SBMA that computers, electronics and electrical equipment manufacturers, and the related component suppliers and support industries, can take full advantage of the infrastructure and technically trained labour. These industries are also in line with the government’s “Industry Plan 2000”.

CONCLUSION

Over the last two years, the SBMA under the leadership of Mr. Gordon, has been trying to turn the military base into a prosperous free port and SEZ. To date, total investment in the sprawling free port is more than US$650 million. SBMA expects 30,000 jobs to be generated by the end of 1995, three years after the departure of the United States.

In our opinion, SBMA has been doing a solid job in reviving Subic Bay. However, it is patently clear that many challenges still lie ahead.

APPENDIX 18–1

List of Investors in Subic Bay
Subic Bay Freeport and Special Economic Zone Approved Projects
as at 11 March 1994

Company	Project	Nationality
Asia Pacific Merchandise Mart, Inc.	Retailing	Filipino
Chern-Lih Industrial Co. Ltd.	Moulding, Design and Manufacturing. of PVC Pipes and other Plastic Products.	Taiwanese
Coastal Subic Bay Terminal, Inc.*	Petroleum Products	American
DFS Sports Unlimited, Inc.*	Retailing	Filipino
Duty-Free Commodities*	Retailing	Filipino
Eastern Telecoms**	Telecommunications	Filipino
Electruck Private Limited*	Industrial Lifts, Cranes, Spreaders Manufacturing	Australian
	Computer Cards Manufacturing	Swiss
Entron Subic Power Corporation*	Electric Power	American
Far East Bank & Trust Company*	Banking	Filipino
Fluor Daniels Pacific, Inc.*	Construction Services	American
Genting International Casino Hotel Resort (1990) Limited*	Casino, Hotel and Resort	Malaysian
Good Speed Garments	Garments Manufacturing	Filipino
International Freeport Traders, Inc.*	Retailing	Hong Kong
Kace Philippines, Inc.	Electronics Product Manufacturing	Korean/ Hong Kong

APPENDIX 18–1 (Cont'd)

K.O.G. International Phils, Inc.	Heavy Equipment Leasing	American
Kinberg Leder, Inc.	Leather Goods Manufacturing	Filipino
88 Mart Duty Free, Inc.	Retailing	Filipino
Metropolitan Bank & Trust Company	Banking	Filipino
Olongapo Food Corporation	Restaurant	Filipino
Pacific Hollywood Corporation	Restaurant	Filipino/ American
Pacific Clothing Corporation	Garments Manufacturing	Filipino
PCI Bank	Banking	Filipino
PLDT Company, Inc.	Telecommunications	Filipino
Powerich Industrial Corporation	Garments Manufacturing	Taiwanese
Prudential Bank	Banking	Filipino
Ritchie Bros. Auctioneers Limited*	Industrial Equipment Auction	Canadian
Royal Cargo Corporation*	Forwarding Services	German
Royal Duty Free Shops Inc.*	Retailing	Filipino
Security Bank & Trust Company*	Banking	Filipino
SGS (Subic Bay), Inc.*	Fuel Testing	Swiss
SR Telecoms, Inc. – Subic Bay*	Telecommunications Equipment Repair	Canadian
Shamburgh Imports, Inc.*	Retailing	Filipino

APPENDIX 18–1 (Cont'd)

Shell Gas Trading (Asia Pacific), Inc.*	LPG Trading	Dutch
Subic Bay Apparel Corporation*	Garments Manufacturing	Filipino
Subic Bay Aqua Sports, Inc.*	Tourism/Retailing	Filipino
Subic Bay Clothing, Inc.*	Garments Manufacturing	Australian
Subic California Clothing, Inc.	Retailing	Filipino
Subic Chow Food Corporation	Restaurant	Filipino
Subic Duty Free Shop, Inc.	Retailing	Filipino
Subic Duty Free Shoppers, Inc.	Retailing	Filipino
Subic International Cargo Centre, Inc.	Transshipment Services	Hong Kong
Subic International Hotels, Inc.	Hotel/Restaurant	Filipino
Subic Park and Shop, Inc.	Retailing	Filipino
Subic Resort Corporation	Hotel and Beach Resort	Filipino
Subic Star, Inc.	Shoe Manufacturing	Taiwanese
TST Subic Boat Works	Small Boat Manufacturing	Japanese
United Coconut Planters Bank	Banking	Filipino
United Distillers Subic, Inc.*	Warehousing and Distribution	Filipino
Wimpy's Food Corporation*	Restaurant	Filipino

* Fully Operational
** Pre-existing Locators

REFERENCES

"Philippines 1994 Investment Priorities Plan", Board of Investments, Philippines, 1994.

"Primer on Investment Policies in the Philippines", Department of Trade and Industry, Board of Investments, Philippines, 1994.

"Subic Bay Freeport, Philippines – A Guide for the Foreign and Local Investors", Joaquin Cunanan & Company, Price Waterhouse, 1993.

"The Philippine Export Processing Zones", The Export Processing Zone Authority, Philippines, 1994.